COMPUTE!'s
MAPPING the
IBM PC and PCjr

Russ Davies

COMPUTE! Publications,Inc.abc

One of the ABC Publishing Companies

Greensboro, North Carolina

Printed in the United States of America

10 9 8 7 6 5 4 3 2 1

ISBN 0-942386-92-2

COMPUTE! Publications, Inc., Post Office Box 5406, Greensboro, NC 27403, (919) 275-9809, is one of the ABC Publishing Companies and is not associated with any manufacturer of personal computers. IBM PC, PCjr, PC/XT, XT/370, Portable PC, PC AT, and 3270PC are trademarks of International Business Machines, Inc.

Contents

Contents

Figures, Tables, and Programs

Figures

Tables

Programs

Foreword

If you've programmed in BASIC or machine language on the
IBM PC, you're aware of the many features that the computer
offers. You've probably also discovered that there are capabilities which are difficult for the average programmer to learn
and use. *COMPUTE!'s Mapping the IBM PC and PCjr* is a memory map and guide to the inner workings and structure of the
IBM PC and PCjr. It will show you how to take advantage of
the vast and powerful abilities of your computer's built-in
hardware and software.

Through examples and illustrations, you'll be introduced
to the techniques that professional programmers use to add
polish to commercial software. By studying these keyboard,
sound, and screen techniques, you'll learn the skills needed to
design attractive and effective programs in any language.

Sample programs show you how to read the keyboard,
screen flip, call DOS commands from BASIC, and even define
the function keys to automatically execute the tasks you use
most often.

COMPUTE!'s Mapping the IBM PC and PCjr contains a series of detailed Appendices, including extensive memory and
port maps, a handy listing of interrupts and DOS function
calls, cross references to IBM documentation, and details of the
differences between each version of DOS and BASIC.

Whether you're new to machine language on the IBM or
are a veteran 8088 programmer, you'll find that *COMPUTE!'s
Mapping the IBM PC and PCjr* is the most clearly written and
easy-to-use guide to the IBM PC memory available.

Acknowledgments

My thanks to personal and professional acquaintances who
provided valuable suggestions and especially to those who
were tolerant of my absent-mindedness and lack of social
graces during yet another book-writing marathon. I promise
not to talk to myself anymore or scribble on tiny scraps of
paper in the middle of conversation—at least until the next
project. My warmest gratitude to Doug Martin, Lester
Kooyman, Greg Grimm, Guy Moore, and Jim Cady, each for
his own unique contribution.

Special thanks go to Orson Scott Card, who first gave me the opportunity to express myself through this medium. The good cheer and wisdom of Stephen Levy and enthusiasm of Gregg Keizer have made my relationship with COMPUTE! Books a joy through two long projects.

My family have been dears through both projects. Thanks for waiting, Mom; I can talk now. And finally, I am indebted once more to Cindy King, who made this book happen. I simply could not have persevered through it without her unselfish sacrifices, constant support, good cheer, tender warmth, and unfailing belief. "You know I'd like to, but I have to work on the book" is finally over.

This book is dedicated with love to Earl, George, and Jamie.

Introduction

Whether you use an IBM PC, XT, PCjr, XT/370, Portable PC, or 3270PC, this book will help you get more from your computer. In each chapter we'll explore the way the PC operates and show how to make it work to your advantage. IBM documentation just doesn't say enough about the things the typical user wants to be able to control and use.

Have you noticed that no DOS or ROM BIOS services are available for the production of sound and that the *Technical Reference* manual (TRM) doesn't explain how to produce sound on the PC? Sound is left uncovered except for the BASIC manual.

Wouldn't it be nice to be able to call ROM BIOS and DOS functions from your BASIC program? Or to be able to determine, from your program, which version of DOS and BASIC is being used? How can you program the function keys so that they stay active even when you leave BASIC? Did you ever wish that you could turn off the Break key in BASIC? Or set the Shift keys on or off from your program? How do you determine the best place to BLOAD or POKE a machine language routine for BASIC?

Did you know that there's a third palette available in 320 × 200 mode on the PC? Do you understand the various video modes? Would you like to be able to smooth-scroll and perform seemingly instantaneous full-screen writes? Would batch file in-process modification or a secondary COMMAND.COM be the best technique for nesting .BAT file calls? We'll explore these topics and many more in this book.

These techniques and tricks will make your programs more impressive, but what's more important is the knowledge you'll gain about the way memory and ports are used on the PC and PCjr. From this understanding you'll have a clear picture of the way the PC works from the ground up, through ROM BIOS, DOS, BASIC, and application programs.

IBM documentation will be enhanced by the many references you'll find to the proper sections for additional details. Have you had problems finding information you need in the *Technical Reference* manual? Quick—where can you look to determine the cursor position for video page 3? How about the port address associated with COM2? If you see a POKE to location &h20, what is the program doing? Why would an INP(&h321) be in a program? Not the easiest things to find in the existing IBM documentation, but this book's memory map and port map will answer such questions quickly.

What You Need to Know

Although it is not imperative that you know BASIC or 8088 machine language, an understanding of them will be helpful if you are to gain the most from this book.

You should have a fundamental knowledge of how to operate the computer and how to enter a program. If you are unfamiliar with batch files or the use of DEBUG, you may want to review those sections of the DOS manual. In addition, experience using the most common DOS commands will be useful.

What You Need to Have

You'll need to have access to an IBM PC or PCjr. Most of the information in this book also applies to many of the IBM-compatible work-a-like computers. The greater the compatibility with an IBM PC, the more useful this book will be for a non-IBM computer.

The PC, PCjr, XT, XT/370, Portable PC, and 3270PC will run the sample programs without modification. The majority of the sample programs require no modification for the PC AT.

It doesn't matter what amount of memory is present on the computer, which display adapter you're using, or what additional peripherals you have. You'll be able to learn a great deal regardless of your configuration. A 384K PC, 384K XT, and 128K PCjr (with 256K additional RAM sometimes used) and both monochrome and RGB color monitors (only RGB for the PCjr) are used for example purposes, but the principles explored are common to any memory size or display configuration.

The level of DOS that you are currently using is not critical. DOS versions come and go, and this material is presented in a way that makes it relatively independent of the release level of DOS. DOS 2.0/2.10 is used in this book for example's sake, but DOS 1.1 through DOS 3.0/3.10 features are discussed.

Three IBM manuals are referenced in this book: the BASIC manual, the DOS manual(s), and the system unit *Technical Reference* manual. If you have all three and are generally aware of the range of information contained in each, you're in the best possible position to learn the most from this book. But you needn't have the *Technical Reference* manual to gain substantial knowledge. You'll need the *Technical Reference* manual only to pursue the finer points of the concepts discussed here.

The primary *Technical Reference* manual address and page references are for the XT and PCjr (see below for the exact edition of the manuals used). The XT was selected as a common denominator because of the vast number purchased for business use, the likelihood that serious users will eventually be drawn to it as the price continues to erode, and the many other configurations based on it (such as the 3270PC and XT/370). The XT 2.02 *Technical Reference* manual contains more information than any of the other TRMs, including the PCjr. The Memory Map Appendix clearly lists the differences in PC2 and XT routine addresses. These are primarily confined to two areas of ROM BIOS.

For those unfamiliar with the differences between PC1/2/XT models, here is a summary of the major differences.

	PC1	PC2	XT	PCjr
System board RAM capacity	64K	256K	256K	128K
Minimum RAM	16K	64K	128K	64K
Expansion slots	5	5	8	3 dedicated
256K chips usable	no	no	yes	no
Cassette	yes	yes	no	yes
ROM pins	24	24	26	26
Config switches	2	2	1	0

The *Technical Reference* manuals have undergone a major change from the PC1, PC2, XT, and PCjr versions. The *Options and Adapters* addendum volumes (1 and 2) are now used to contain the information for optional adapters. Here is a list of the versions of system unit *Technical Reference* manuals that I have found available:

Computer	Part Number	Dated
PC1	6025008	7/82
XT	6936808	4/83 with "2.02" sticker
Jr	1502293	9/83
PC2	6322507	4/84
All	6322509	4/84 (*Options and Adapters*, vol. 1 and 2)

It's extremely unlikely that all these versions are available to you. This book uses the XT and the PCjr *Technical Reference* manuals (listed above) as standard references.

Unfortunately, this book cannot cover every aspect of the PCs. Time and space requirements preclude the in-depth examination of Cassette BASIC routines, DOS internals, disk, printer, RS-232, cassette tape, expansion unit, game adapter, and system board support chips. However, the memory and port maps include detailed information about these subjects. I'm sure you'll find that this volume contains the most important and usable information that could be placed in a single book.

The sample programs, diagrams, routine references, and *Technical Reference* manual references reflect the results obtained on several different configurations of PC models. The PC values are derived from a computer with 384K, both color and monochrome displays, and a parallel printer adapter. The PC/XT used had the same memory and peripheral configuration. The PCjr used contained the 64K display and memory enhancement and an additional 256K to bring the system to parity with the others. Although no particular configuration is required, it is assumed throughout that there is a disk drive attached and that some level of DOS is in use. The lack of these would not preclude the bulk of information presented here, but it would somewhat reduce the number of sample programs that you would find useful in your situation.

I recommend DOS 2.10 as the standard operating system for your PC (assuming the 24K of memory used is tolerable), because it is far more powerful than any DOS 1.x versions, with its redirection, pipes, filters, and built-in miniassembler in DEBUG. Some problems with DOS 2.0 were fixed in 2.10, and 2.10 is usable for all members of the PC family (except the AT).

What You'll Find in This Book

The first chapter will introduce you to the memory architecture of the PC and PCjr, and will explain the BASIC, DOS, and ROM BIOS use of memory. It will also summarize the cold start process and give you a powerful tool for invoking DOS and BIOS services from within your BASIC programs. This base of knowledge will be used in later chapters.

Because the keyboard, sound, and video image form the interface between humans and computers, the primary focus of the next three chapters is on using these devices to their full potential. Through many sample and demonstration programs you'll come to know the potential and limitations of each of these devices. We'll also use nearly every feature that they are endowed with, many of which are not explored in other works.

The Appendices include a comprehensive memory map, port map, DOS and BASIC version differences, an interrupt and function guide by device type, and a BASIC token reference. I simply can't imagine how serious programming can exist without decent memory and port maps. They seem fundamental. You can do so much more and use all the power of the computer system only if you are aware of how it is structured and organized. The lack of such information makes understanding other people's programs much more difficult, especially if they are using advanced techniques or all the available system resources.

Sample programs are included to demonstrate the methods that may be employed to use the features under discussion. They are not intended to be examples of clever programming, optimization of speed or memory usage, or models of programming form or technique. Additionally, examining and trying the accompanying programs may clarify finer details of the discussions.

Your involvement at the instructional level will solidify your understanding of the concept being discussed. I encourage you to modify and experiment with the programs to suit your needs. You will ultimately learn much more by trying to change the samples (once the programs are entered and working correctly) than you would from merely observing their original purpose and then moving on to the next subject. The programs have been intentionally written in a straightforward, easy-to-follow manner so that you will find them easy to tailor, adapt, incorporate, and understand.

1
Memory Organization and Management

1
Memory Organization and Management

Your PC or PCjr can address up to one megabyte of memory which is a whopping 1,048,576 bytes for data and programs. There are some programs and data already in the machine before you turn it on. The ROM BIOS, BASIC ROM, and (if you have an XT) Hard Disk ROM BIOS each take away a chunk of the space. These programs need some RAM data areas since ROM can't be written to, so another small chunk is reserved for that purpose. Video mapping requires a healthy section of storage, and memory reserved for future video usage is even larger.

Then there are some areas reserved for future ROM. And let's not forget the memory used to hold the Disk Operating System (assuming that you have a disk drive). That leaves a PC with maximum memory of about 600K for our use, give or take 20K depending on the version of DOS. That's still a healthy amount for programs. And we can always use overlays and disk files to reduce the amount of memory required. CP/M machines have been limited (in general) to 64K, minus the system and operating system overheads. PCs have 16 times the storage capacity.

Incidentally, some of the older PCs (referred to as PC1's and identified by only 64K of memory on the motherboard) do not have the ability in ROM BIOS to use memory above 544K. We'll be exploring ways to overcome that limitation in this chapter. ROM BIOS manufactured after October 27, 1982 doesn't have this limitation. We'll see how to obtain the ROM BIOS date in a moment.

Figure 1-1 shows the memory allocation of the one-megabyte PC address space in 64K blocks.

Figure 1-1. Allocation of PC Memory Address Space in 64K Blocks

Hex	****** 64K Block Memory Map ******
00000 0K	
10000 64K	Vectors, data, DOS, Disk/Advanced BASIC
20000 128K	User program RAM, if filled *
30000 192K	User program RAM, if filled *
40000 256K	User program RAM, if filled *
50000 320K	User program RAM, if filled *
60000 384K	User program RAM, if filled *
70000 448K	User program RAM, if filled *
80000 512K	User program RAM, if filled *
90000 576K	User program RAM, if filled *
A0000 640K	User program RAM, if filled *
B0000 704K	Future video reserved
C0000 768K	Mono/color video
D0000 832K	Future ROM / XT fixed disk ROM
E0000 896K	Future ROM / jr cartridges
F0000 960K	Future ROM / jr cartridges
FFFFF 1024K	Tests, ROM BASIC, ROM BIOS

* BASIC programs are limited to a 64K workspace

Memory Segmentation

Before exploring the boot process and the resulting configuration of software in memory, let's discuss the concept of storage segmentation, since from here on we'll be speaking in terms of offsets within segments or absolute addresses. Since the 8088 microprocessor in the PC or PCjr can access a memory address space of one megabyte (1024K), a memory address can reach as high as FFFFFh, requiring 20 bits to express. This is obviously half a byte more than can fit into the two-byte, 16-bit registers in the 8088. So how does the PC manage to address memory which needs more than two bytes to express over FFFFh (64K)? And how are 20-bit interrupt vector addresses stored in memory? What are segment registers and why do we need to use the DEF SEG statement to look into video memory? If you can confidently answer these questions in your own mind, then feel free to skim ahead to the next section.

Figure 1-2 illustrates the process that the 8088 microprocessor uses to develop an address that spans the memory address range of 0h to FFFFFh. A two-byte *offset* is added to an adjusted two-byte *segment* value to derive the memory address. This is performed very quickly by the 8088 itself, and we need take no special action to have it done; we need only to insure that the segment register is loaded with the correct segment number, then set the offset to the number of bytes beyond the start of the segment.

The segment register is adjusted by adding a low-order zero, which changes the segment number to the address of the nearest-but-not-after memory location that ends in 0h. In other words, B800h segment number is changed to B8000h address. There's no sense carrying around the trailing zero in the segment number since we need the space in the register just to specify the full range of possible segments: 0–FFFFh. The 8088 adjusts the segment number, logically adding a low-order zero to it, adds the offset value, and out pops a memory address.

Thus, every address that ends in 0h is potentially a segment number, and a segment number does not include the low-order 0h. For address FFFF2h, the segment register could contain FFFFh and the offset would be 2h. Sometimes it's helpful to specify an address by indicating the segment and the offset separated by a colon. For example, address FFFF2h could be written as FFFF:2.

Figure 1-2 diagrams the segment:offset address computation process that the 8088 carries out for us.

Your PC *Technical Reference* manual (as discussed in the Introduction, all page references are for the XT manual) illustrates the memory address resolution method shown in Figure 1-2 on page B4, but the PCjr *Technical Reference* manual has strangely omitted this 8088 reference material. This lends credence to the rumor that IBM had planned to use another microprocessor in the PCjr, but problems precluded that, delaying the availability of the PCjr for many months. Since

5

Figure 1-2. Calculation of Memory Address from Segment:Offset

			Contents	Effectively
	0000 | 16-bit offset		10B2h	010B2h
bit	19 15	0		
+	16-bit segment | 0000		E0A6h	E0A60h
bit	19 4	0		———
=	20-bit address			E1B12h
bit	19	0		

that 8088 material isn't available to PCjr users, the diagrams in this section will recap some of the 8088 material in the PC *Technical Reference* manual.

Since an offset can range from 0 to FFFFh, you can see that it would be possible to reference a memory address using many different segment:offset combinations. For example, 12345h would be the address resulting from any of the following segment:offsets—1234:5, 1230:45, 1200:345, 1000:2345, or even 1233:15, 1190:A45, 430:E045, or 235:FFF5. An offset can address any byte in 64K of memory, and there's no reason that the segment can't start at any address ending with zero (called a *paragraph boundary*), as long as the segment:offset combination adds up to the needed address.

Actually, PC users have adopted the convention of only starting segments that end with zero (such as segment number 40h) and that refer to the beginning of a major block of data or instructions (such as segment B800h or F600h).

For the sake of clarity, all addresses in this book (except where counterproductive to the discussion at hand) will be in the *absolute* form, with the 8088 addition already done and referring to a memory address between 0 and FFFFFh. So when you see the address B8000h, you know that it may easily be expressed in segment:offset form as B800:0 or any other handy combination. Even though you often see an address like 40:11 in other references, we'll refer to it as 411h, and you can express it as any segment:offset that you prefer.

The first 64K of memory on the PC contains many vectors to routines and data tables. These vectors are normally four

6

bytes and are formatted as shown in Figure 1-3. The format
may take a little getting used to, but it soon becomes familiar.
This concept of the Least Significant Byte (LSB) followed by
the Most Significant Byte (MSB) is used throughout the PC
and PCjr with only a few exceptions. You'll quickly become
adept at working with the format, and the VECTORSB,
VECTORSD, and VECTCMPR (Programs 1-8, 1-9, 1-10) presented in this chapter will ease the task of constructing absolute addresses from memory vectors, as well as demonstrate
the process of determining the resulting absolute addresses.
DEBUG can also be used to examine these vectors in memory.

Figure 1-3. Vector Format and Example of Contents

Offset		Segment	
LSB	MSB	LSB	MSB
A4	14	23	FE

Byte: 0   1   2   3

Offset: 14A4h
Segment: FE230h

Address: FF6D4h

Sometimes you'll encounter a segment number stored in
memory with no associated offset. We'll see these during the
discussion of storage block chains later in this chapter. This
format conserves data storage space and is used for addresses
that always occur on a 10h byte boundary. They also use the
LSB/MSB format, so you'll need to add a low-order zero to
derive the absolute address. The BASIC DEF SEG= statement
is this type of segment number. The statement is used to adjust BASIC's CS segment register so that memory outside BA-
SIC's 64K segment can be accessed. The offset is set with a
PEEK, POKE, BLOAD, BSAVE, CALL, or USR instruction. See
pages 4-71 and C-8 of the BASIC manual or PCjr BASIC,
pages 4-88 and C-9.

When using DEBUG, be aware that while memory is in
LSB/MSB format, the 8088 registers are in MSB then LSB format. Figure 1-4 illustrates the effect of moving data between
memory and registers. This demonstrates that memory is actually designed to hold data in the LSB/MSB format.

Figure 1-4. Format Change During Register/Memory Moves

AX Register			Memory		
MSB	LSB	← MOVE →	LSB	MSB	
AH	AL		0	1	byte
FE	53	← Contents →	53	FE	

When using DEBUG or the Assembler, the registers shown in Figure 1-5 are available for your use. Some registers are designed to be used as segment registers, while others may be used as general work areas or base/index registers. The figure shows each register available and its assumed usage in certain instruction types. Registers that are split may be used as two 8-bit registers or as a single 16-bit, two-byte (called *word*) register.

Addressing Modifiers

From DEBUG and the Assembler, the base and index registers can be specified for use in the calculation of the final absolute address, as shown in Figure 1-6. You can experiment with using base and index registers by entering assembly language statements in DEBUG, setting the registers, and tracing the instruction to see the resulting memory address referenced.

As Figure 1-6 demonstrates, the Assembler and DEBUG make assumptions about which segment register is to be used when performing address calculations. This assumption is then reflected in the 8088 instructions generated. Whenever the next instruction to be executed is referenced (by a JMP or CALL), the registers CS:IP are used. The SS:SP pair is used to reference the stack, which we will be discussing in more detail. The source and destination segment register is assumed to be DS, while the destination for string operations is assumed to be and must use ES:DI. If the BP register is used in an instruction, the segment register is assumed to be SS.

A program can override the assumption that DS is the source and destination and SS is the segment register when BP is used in an instruction. The PCjr *Technical Reference* manual does not document these segment register assumptions, but the PC *Technical Reference* manual has a figure on page B-4.

Figure 1-5. 8088 Segment, Base/Index, and Miscellaneous Registers

Data Registers

AH	AL
BH	BL
CH	CL
DH	DL

AX Accumulator

BX Base

CX Count

DX Data

Assumed Usage:

AX multiply and divide word, I/O
AH multiply and divide byte
AL multiply and divide byte, I/O, decimal mode, translation
BX base register
CX string and loop
CL rotate and shift
DX multiply and divide word, I/O

Pointer and Index Registers

SP Stack Pointer

BP Base Pointer

SI Source Index

DI Destination Index

Assumed Usage:
SP stack index
BP base index
SI strings
DI strings

Segment Registers

CS Code Segment

DS Data Segment

SS Stack Segment

ES Extra Segment

Miscellaneous

IP Instruction Pointer

			flags →				O	D	I	T	S	Z		A		P		C

```
        1 1 1 1 1 1                              bit
        5 4 3 2 1 0 9 8 7 6 5 4 3 2 1 0 no.
```

FH	FL

9

Figure 1-6. 8088 Address Calculation with Base/Index

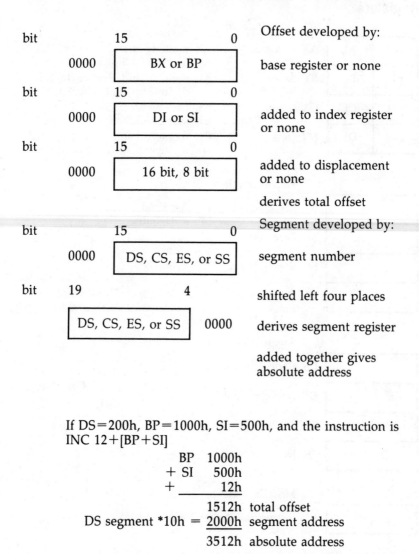

bit   15   0   Offset developed by:

    0000 | BX or BP | base register or none

bit   15   0

    0000 | DI or SI | added to index register
                                                          or none

bit   15   0

    0000 | 16 bit, 8 bit | added to displacement
                                                          or none

                                                          derives total offset

bit   15   0   Segment developed by:

    0000 | DS, CS, ES, or SS | segment number

bit   19   4   shifted left four places

    | DS, CS, ES, or SS | 0000   derives segment register

                                                           added together gives
                                                           absolute address

If DS=200h, BP=1000h, SI=500h, and the instruction is
INC 12+[BP+SI]

$$
\begin{array}{rl}
\text{BP} & 1000\text{h} \\
+\ \text{SI} & 500\text{h} \\
+ & \underline{12\text{h}} \\
& 1512\text{h} \quad \text{total offset} \\
\text{DS segment *10h} = & \underline{2000\text{h}} \quad \text{segment address} \\
& 3512\text{h} \quad \text{absolute address}
\end{array}
$$

A caution about segment overrides: When a REP or REPZ is used for a string operation and an interrupt such as an NMI occurs, only the segment override nearest the string operation code will be "remembered" and restored. The moral is that segment overrides are not prudent for string operations using REP or REPZ.

Segment registers can point to segments whose 64K range overlaps other 64K segments specified by other segment registers. Of course, segment registers may each point to entirely separate 64K segments of memory. The PC *Technical Reference* manual illustrates a discrete segment example on page B-4.

Stack

The 8088 provides instructions to manage a last-in, first-out (LIFO) stack area that is used to store and restore data. Stacks are used by all programs. The current stack area is typically used to save registers and other program control information. But there's no reason that any data you wish could not be saved on the stack, as long as you're willing to remove it later. The Assembler instruction PUSH places data on the stack and POP recalls it. These instructions are used with a word of data.

The stack area is actually any area in RAM that the stack segment register (SS) has been set to point to. Because the stack grows downward toward offset 0 from offset FFFFh in the SS segment, the correct setting of SP for an entirely empty stack segment is FFFFh. A PUSH of a word of data onto the stack causes SP to be decremented by two. Then the MSB is placed on the stack, followed by the LSB, maintaining the same LSB/MSB format as we've seen used in memory. So SP always points to the last byte that was placed on the stack.

The POP of a word of data from the stack copies the data pointed to by SS:SP to a location indicated by the instruction and increments SP by two. The data on the stack is not erased, but SP is adjusted so that it will be overlayed by the next PUSH of a data word.

Besides accessing data at the top of the stack with SS:SP, you can also obtain information from within the stack segment by using BP with its default segment register of SS. This method is employed to pass parameters to machine language programs from BASIC. See either computer's BASIC manual, page C-11. When moving data from the stack, other than POPing, it, the original data remains on the stack.

11

Since DOS and BIOS use your stack area when you request one of their services, the DOS manual recommends that your stack area be at least 80h larger than your program requires. The INT instruction uses three words of the stack to save the current CS:IP and flag register. CALL pushes the IP word, and CS if a FAR CALL is used, onto the stack. RET (or RET FAR) restores these registers by POPing them from the stack. The *n* parameter for RET specifies the number of **bytes** (*not* words) to be discarded off the stack before the CS:IP location on the stack. That's why *n* is typically twice the number of parameters passed by BASIC to a machine language program.

As we shall see later, DOS has a few places where SS and SP are set in the wrong order. SS should be set before SP, since any interrupt that occurs after the setting of SP and before SS would cause the wrong stack segment to be used, possibly destroying vital information and certainly using an incorrect return address. We could disable interrupts during the setting of these registers, but an NMI (Non-Maskable Interrupt) on the PCjr generated by the keyboard cannot be disabled and would create havoc.

ROM BIOS Versions

Since there are different versions of DOS, BASIC, and even ROM BIOS that include support for additional or enhanced commands (as well as known bugs), you may want to determine the release level of the software on a PC before issuing a command in a program. For example, the LOF function in BASIC is helpful in determining the size of a file. But LOF is not available in Cassette BASIC. In addition, BASIC 1.0 and 1.1 return the file size as the next higher multiple of 128 bytes, whereas BASIC 2.0 and above return the actual number of bytes in the file. VARPTR$ didn't exist before BASIC 1.1, and ON TIMER is new with BASIC 2.0. LABEL is a new DOS command on DOS 3.0, redirection is new in DOS 2.0, and all x.0 releases of DOS feature additional and enhanced function calls.

It's therefore important to understand which version of software is in the environment so that your programs can take advantage of the power of provided facilities and avoid errors caused by attempting to use nonexistent features. Program 1-1 determines the machine type, the ROM BIOS release date, and the ROM part number. The release date and part number can be used to distinguish early XTs which had the same machine-type code as a PC. Your PC *Technical Reference* manual BIOS listing may be back-level. Compare the date on the last page of the BIOS listing to that found in ROM.

Program 1-1. ROM BIOS Version

For error-free program entry, be sure to use "The Automatic Proofreader," Appendix H.

```
HM 100 'MEMROMVR; Decode machine type, part num,
        version date from ROM BIOS
HA 120 DEFINT A-Z
OL 130 DEF SEG=&HFFFF: MACHINE=PEEK(&HE)
EF 140 MACHINE$="n unknown machine"
GJ 150 MACHINE=MACHINE-&HFB:ON MACHINE GOSUB 240,
        250,260,270
HA 160 '
QM 170 FOR X=5 TO 12: VER.DATE$=VER.DATE$+CHR$(PE
        EK(X)): NEXT
HE 180 '
LN 190 DEF SEG=&HF000: FOR X=0 TO 7: PART$=PART$+
        CHR$(PEEK(&HE000+X)): NEXT
GF 200 '
IP 210 CLS:PRINT"This is a"MACHINE$" with ROM dat
        ed "VER.DATE$", part num "PART$
LP 220 END
HL 230 '
JH 240 MACHINE$=" PC/AT": RETURN   '&hFC
CL 250 MACHINE$=" PCjr": RETURN   '&hFD
CL 260 MACHINE$=" PC/XT, XT/370, OR 3270 PC": RET
        URN   '&hFE
MB 270 MACHINE$=" PC": RETURN   '&hFF
```

Running Program 1-1 has shown the following versions of ROM BIOS:

Date	Part	Machine
04/24/81	5700051	PC
10/19/81	5700671	PC
08/16/82	5000026	XT, XT/370
10/27/82	1501476	PC
11/08/82	1501512	XT, XT/370, and 3270PC
06/01/83	1504037	JR
01/10/84	6181028	AT

It's likely that other ROM BIOS versions exist, and it's certain that more will be released in the future.

DOS Versions

The version of DOS that is being used on a PC can be obtained by using the VER command, DOS function 30h, the BASIC SHELL command on DOS 3.0 and higher, or Program 1-2 that allows SHELL to work on BASIC 2.0 or 2.1 (Program 1-2 will not work on the PCjr). In the Appendices of this book you will find a list of the new and enhanced commands on each level of DOS from 1.1 through 3.1.

You can use a machine language routine in BASIC to call DOS function 30h for the version of DOS as illustrated by Program 1-3 (Program 1-3 will work on the PCjr). We'll soon explore a generalized machine language routine that can be used for many other DOS functions and INT calls as well.

If 0.0 is shown as the DOS version, then DOS is previous to 2.0.

Program 1-2. Determining the DOS Version Using SHELL

For error-free program entry, be sure to use "The Automatic Proofreader," Appendix H.

```
DP 100 'MEMDOSVR; Obtain version of DOS from BASI
       C
DG 110 'will not work on JR
HI 120 '
GN 130 PL=PEEK(&H30): PH=PEEK(&H31) 'save data fr
       om BASICs non-PSP
JK 140 SHELL "ver >temp.ver"  'create a file with
        VER return message
OO 150 POKE &H30,PL: POKE &H31,PH 'restore saved
       data
HA 160 '
CD 170 OPEN "temp.ver" FOR INPUT AS #1 'show the
       VER message
CE 180 INPUT #1,X$,Y$
FF 190 PRINT Y$
GF 200 '
LJ 210 VER$=RIGHT$(Y$,4): PRINT VER$ 'set a strin
       g to the DOS version
HM 220 CLOSE #1: KILL "temp.ver" 'erase the tempo
       rary file
```

Program 1-3. Determining the DOS Version Using DOS Function 30h

For error-free program entry, be sure to use "The Automatic Proofreader," Appendix H.

```
DD 100 'MEMDOSVS; Call DOS function 30h for versi
       on number
GG 110 '
```

```
OB 120 GOSUB 160: CALL ASMROUT!    'load and call
        the assembler routine
QM 130 PRINT"DOS Version"PEEK(&HB)"."PEEK(&HC)
LC 140 END
LC 150 ' --- LOAD ASSEMBLER ROUTINE ---
QN 160 DEF SEG=&H1800: I=0 'starting address for
        assembler routine
EP 170 ' outside of BASIC's segment
JA 180 READ X$: IF X$="/*" GOTO 200 'read loop
OH 190 POKE I,VAL("&H"+X$): I=I+1: GOTO 180 'cons
        truct the routine
KC 200 ASMROUT!=0          ' address of the routine
MO 210 RETURN
KJ 220 ' --- Assembler routine ---
MH 230   DATA B4,30   : MOV AH,30        ;REQUEST
        DOS VERSION FUNCTION
IG 240   DATA CD,21   : INT 21           ;CALL DO
        S
IN 250   DATA 2E      : CS:              ;SAVE IN
        THIS SEGMENT
BJ 260   DATA A3,0B,00 : MOV [0B],AX     ;SAVE DO
        S RETURN INFO
ED 270   DATA CA,00,00 : RETF 000        ;RETURN
        TO BASIC
CJ 280   DATA 00,00   ' : AL, AH FROM DOS ; MAJOR,
        MINOR VERSION
OJ 290   DATA /*
```

BASIC Versions

The version of BASIC that the program is currently running under may also be of interest. The BASIC version together with the DOS version gives a clear picture of which BASIC commands are supported. See the Appendices for a table of which BASIC commands are not supported in which releases of BASIC, and which releases enhanced the BASIC commands.

Cassette BASIC is an anomaly because, by definition, no DOS is present. None of the new or enhanced BASIC commands are available—only those commands that are in the BASIC ROM. The PCjr BASIC cartridge is required for BASIC(A) when running any level of DOS on the PCjr. So for the PCjr, Cartridge BASIC is always at a DOS 2.1 level, regardless of the DOS version. By renaming BASIC or BASICA, you can run the disk versions of BASIC on the PCjr. (But you'll still need the cartridge inserted.) A higher level of Cartridge BASIC will undoubtedly be available in the future.

The level of DOS is meaningless for Cassette BASIC and largely irrelevant for compiled BASIC programs. Of more interest would be the level of the BASIC compiler.

Program 1-4 can be used to determine the version of BASIC that is in use. Cassette BASIC is included for those users who may be writing for systems that use a cassette tape drive.

Program 1-4. Determining the BASIC Version

For error-free program entry, be sure to use "The Automatic Proofreader," Appendix H.

```
HE 100 'MEMBASVR; Determine version of basic
GG 110 '
OD 120 ON ERROR GOTO 230
MP 130 CV$="12":TEST=1:X=CVI(CV$)   'if bad, casse
       tte
GC 140 TEST=2:ON ERROR GOTO 150: SOUND OFF: GOTO
       230 'if good, PCjr
EB 150 RESUME 160
PL 160 ON ERROR GOTO 230
FF 170 TEST=3:ON STRIG(4) GOSUB 180:GOTO 190  'if
        bad, disk BASIC
NL 180 RETURN
FH 190 TEST=4:ON ERROR GOTO 200:X$=SPACE$(256):GO
       TO 230  'if good, compiled
AD 200 RESUME 210
BP 210 VERSION$="A":PRINT"Advanced Basic":END
HJ 220 '
GB 230 ON TEST GOSUB 250,260,270,280:END
HN 240 '
NA 250 VERSION$="C":PRINT"Cassette Basic":RETURN
IF 260 VERSION$="J":PRINT"PCjr Basic":RETURN
PA 270 VERSION$="D":PRINT"Disk Basic":RETURN
KC 280 VERSION$="O":PRINT"Compiled Basic":RETURN
```

We could have determined the version of BASIC by reading the copyright line that is presented on the screen when BASIC is started. The SCREEN(x,y) command can perform this for us. But the command BASIC PGM can be entered to cause PGM.BAS to be run without the copyright line being displayed. So PGM would have no copyright information line to retrieve from the screen.

The copyright information is stored in various places within each BASIC, not at the same offset into the programs. So we would need to know which version of BASIC we are using before we could find the version number. That's not helpful. I have to believe that there is an indicator at some uniform location within each BASIC, but try as I might, I have been unable to locate it.

Incidentally, you can throw the user into Cassette BASIC and provide no method of exit by using JMP F600:0. Normally, INT 18 could be used, but the PCjr BASIC cartridge causes INT 18 to point to itself at E8177h.

Table 1-1 summarizes the sizes of various versions of DOS and BASIC. This may be helpful in planning the machine/DOS/BASIC versions to be supported by your programs.

Table 1-1. Sizes of DOS/BASIC Versions

	3.0	2.1	2.0	1.1
DOS Sum	36K	24K	24K	12K
IBMBIOS	8964	4736	4608	1920
IBMDOS	27920	17024	17152	6400
COMMAND	22042	17792	17664	4959
BASIC	17024	16256	16256	11392
BASICA	26880	26112	25984	16768

From DOS Requests to BIOS Requests

The PC and PCjr PC/DOS operating system provides a set of generalized service requests for machine language applications such as .COM or .EXE programs (including BASIC). DOS also provides a set of internal commands (such as DIR, TYPE, and .BAT file processing) that can be requested directly by the user or from within programs. DOS can search for, load, and execute machine language programs at the request of a program or a user. Some of the programs are supplied with DOS (*external* commands such as FORMAT, DEBUG, BASICA), while other programs are user supplied. DOS currently makes no distinction between user and provided programs.

Service requests (functions and interrupts) for DOS are usually translated by DOS to the appropriate service requests (interrupts) of the ROM BIOS device-level routines. By changing the interrupt vectors to these routines, you can replace them or add additional front-end routines. When needed, DOS and ROM BIOS call their own internal service requests to help with the work at hand. Extensive use of subroutines within DOS and BIOS allows service requests to use routines that are also needed by other services. Generally transparent to the user (and even the requesting program) are the myriad of routines checking to be sure that all went well and just waiting for the chance to handle an error situation.

As you can see, what your program may consider to be a simple request at your level causes a spreading flurry of activity as it gets passed on to helper routines at the same level and down to lower-level routines where all the messy details get handled. A diagram (see Figure 1-7) of the activity looks much like a drawing of a tree's root system. There really is no such thing as a simple request for DOS or BIOS, especially for any type of I/O activity.

Figure 1-7. Levels of DOS and BIOS Service Requests
Width of box suggests increasing path length. Figure not to scale.

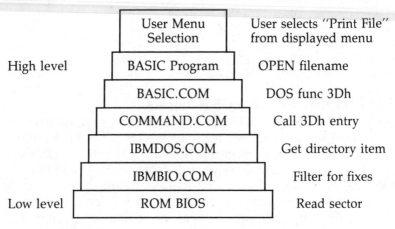

High level	User Menu Selection — User selects "Print File" from displayed menu
	BASIC Program — OPEN filename
	BASIC.COM — DOS func 3Dh
	COMMAND.COM — Call 3Dh entry
	IBMDOS.COM — Get directory item
	IBMBIO.COM — Filter for fixes
Low level	ROM BIOS — Read sector

Memory Usage: Loading the OS and BASIC

When you turn on your PC or PCjr with a DOS disk in the drive, DOS is loaded into your computer and you receive either a Date/Time prompt or an AUTOEXEC.BAT file sets up the environment for you. Your DOS manual or DOS *Technical Reference* manual contains a brief overview of the boot process, starting on page B-1 for DOS 2.0, or page 1-3 of the DOS *Technical Reference* manual for DOS 2.10 and 3.0. We'll be adding important new information to those synopses.

Figure 1-8 shows the memory usage results of loading the operating system into your computer and starting BASIC. We'll be discussing each component shown in the diagram, but let's start with a description of the boot process itself, as we'll gain valuable insight by exploring that subject first. Use the diagram in Figure 1-8 as a reference as we discuss the method by which the system is prepared to perform productive work for the user.

This discussion won't detail the various self-test procedures that the PC and PCjr ROM BIOS perform during the initial stages of the power-on sequence; these are adequately documented in the *Technical Reference* manual. Those steps that result in decisions about the eventual memory usage configuration will be discussed.

Cold/Warm Starts

When a boot is performed by switching on the computer (called a cold start) or Ctrl-Alt-Del (called a system reset or warm start), an instruction at location FFFF0h (by 8088 convention) is executed that causes the Power On Self Test (POST) routines to begin component tests. If bytes 472–473h are found to contain 3412h, a reset via Ctrl-Alt-Del has been requested. If so, the POST actions are skipped and memory will not be tested. Memory will simply be cleared to all zeros. The time difference between a cold start and a reset is dependent on the amount of memory installed, but worst case is over two minutes for a cold start of 640K compared to around 20 seconds for a warm start.

Programs 1-5 and 1-6 show methods that can be used within BASIC to call for cold and warm starts. The difference between the two programs is the dependence on the presence of the restart code in locations 472–473h. As written, the programs will perform a cold start (Program 1-5) or a warm start (Program 1-6); be sure to save the programs before running, since both warm and cold starts zero out memory.

Incidentally, the PCjr keeps 3412h in location 472–473h after power-on so that inserting or removing a cartridge will cause a warm start rather than a cold start.

Figure 1-8. Map of Typical PC Memory Usage

Using DOS 2.10, no CONFIG.SYS or AUTOEXEC.BAT, 384K memory
All numbers (except K) are hexadecimal

0K		Trap vectors INT 0–7 8259 vectors INT 8–F BIOS vectors INT 10–1F DOS vectors INT 20–2F Assignable INT 40–FF	
1K	400	ROM BIOS communications area	
	500		
1.5K		DOS data areas	
	700		
3.5K		IBMBIO 72F of 1280	DEBUG Search Pattern "VER 2.15"
	E30		
		IBMDOS 3F89 of 4280 Storage chain anchor →5100	DEBUG Search Pattern E9 87 3F 03 44 45 56
19K			← INT 20,25,26,27
	4DB9		
		Device drivers User extensions of IBMBIO such as ANSI.SYS CONFIG.SYS: buffers, files	
21K	53F0	*P Resident COMMAND	← INT 21,22,23,24
24K	5FD0		
		* Master ENVIRONMENT for COMMAND A0h bytes, expandable to 32k if no programs have been made resident	
24.1K	6080		
		* ENVIRONMENT for next program	
	60B0		
		*P Application program or BASIC BASIC Extensions Disk=12k, Advanced=22k	
		Start of BASIC 64k workspace: DS:0 4K interpreter work area	BASIC ← redirected INT 0,4,9,B
		Communications/file buffers	1B,1C, 23,24
		DS:30–31> BASIC program	
		DS:358–9> Scalars, toward FFFF	
		Arrays, toward FFFF	

```
                    ┌─────────────────────────────────────────┐
                    │ Free space                              │
                    │·········································· │
                    │ Strings, toward 0000               ↑    │
                    │·········································· │
                    │ Stack 200 bytes toward 0000             │
      end−3410      ├─────────────────────────────────────────┤     DEBUG Search Pattern:
      Jr:end=112K   │       Transient COMMAND                 │     B4 0E CD 21 2E 8E 1E
          end−FA8   │       error messages                    │
          end−B10   │       internal command table            │
          end−9F6   │       length of last command            │
          end−9F5   │       last command text                 │
          end−8AE   │       formatted filespec                │
      1C000         ├─────────────────────────────────────────┤
      Jr:128K−16K   │       Video buffer in Jr                │
                    ├─────────────────────────────────────────┤
                    │ ::::::End of RAM memory expansion::::::  │
  640K  A0000       ├─────────────────────────────────────────┤
                    │       Video buffers                     │
        C0000       ├─────────────────────────────────────────┤
                    │       PC: ROM expansion                 │
                    │       C8000 XT: Hard disk ROM           │
        D0000       ├─────────────────────────────────────────┤
                    │       Jr: cartridges                    │
                    │       PC: ROM expansion                 │
        E0000       ├─────────────────────────────────────────┤
                    │       Jr: cartridges                    │
                    │       PC: ROM expansion                 │
        F0000       ├─────────────────────────────────────────┤
                    │       Jr: POST/keyboard adventure       │
                    │       PC: ROM expansion                 │
                    │       Jr: cartridges                    │
        F6000       ├─────────────────────────────────────────┤
                    │       Cassette BASIC                    │
                    │       Jr: cartridges                    │
        FE000       ├─────────────────────────────────────────┤
                    │       ROM BIOS                          │
                    │       Jr: cartridges                    │
        100000      └─────────────────────────────────────────┘
```

* = Storage chain block, 10h bytes
P = Program segment prefix, 100h bytes

Program 1-5. Cold Start Invocation

```
100 'MEMCOLD; Call for Power On Self Test (Col
    d Start)
110 '
120 DEF SEG=0:POKE &H472,&H0 :POKE &H473, &H0
    'insure no warm start code
130 DEF SEG=&HFFFF: POST=0 'address of 8088 re
    st jump
140 CALL POST
```

Program 1-6. Warm Start Invocation

```
100 'MEMWARM; Call for Ctrl-Alt-Del (Warm Star
    t / System Reset)
110 '
120 DEF SEG=0:POKE &H472,&H34 :POKE &H473,&H12
    'insure warm start code
130 DEF SEG=&HFFFF: WARM=0 'address of 8088 re
    set jump
140 CALL WARM
```

On the PC and XT (but not the PCjr), both cold and warm starts use the configuration switch(es) to set the configuration and memory size information in locations 410–413h. Locations 415–416h are set to the total amount of memory found by scanning the entire address space for contiguous RAM. The memory configuration switch usage is quite different for the PC1/2 and XT. See the explanation of ports 60–62h in the Port Map Appendix and memory locations 410–416h in the Memory Map Appendix. PCs with a ROM date before October 27, 1982 are not designed to recognize memory above 544K. You can correct this shortcoming. Also, you may want to reduce the time needed to test the entire range of memory with five different bit patterns (see *Technical Reference* manual, page A-15) by setting the configuration switches to some value lower than the amount of memory that is present in the computer.

Once the PC has been booted, replace the values in 413–416h with the true memory sizes, and clear the POST-unseen memory to zeros to prevent parity errors. Then use INT 19 for a hot start, causing DOS to be loaded using the adjusted memory size, without reobtaining the configuration switch settings. More about INT 19 in a minute.

The PCjr and AT don't use configuration switches to determine the amount of memory installed, so we won't be able to speed up their cold start process in this way.

When adding memory to your PC, insure that the motherboard sockets are all filled before adding expansion (I/O channel) memory. Otherwise, intermittent memory parity and disk errors may occur. The chance of parity errors is reduced by using 150 nanosecond RAM rather than the less expensive 200 nanosecond chips.

ROM Expansion

Next, the ROM expansion areas from C0000h through F5800h are checked in 2K increments to determine if any of those areas are filled with ROM-resident programs. They are recognized by the signature of 55AAh in the first two bytes (offsets 0 and 1). The length of the program divided by 512 is stored in byte 2 and is used to compute a checksum of the ROM in 512-byte increments. Then the ROM initialization routine, whose instruction is stored in bytes 3, 4, and 5, with the offset in bytes 4 and 5, is given control. This method is used to cause the hard disk BIOS to be used during the boot of a PC with a hard disk. In the PCjr the BASIC cartridge overlays the address of Cassette BASIC at INT 18 by using this initialization routine.

A PCjr cartridge may contain a list of DOS commands that are scanned when a DOS command is entered. This list redirects a DOS command to the cartridge version. The PCjr BASIC cartridge has the BASIC and BASICA commands in this table to intercept the disk versions of these programs. So by renaming the disk versions of BASIC, you can still get to them if you should want to, but the PCjr BASIC cartridge is still required. IBM PCjr *Colorpaint* uses this table to add the DOS command G to activate the cartridge. PCjr cartridges are designed so that even ROM BIOS may be replaced by a cartridge version since cartridges may occupy whatever address above D0000h they are designed for. The three types of PCjr cartridges are IPLable (automatically started when inserted or power on), DOS (containing commands or programs), and BASIC (programs written in BASIC that start automatically when Cartridge BASIC is started). The PCjr *Technical Reference* manual has an in-depth discussion of cartridge concepts and requirements (see page 2-107).

The Boot Record

Once the POST and memory-clearing routines have finished their tasks, a short beep is sounded and INT 19 is called to load the disk boot record into memory. The PCjr first insures that there is a disk drive and jumps to Cassette or Cartridge BASIC if not. Both the PC and the PCjr try four times to read the disk, then give up and branch to Cassette (or Cartridge) BASIC. If the boot record is missing from the disk (the disk hasn't been formatted), then Cassette or Cartridge BASIC is invoked.

When the INT 19 routine reads the disk, it's using INT 13 to load the special 512 (200h) byte boot sector into location 7C00h. This sector was placed on side 0, track 0, sector 1 by the DOS FORMAT command.

For the XT, INT 19 has been replaced by the initialization code in the hard disk BIOS at C8000h to point to a version of INT 19 in the hard disk BIOS ROM. The INT 13 vector also is replaced with a new INT 13 routine for hard disk I/O that passes disk I/O on to INT 40. The hard disk version of INT 19 attempts to load from the disk first, then the hard disk (cylinder 0, track 0, sector 1 of the DOS partition), then finally jumps to Cassette BASIC.

Now that the boot sector has been loaded into location 7C00h, the INT 19 routine jumps to that location to start the DOS level-dependent boot process. There's nothing that keeps you from having your own version of a boot record that supports your particular needs. You could even have a custom boot record that causes your own disk-resident programs to be loaded instead of DOS, assuming that you have no requirement for DOS.

Figure 1-9 describes how to load the boot record into memory and display its contents using DEBUG.

Figure 1-9. Loading and Displaying the Boot Record Contents

```
l  cs:7c00 0 0 1
u  7c00   7c02    jump to entry point
d  7c03   7c2b    DOS version, disk parameters
u  7c2c   7d7d    main routine, using INT 13 for disk I/O
d  7d7e   7dff    error messages and filenames
```

IBMBIOS and IBMDOS

Once the boot record has been loaded, its task is to initiate a fairly lengthy process of loading the disk-resident BIOS and DOS program modules into the computer to perform their start-up duties. This occurs between the time you hear a beep from the system to when the first A> prompt is seen. Actually, some of this time period is spent in initializing COMMAND.COM, as we shall see in the next section.

The activities that occur during this time are the subject of this section. The DOS 2.0 manual contains a brief description of the actions taken during the boot process by the IBMBIO.COM and IBMDOS.COM modules on page B-1, or page 1-4 of the DOS 2.10 TRM. The additional insight provided by this section complements and enhances that information. You may wish to read the short description in the DOS manual before continuing here, but it's not necessary.

If you used DEBUG to load and examine the contents of the boot record (as described in the previous section), you saw the filenames of IBMBIO.COM and IBMDOS.COM near the end of the boot record. The boot program will check that the files listed there are the first two files in the disk directory, insure that they are in the proper order, and load them into memory.

We'll be using IBMBIO as a nickname for IBMBIO.COM, and IBMDOS for IBMDOS.COM in the remainder of this section. Incidentally, for IBM PC work-a-likes that use Microsoft MS DOS rather than PC DOS, use the name IO.SYS instead of IBMBIO.COM, and MSDOS.SYS instead of IBMDOS.COM.

If you wanted to load different files into memory to serve as your operating system, the filenames for IBMBIO and IBMDOS within the boot record could be changed with DEBUG to reflect the desired files. The files must be the first names in the disk directory; otherwise, a *Nonsystem disk or disk error* message will be displayed by the boot program, and it will not be able to continue the boot process until a correct disk is provided.

Although the FORMAT program sets some special attributes for the IBMBIO and IBMDOS files, they really don't need them. The attributes set by FORMAT make IBMDOS and IBMBIO hidden files (from most commands), read-only (can't be written to), and system files (a system file as opposed to a user file) for them to be used properly by the boot program. IBM has chosen to make them invisible and read-only files so that they will not be inadvertently erased.

The file attribute byte is the byte following the filename in the disk directory. You can use DEBUG to load the disk directory (syntax: **L cs:100 0 5 1**) from a copy of your DOS disk and see the attribute byte of 27h immediately after the IBMBIO.COM filename. By entering 20h into this byte (syntax: **E 10B** then **20**), you can remove the hidden, read-only, and

system file attributes. Then use **W 100 0 5 1** to write the modified directory sector back to the disk and exit DEBUG with **Q**.
Issue a **DIR IBM*.*** command to confirm that the change has
caused the file to now be visible.

The boot record program loads the IBMBIO file into memory starting at absolute location 700h, follows it with the
IBMDOS file, and then jumps to the IBMBIO program's starting point at absolute location 700h so that it may perform its
initialization tasks. Since the contents of these two programs
vary among the versions of DOS, we'll explore them from a
conceptual level rather than getting into the details of each
version.

IBMBIO begins its duties by initializing the devices associated with CON:, AUX:, PRN:, NUL:, COM1:, COM2:, and
LPT1 through LPT3:. These names are established by DOS to
allow the user to refer to standard peripheral devices by name.
For instance, **COPY AUTOEXEC.BAT CON:** causes the
AUTOEXEC.BAT file to be listed on the console (display
screen).

Your DOS manual contains a short description of these
names near the beginning of the manual, in the same section
as the description of filenames. These device names are an
inheritance from the predecessor CPM's CRT:, PTR:, BAT:,
and LPT: names. DOS initializes the devices associated with
the names by calling a set of DOS-provided device driver
routines. A device driver is a special program that is designed
to manage the data flow and control of a peripheral device beyond the level provided in BIOS. You can provide your own
device driver routines for special peripherals that you wish to
attach to your computer.

Next, IBMBIO processes the parameters contained in the
CONFIG.SYS file, if the file is found on the disk. If the file
can't be located, certain defaults are assumed by IBMBIO. The
meaning and defaults for the various CONFIG.SYS parameters
are shown in your DOS 2.0 manual on page 9-3, or DOS
2.10/3.0, page 4-3. Any memory space required to satisfy the
CONFIG.SYS parameters will be reserved from the memory
immediately following the IBMBIO and IBMDOS programs.

A word of caution: *Do not use* the undocumented, but
legal, CONFIG.SYS parameters SWITCHAR and AVAILDEV,
as they are no longer supported in DOS 3.0 and have been
shown to be particularly bug-laden. See the Appendices for a

list of the features and commands added by each release level
of DOS from 1.0 on.

Next, any device driver routines that are specified in
CONFIG.SYS DEVICE= statements are loaded into memory
from disk. Then, each device driver routine is called by
IBMBIO to perform any initialization tasks. The provided pro-
gram ANSI.SYS is an example of a device driver for the con-
sole. You can read more about device driver routines in the
DOS manual (page 14-1 for DOS 2.0, or 3-4 of the DOS 2.10
TRM).

IBMBIO provides an IRET (return from interrupt) instruction at absolute location 847h that is used as a dummy routine
for interrupts that are not used by DOS. This technique allows
the unused interrupt routine to simply do nothing (by virtue
of the IRET instruction) until a user's interrupt routine address
is placed in the interrupt vector. IBMBIO sets INT 1, INT 3,
and INT F to point to this IRET instruction. See the description of these interrupt vectors in the Memory Map Appendix
of this book.

Finally, IBMBIO moves the program IBMDOS down over
the completed IBMBIO initialization routines to minimize
memory space requirements and jumps to the IBMDOS program to perform its own initialization tasks.

IBMDOS begins by initializing the vectors for INT 20–2F
to their proper values.

The next actions performed by IBMDOS are related to
DOS storage and program management functions. This topic
will take us deep into the technical intricacies of DOS program
control blocks. You may wish to only skim the following paragraphs if you are not particularly interested in the details of
this subject. Programmers (both BASIC and machine language)
can gain some powerful techniques by understanding the
structure of the DOS storage and program management control blocks and learning to use the information contained in
them.

A *storage chain anchor* is built by IBMDOS at absolute
location EBCh for DOS 2.0, or F28h for DOS 2.10 (add 70h
for the PCjr, and 80h if a hard disk is installed). This storage
chain anchor is located within IBMDOS and contains the segment number of the first *storage block*. Storage blocks are used
by DOS to record the amount and location of *allocated* memory within the PC and PCjr memory address space. Let's

digress for a moment to look at the control areas (including the storage block) used by DOS to manage programs.

A storage block, a Program Segment Prefix (PSP), and an ENVIRONMENT area are built and maintained by DOS for each program currently resident in the memory address space. The storage block is used to record the address range of memory allocated to the program. It is used by DOS to find the next available area to load a program and to determine if there is enough memory remaining to load the requested program. When an area of memory is in use by a program, it is said to be *allocated*. When the program ends (or explicitly requests less memory), all (or some) of the address range is *deallocated*. Several DOS services support memory allocation and deallocation functions. These will be discussed in a later section.

A storage block contains a pointer to the Program Segment Prefix (PSP) associated with each program. This control block is constructed by IBMDOS for the purpose of providing standardized areas for DOS/program communications. Within the PSP are areas that are used to save interrupt vectors, pass parameters to the program, record disk file directory information, and buffer disk reads and writes. This control block is 100h bytes in length and is followed by the program module loaded by DOS. The contents of the PSP are described in the DOS 2.0 manual on page E-8, or DOS 2.10/3.0 TRM, page 6-5. A following section will discuss the PSP in more detail.

The PSP contains a pointer to an ENVIRONMENT area for the program. This area contains a copy of the current DOS SET, PROMPT, and PATH specified values. The program may examine and modify this information as desired. We'll soon be learning more about this ENVIRONMENT area which follows the program module in memory. But let's return to our examination of storage blocks.

Each storage block is 16 (10h) bytes long, although only 5 bytes are currently used by DOS. The first byte contains 4Dh (a capital *M*) to indicate that it contains a pointer to the next storage block. A 5Ah (capital *Z*) in the first byte of a storage block indicates that there are no more storage blocks following this one (it's called *the end of the chain*). This identifier byte is followed by a 2-byte segment number of the associated Program Segment Prefix (PSP) for the program. The next 2 bytes contain the number of segments that are allocated to the program. If this isn't the last storage block (4Dh *M* is in the indicator byte), then another storage block follows the allocated memory area.

When the storage block contains zero for the number of allocated segments, then no storage is allocated to this block and the next storage block immediately follows this one. This can happen when memory is allocated and deallocated repeatedly during your session on the PC. If the PSP segment number is zero, then the memory described by the storage block is available (deallocated) rather than allocated.

To finish its work, IBMDOS constructs a storage block and PSP for the soon-to-be-loaded COMMAND.COM program. Finally, IBMDOS returns to IBMBIO to cause the COMMAND.COM program to be loaded and jumped to. IBMDOS remains resident in memory to provide high-level function services for the COMMAND.COM program. IBMDOS will do its part in satisfying these requests and will call IBMBIO for lower-level device-oriented functions.

After it jumps to the COMMAND.COM program, IBMBIO stays in memory to provide an interface from IBMDOS to ROM BIOS. Corrections to ROM BIOS errors are implemented in IBMBIO. IBMBIO also includes some error recovery routines and implements the "phantom" disk drives (such as drive B: on a one-drive system).

COMMAND.COM

Normally, COMMAND.COM is loaded and given control of the system by IBMBIO. However, if SHELL was found in CONFIG.SYS, then the program named by that parameter would be used in place of COMMAND.COM. It is permissible to have more than one COMMAND.COM active at one time. Any COMMAND.COM other than that loaded at boot-time is called a *secondary* COMMAND.COM. The next section will explore the reasons for using a secondary COMMAND.COM.

Assuming that this is not a secondary COMMAND.COM (the lack of an ENVIRONMENT address at PSP + 2Ch is what tips off COMMAND.COM that it is not a secondary copy), the program loads the transient portion of itself at the high end of memory. This portion can be overlaid by an application program and is automatically reloaded by the resident portion of COMMAND.COM. The associated master ENVIRONMENT address is built after the resident portion of

COMMAND.COM, the keyboard buffer is cleared, the disk directory is selected, the logged (booted) disk ID is retrieved, and the familiar A> prompt is given. The Break key is now recognized from this point onward.

Finally, either DATE and TIME are executed and the copyright information is displayed, or the AUTOEXEC.BAT file is processed. You can change the name of the .BAT file to be executed by using DEBUG and searching for the string AUTOEXEC.BAT in capitals. You could also make this a hidden, read-only, system file by altering the disk director attribute to 27h rather than 20h. In COMMAND.COM, just above "AUTOEXEC.BAT", you'll find the copyright information to be displayed. You can change these messages to greet your user as appropriate.

Now our PC has been booted and is ready to work for us. COMMAND.COM stays in memory and interacts with the user when a DOS command is entered. INT 22, 23, and 24 vectors point within the resident portion so that the termination of a program can trigger the transient portion to be reloaded if needed. The resident portion also provides the bulk of the error recovery messages such as *Terminate batch job (y/n)?*, *Abort, retry, or ignore?*, *Invalid COMMAND.COM*, and the like. COMMAND.COM implements the redirection of standard input/output devices and piping files.

An unfortunate aspect of COMMAND.COM is its blind desire to reload the transient portion from the booted drive rather than the currently logged drive. By changing the COMSPEC parameter of the ENVIRONMENT using the SET command, you can change the disk and path that are used to reload the transient portion. The concept of a resident and a transient portion is a powerful feature because it allows a full-function user interface module to be available, while not requiring dedicated storage to contain the module and internal commands while they are not being used.

The transient portion prompts the user (using the default or PROMPT specified characters), parses the user- or batch file–entered line, processes the batch commands, executes the internal commands, and contains (in about the last 1600 bytes of memory) the program loader. This portion searches for .COM and .EXE files to be loaded and executed for the user. The scan order for commands is such that Cartridge DOS commands are searched for, then the internal command table,

.COM files, .EXE files, and finally .BAT files. So XYZ.BAT will never be found if it is on a disk with XYZ.COM, and DIR.COM could never be found since DIR is an internal command.

The loader uses DOS function 4Bh to load and execute the requested program. It's possible to use this function in your programs to cause another program to be loaded and executed ("spawned"), using your files if desired, then return to your program. We'll be discussing this feature more in a moment.

Secondary COMMAND.COM

One of the problems with batch files is that you can't execute nested batch files. Try creating these two batch files and executing the first as follows ([F6] means to press the F6 function key):

A>COPY CON 11.BAT
chkdsk
22
date [F6]

A>COPY CON 22.BAT
set [F6]

A>11

We would like to see the following order of commands: chkdsk, set, date. But, in fact, the 11.BAT date command is never issued because once the 22.BAT set command was processed, COMMAND.COM found that the batch file that it was tracking reached the end of file. COMMAND.COM can only track one batch file at a time.

The ability to nest batch files can be gained by invoking another copy of COMMAND.COM to track the lower level of batch file. The method used to invoke this "secondary" COMMAND.COM is documented in the 2.0 DOS manual starting on page 10-9, DOS 2.10, page 1-11, and DOS 3.0, page 6-9. The DOS manual does not, however, mention that it is useful in nesting batch files. The only mention of invoking another batch file is that it can be done at the end of a batch file being processed. That's not nearly as powerful.

To apply the method to the above example, try the following revision:

```
A>COPY CON 11.BAT
chkdsk
command /c 22
date [F6]
A>COPY CON 22.BAT
set [F6]
A>11
```

That solved the problem, and now the 11.BAT date command is performed.

You should know a few facts about using multiple copies of COMMAND.COM. Obviously, COMMAND.COM will need to be available on the same disk as the nested batch files; otherwise, you'll receive a *Bad command or file name* error message. Each level of COMMAND.COM that is invoked in this manner requires 17K (DOS 2.0/2.10) or 22K (DOS 3.0) of memory while that copy is in memory. The copy is discarded after processing its parameter line, assuming that the /C parameter is used. COMMAND.COM detects that it is a secondary copy by observing that the pointer to an ENVIRONMENT has been filled in at PSP+2Ch.

It is also possible to invoke a secondary COMMAND.COM from within an application program. This allows the execution of a batch file (which in turn may cause other batch files or programs to be executed) by an application program with eventual return to the program. You can read more about invoking a secondary COMMAND.COM from your program on page F-1 of the DOS 2.0 manual and page 7-3 of the DOS 2.10 DOS *Technical Reference* manual. DOS function 4Bh is discussed on page D-44 of the DOS 2.0 manual, 5-42 of the DOS 2.10, and page 5-124 of the DOS 3.0 *Technical Reference* manuals.

Batch File Modification
Another useful tool with batch files is the ability to modify a batch file that is currently being processed by using a program executed in the batch file. The modifications would logically occur on lines that are yet to be executed. Of more practical use is the addition of lines on the end of a temporary copy of the master batch file.

Another technique to consider is the execution of another batch file that the program has built by including its name after the program's name in the batch file. This has the advantage of allowing the master batch file to remain unaltered by the program, but it is more limited in the number of programs that can be called. Another disadvantage is that the associated temporary batch filenames can get unmanageable in a complex situation. The addition-to-a-copy method is my preference.

Figure 1-10 and Program 1-7 demonstrate this batch file modification technique. The COPY statement in the batch file is used to make a copy of itself so that the original batch file won't be changed. Then it invokes this temporary copy (passing any entered parameters) *without* using the command so that the master batch file will not be returned to when the temporary copy ends. We are now using a previous limitation to our advantage. The IF statement before the COPY skips the copy and invocation process in the temporary version.

A batch file can be coded to perform the function shown here, without the need for the program at all. Also the date sort does not optimally handle the month-date-year format. You may want to add another program to read and format the date before sorting. The point here is not that this is the only way to achieve the function provided by the batch file and BASIC program combination. Rather, a BASIC program can be used to modify a temporary copy of a batch file while it is executing. This opens up a whole new realm of possibilities since the batch file facility does not provide many functions that BASIC has, including prompting and acting upon the response.

Enter the batch file, Figure 1-10, using your word processor, EDLIN, or the DOS COPY function; enter Program 1-7 while in BASIC. Note that you must have the DOS files SORT.EXE and MORE.COM present on the disk and you must name the BASIC program MEMBAT.BAS and the batch file MEMBAT.BAT. To see the demonstration, enter MEMBAT from the DOS A> prompt.

Be aware that DOS 3.0 has tightened the rules about comment lines in batch files. Periods, quotes, and brackets are no longer recognized as REM substitutes at the beginning of a line.

Figure 1-10. MEMBAT.BAT

echo off
if %0 == tempbat goto :tempbat
copy %0.bat tempbat.bat
tempbat %1 %2 %3 %4 %5 %6 %7 %8 %9
rem *** temporary, will not return to this master
:tempbat
rem *** this must be the temporary batch file
basic membat
rem *** above program will add needed lines[F6]

Program 1-7. MEMBAT.BAS

For error-free program entry, be sure to use "The Automatic Proofreader," Appendix H.

```
HC 100 'MEMBAT; Demonstrate BASIC adding to batch
       file
GG 110 '
KO 120 OPEN "tempbat.bat" FOR APPEND AS #1
HG 130 ' PRINT#1,CHR$(13);CHR$(10) ' only needed
       if "copy con" created .bat
PF 140 CLS: PRINT"SORTED DIRECTORY WANTED BY WHIC
       H FIELD?"
HK 150 LOCATE 3,10: PRINT"D = Date"
DM 160 LOCATE 5,10: PRINT"S = Size"
NE 170 LOCATE 7,10: PRINT"N = Name"
JO 180 INPUT K$: K=INSTR("SsDdNn",K$): ON K GOTO
       210,210,220,220,230,230
HF 190 BEEP:GOTO 180
GF 200 '
MK 210 PRINT#1,"dir %1!sort /r /+16!more";: GOTO
       240
LF 220 PRINT#1,"dir %1!sort /r /+24!more"; :GOTO
       240
MN 230 PRINT#1,"dir %1!sort /+1!more";: GOTO 240
FK 240 CLOSE 1
IK 250 CLS: SYSTEM
```

Application Program Environmentals

We'll be discussing the BASIC program's environment in a
following section, but first let's understand the memory
environment that BASIC and our own .COM and .EXE programs inherit when invoked by COMMAND.COM or another
program.

The loader portion of COMMAND.COM is used to load
.COM and .EXE modules into memory, prepare the environ-

ment for the program, and execute the module. It is possible to invoke this function from a program by using DOS function 4Bh and to specify whether the loaded module is to be executed. This feature allows a program to cause overlays of routines or data tables to be made available to a program.

The loader always allocates memory for a module (.COM or .EXE) from the lowest numbered unallocated segment. All remaining memory is then available to the new module. The storage block for the new module (at PSP − 10h) and the PSP itself contain the amount of memory available. The storage block has a count of allocated segments in the fourth and fifth bytes, while the PSP contains the number of available bytes in the current segment at offset 6. There are additional memory considerations for invoked modules (see DOS 2.10 *Technical Reference* manual, page 10-1, and DOS 3.0 *Technical Reference* manual, page 10-3).

In order for the module to execute another module, some memory must be freed by using DOS function 49h or 4Ah. This action causes a storage block to be created that marks the freed area as unallocated. Then, DOS function 4Bh (load and execute module) will allocate and use that area of memory. For the *load-but-don't-execute* overlay option of function 4Bh, the invoker must preallocate the memory for the module to be loaded.

A "well-behaved" invoked module (not an overlay) will free as much storage as possible so that other modules will fit in memory, will free all memory allocated by it before exiting, and will exit using DOS function 4Ch, passing a return code to the invoking module. The invoker can retrieve this return code by using DOS function 4Dh. See DOS 2.0 manual, pages D-43 through D-48; DOS 2.10 *Technical Reference* manual, pages 5-41 through 5-45; and DOS 3.0 *Technical Reference* manual, pages 5-121 through 5-130.

When the loader processes an .EXE module, the loader resolves all necessary relocation and loads the module at the low or high end of the needed memory size for the module. .EXE modules do not necessarily own the remainder of memory, only the amount required to contain the module. For additional .EXE file information, see DOS 2.0 manual, page H-1, and DOS 2.10/3.0 *Technical Reference* manual, page 9-3.

A resident COMMAND.COM causes a loaded module to follow it in memory as illustrated in Figure 1-8, "Map of

Typical PC Memory Usage." If the loaded module executes another module, that second module will follow the first in memory, and so forth. Whenever the lowest module is finished, it returns to the invoking module because PSP + Ah has been set to point to the next instruction in the invoker module. The PSP of the invoked module is used to save the invoker's INT 22–24 vectors, which are restored when the invoked module ends.

Several control blocks are formatted and made available to the invoked (nonoverlay) module by DOS function 4Bh (which COMMAND.COM uses to invoke our modules). Foremost of the control blocks is the PSP which is pointed to by the DS register. This control block is 100h bytes long and is preceded by a 10h byte storage block. Your program module normally follows this control block. A layout of the PSP can be found in your DOS 2.0 manual on page E-8, or DOS 2.10/3.0 *Technical Reference* manual, page 6-5. This section of your DOS manual provides valuable information about the program environmentals.

The PSP contains a default disk buffer (DTA), two file control block (FCB) areas, a formatter parameter area, a pointer to the ENVIRONMENT area for the program, a long call to DOS (for portability), and save areas for the invoker's INT 22–24. A few amplifications on the layout of the PSP are needed.

BASIC uses the PSP for its own data storage purposes, and some fields are not as described in the PSP layout. (See the BASIC memory map in the Appendices.) The top-of-memory word at offset 2 is normally the segment number of the last segment usable, until memory is freed by an explicit DOS call or when the program is made resident using function 31h. The long call to DOS (five bytes) is actually at offset 50h, not at offset 6 as shown in the *Technical Reference* manual. The word at offset 6 that contains the number of bytes available in the segment is usually FFF0h, because of the 10h bytes used by the storage block. The word at offset 16h is normally the invoker's PSP segment. In DOS 3.0, the zero marking the end of the ENVIRONMENT is followed by a path and filename that was used to load the program. This makes it easier for the program to locate its data files. Changes made to a program's ENVIRONMENT will not be reflected in the master ENVIRONMENT, but they will be present for invoked modules.

Resident Programs

INT 27 (or preferably DOS function 31h so that a return code can be set) can be used to cause a program to stay resident after it has finished execution. The size of the module is passed back from the program and COMMAND.COM insures that this program becomes logically a part of DOS. This simply means its storage block, PSP, and program module remain in memory and the area is not reassigned.

This is a powerful facility that can be used by modules that are intercepting other INT vectors in order to preprocess the interrupt. CHAR28, in Chapter 4, illustrates the use of this function for the purpose of loading video PEL (picture element) map information.

A few considerations apply to resident programs. To prevent the module from being made resident more than once per session, leave a signature somewhere that will be detected by the module, causing it not to reinstall itself again. INT 60–67 can be used for this type of information. If INT vectors are being intercepted, you will probably want to save the original contents of the vector so that you can branch to it after your routine finishes processing. DOS allows larger programs to be made resident if function 31h is used. You will want to provide a stack area for the program since the default size of eight words is probably not enough. Obviously, care must be taken to save and restore the registers since the use of the routine must be transparent. DOS cannot be called from a resident program that processes a timer interrupt.

If you install a resident program, it is wise to provide a switch that will allow the program to deactivate itself, since you may want to turn it off during your session. At that time, release the storage used by the program by using function 4Ah. This will allow the ENVIRONMENT to expand if no other resident programs are currently loaded (PRINT, GRAPHICS, and MODE are resident programs). If any other resident programs exist, releasing memory may have no apparent effect since resident programs might be after the released memory. Programs that use this feature must not be linked with the /HIGH option.

Memory Mapping Programs

To help you better understand vectors and allow them to be compared to vectors from a previous hardware or memory environment, some sample programs are provided. With these programs, you can examine the changes to memory that take place as you add hardware to your computer, specify different CONFIG.SYS options, or use a different version of DOS, BASIC, or even an application program.

The programs should be used to determine the vector contents when consulting the Memory Map Appendix, since differing hardware/software configurations will affect the contents of low memory. I keep a VECTORSD and several VECTCMPR listings (with BASIC, with different DOS versions, with differing hardware/memory options) right next to my computer for instant access to this information.

The programs map each four bytes of a memory range in hexadecimal starting with the address, the contents of the four bytes, the segment:offset represented, the absolute address, and the ASCII translation of the characters. The segment:offset and absolute address are useful in determining if the four bytes actually contain a vector. If not, the hex and ASCII representation of the bytes can be used to examine the contents of the four bytes. Figure 1-11 shows a sample listing. In all these programs, the output may be directed to SCRN, LPT1, or PRN rather than to a file. To compare vector images, an output file must be created.

Figure 1-11. Sample Vector Program Output

```
Segment=0h; Environment description placed on this line
0000   F6  06  0C  06   060C:06F6  0067B6   'y,:.'
0004   D6  FE  00  F0   F000:FED6  0FFED6   'V..p'
0008   E4  FE  00  F0   F000:FEE4  0FFEE4   'd..p'
000C   D6  FE  00  F0   F000:FED6  0FFED6   'V..p'
0010   D6  FE  00  F0   F000:FED6  0FFED6   'V..p'
0014   E6  FE  00  F0   F000:FEE6  0FFEE6   'f..p'
0018   D6  FE  00  F0   F000:FED6  0FFED6   'V..p'
001C   D6  FE  00  F0   F000:FED6  0FFED6   'V..p'
```

Program 1-8 is used to capture the memory image while BASIC is active. Since BASIC changes some low memory vectors (see the Memory Map Appendix), this program captures those changes.

The vectors may be desired in non-BASIC modified form. Program 1-9 will format these vectors from the output created by using DEBUG>*filename*, then the appropriate display command (such as D 0:0 L500), and finally Q to send the data to the file and exit DEBUG. You will have to type blindly while DEBUG output is redirected to a file.

For example, this sequence of keystrokes will produce a file called TEST with the contents of the first 128 bytes of segment 0:

DEBUG>TEST [Enter]
D 0:0 L80 [Enter]
Q [Enter]

Remember, you will be typing the second and third lines blind and you must have DEBUG.COM on your disk. Enter TYPE TEST to see the contents of this file.

Program 1-10, the final program in this series, compares the vectors captured by the other two programs. Usually, the output of this program is substantially shorter than either of the two input files, unless dissimilar areas are compared. It can compare the output of VECTORSD with the output of VECTORSB since both produce output of the same format. Be careful when changing either program to insure that this feature remains. Figure 1-12 shows a sample output from this program. The data is illustrative, not actual. Notice how the

Figure 1-12. Output of Comparing Captured Vectors

file 1 = temp
file 2 = tempd

Segment=0h; From BASIC
From Debug

```
001C E2 30 15 0C 0C15:30E2 00F232 'b0..'
001C 94 FE 00 F0 F000:FE94 0FFE94 ...p

0024 60 30 15 0C 0C15:3060 00F1B0 "0..'
0024 06 01 EF 0B 0BEF:0106 00BFF6 ..o.

006C 27 21 15 0C 0C15:2127 00E277 ''!..'
006C 00 01 D8 05 05D8:0100 005E80 ..X.

007C C0 34 15 0C 0C15:34C0 00F610 '.4..'
007C 00 00 00 00 0000:0000 000000 ....

0088 8B 88 15 0C 0C15:888B 0149DB '....'
0088 4A 02 05 0C 0C05:024A 00C29A J...

0090 65 88 15 0C 0C15:8865 0149B5 'e...'
0090 A8 04 2F 0B 0B2F:04A8 00B798 (./.
```

lines from BASIC-captured vectors have quotes around the ASCII portion, while debug output does not. This is a giveaway to which method was used to capture the data. Another giveaway is *Segment=* in the environment description line.

As can be seen from running the programs, the vectors that BASIC temporarily takes over are INT 0, 4, 9, B, 1B, 1C, 23, and 24.

Program 1-8. Capture Vectors from BASIC

For error-free program entry, be sure to use "The Automatic Proofreader," Appendix H.

```
DN 100 'VECTORSB: read and format low storage fro
        m basic
PG 110 '         output filename can be SCRN:, LPT1:
        , etc
HI 120 '
PL 130 ASCI$="...."
GE 140 INPUT "Output file name? ",FILEO$
DK 150 OPEN FILEO$  FOR OUTPUT AS 2
IC 160 INPUT "Segment (0-FFFF)";SSEG$: SSEG=VAL("
        &h"+SSEG$)
BJ 170 INPUT "Starting offset (0-FFFF)";SOFF$: SO
        FF=VAL("&h"+SOFF$)
ID 180 IF SOFF <0 THEN SOFF=(32769!+(SOFF))+32767
        ' since over &h7fff is neg
PG 190 INPUT "Last Offset (0-FFFF)";EOFF$: EOFF=V
        AL("&h"+EOFF$)
PE 200 IF EOFF <0 THEN EOFF=(32769!+(EOFF))+32767
        ' since over &h7fff is neg
KO 210 INPUT "Enter descriptive line";DESC$
PG 220 PRINT #2,"Segment="HEX$(SSEG)"h;  ";DESC$
KJ 230 MAX=32767*2+1
JL 240 IF SSEG <0 THEN SSEG=(32769!+(SSEG))+32767
        ' since over &h7fff is neg
FK 250 DEF SEG=SSEG
KK 260 FOR ADDR=SOFF TO EOFF STEP 4
HG 270   CSH=PEEK(ADDR+3):CSHC=CSH AND &H7F: IF CS
          HC>32 THEN MID$(ASCI$,4,1)=CHR$(CSHC) ELSE
          MID$(ASCI$,4,1)="."
LG 280   CSL=PEEK(ADDR+2):CSLC=CSL AND &H7F: IF CS
          LC>32 THEN MID$(ASCI$,3,1)=CHR$(CSLC) ELSE
          MID$(ASCI$,3,1)="."
BO 290   IPH=PEEK(ADDR+1):IPHC=IPH AND &H7F: IF IP
          HC>32 THEN MID$(ASCI$,2,1)=CHR$(IPHC) ELSE
          MID$(ASCI$,2,1)="."
EL 300   IPL=PEEK(ADDR+0):IPLC=IPL AND &H7F: IF IP
          LC>32 THEN MID$(ASCI$,1,1)=CHR$(IPLC) ELSE
          MID$(ASCI$,1,1)="."
```

```
AE 310    PRINT #2,RIGHT$("000"+HEX$(ADDR),4);" "
      ;     'current offset
CC 320    IPL$=RIGHT$("0"+HEX$(IPL),2)
IA 330    IPH$=RIGHT$("0"+HEX$(IPH),2)
MN 340    CSL$=RIGHT$("0"+HEX$(CSL),2)
CL 350    CSH$=RIGHT$("0"+HEX$(CSH),2)
DB 360    PRINT #2,IPL$" "IPH$" "CSL$" "CSH$" ";
JF 370    PRINT #2,CSH$;CSL$":"IPH$;IPL$" ";
                  ' cs:ip image
MN 380    SEG=(CSH*256+CSL)
PB 390    DSP=IPH* 256 + IPL
GO 400    VEC=SEG*16+DSP: HI=INT(VEC/MAX): REST=H
      I*MAX: LO=VEC-REST-HI
GG 410    PRINT #2,RIGHT$("000000"+HEX$(HI)+RIGHT
      $("000000"+HEX$(LO),4),6); ' absolute addr
      ess
GD 420 PRINT#2," '"ASCI$"'"
MC 430 '  CC$=INKEY$: IF CC$="" GOTO 345 for line
      -at-a-time
OI 440 NEXT
FJ 450 CLOSE 2: END
```

Program 1-9. Capture Vectors from DEBUG

For error-free program entry, be sure to use "The Automatic Proofreader," Appendix H.

```
KB 100 'VECTORSD: read and format debug output
EK 105 ' WARNING debug must have been run in 80 c
      olumn mode
AB 106 '     for VECTCMPR to properly work
IJ 107 '
PM 110 INPUT "Input file name?   ",FILEI$
GA 120 INPUT "Output file name?  ",FILEO$
CG 130 OPEN FILEO$  FOR OUTPUT AS 2
NN 140 INPUT "Description of environment?",DESC$
NP 160 PRINT #2,DESC$
LC 170 OPEN FILEI$ FOR INPUT AS #1 LEN=80
JO 180    MAX=32767*2+1
IL 190 IF EOF(1) THEN GOTO 410
AA 200 LINE INPUT#1,X$
AG 210 IF LEFT$(X$,1)="-" GOTO 190   'bypass debug
        prompts
KH 220 IF X$="" GOTO 190 'skip blank lines
EH 230 OFFSET$=MID$(X$,6,4)
IK 240 OFFSET=VAL("&h"+OFFSET$)
NC 250 FOR X=0 TO 3
AB 260    CUROFF=OFFSET+(X*4)
CB 270      PRINT #2,RIGHT$("000"+HEX$(CUROFF),4);"
      ";       'current offset
DJ 280      IPL$=MID$(X$,12+(X*12),2):IPL=VAL("&h"+
      IPL$)
```

41

```
PB 290     IPH$=MID$(X$,15+(X*12),2):IPH=VAL("&h"+
           IPH$)
KM 300     CSL$=MID$(X$,18+(X*12),2):CSL=VAL("&h"+
           CSL$)
KN 310     CSH$=MID$(X$,21+(X*12),2):CSH=VAL("&h"+
           CSH$)
ND 320     PRINT #2,IPL$;" ";IPH$;" ";CSL$;" ";CSH
           $;" ";     ' image of 4 bytes
JN 330     PRINT #2,CSH$;CSL$":"IPH$;IPL$" ";
                     ' cs:ip image
LF 340     SEG=(CSH*256+CSL)
PJ 350     DSP=IPH* 256 + IPL
HJ 360     VEC=SEG*16+DSP:HI=INT(VEC/MAX):REST=HI*
           MAX:LO=VEC-REST-HI
HG 370     PRINT #2,RIGHT$("00"+HEX$(HI)+RIGHT$("0
           000"+HEX$(LO),4),6); ' absolute
GJ 380     PRINT #2," ";MID$(X$,62+(X*4),4)    'sh
           ow ascii translation
OB 390 NEXT
GC 400 GOTO 190
EB 410 CLOSE 2: END
```

Program 1-10. Comparing Captured Vectors

For error-free program entry, be sure to use "The Automatic Proofreader," Appendix H.

```
KD 100 'VECTCMPR: compare two vector files, notin
       g differences
HK 110 '       you may use scrn: or lpt1: for outp
       ut file
HI 120 '
PK 130 INPUT "Input file one name?    ",FILE1$
GK 140 INPUT "Input file two name?    ",FILE2$
GG 150 INPUT "Output file name?   ",FILE0$
FM 160 OPEN FILE0$   FOR OUTPUT AS 3
GC 170 OPEN FILE1$ FOR INPUT AS #1 LEN=80
FE 180 PRINT #3,"file 1 = "FILE1$
IH 190 PRINT #3,"file 2 = "FILE2$
MO 200 PRINT #3," "
IE 210 OPEN FILE2$ FOR INPUT AS #2 LEN=80
ID 220     MAX=32767*2+1
DH 230 GOTO 420
LJ 240 'IF LEFT$(X$,1)="-" GOTO 400
BE 250 'IF LEFT$(X$,1)="*" THEN Z$=X$: Z=1: GOSUB
           350: GOTO 400
OL 260 'IF LEFT$(Y$,1)="-" GOTO 410
LK 270 'IF LEFT$(Y$,1)="*" THEN Z$=Y$: Z=2: GOSUB
           350: GOTO 410
FE 280 IF X$="" GOTO 400    'skip empty lines
HC 290 IF Y$="" GOTO 410    'skip empty lines
```

```
GO 300 IF LEFT$(X$,34)=LEFT$(Y$,34) GOTO 420 'omi
       t asci translation in test
HA 310 Z$=X$: Z=1: GOSUB 350
JI 320 Z$=Y$: Z=2: GOSUB 350
IA 330 PRINT #3," ": GOTO 420
QK 340 '--- print selected line ---
PF 350 PRINT #3,Z$
NJ 360 RETURN
MN 370 '--- all done ---
AG 380 CLOSE 1,2,3: END
II 390 '
OK 400 GOSUB 440: GOTO 240      'read #1
CD 410 GOSUB 470: GOTO 240      'read #2
OC 420 GOSUB 440: GOSUB 470: GOTO 240 'read both
BI 430 '--- read file one ---
HA 440 IF EOF(1) GOTO 380
DO 450 LINE INPUT#1,X$: RETURN
BL 460 '--- read file two ---
IC 470 IF EOF(2) GOTO 380
FG 480 LINE INPUT#2,Y$: RETURN
```

BASIC Internal Areas

BASIC partitions the available memory into several discrete
areas that are used to contain certain types of data. The .COM
file that contains the extensions to Cassette BASIC is (as always) located immediately after the PSP. The PCjr contains
the .COM equivalent extensions in the cartridge, leaving more
memory available for the user's BASIC program. This is
particularly important for a 64K PCjr.

   The workspace that BASIC uses to store a program and its
associated variables begins after the BASIC extensions. The
segment number of the beginning of this workspace is stored
in locations 510–511h. Program 1-11 will display this segment
number and set a variable to the value that corresponds to the
default DEF SEG. Even though the CS register is called the
code segment register, BASIC uses this register as its own data
segment register.

Program 1-11. Determining the DEF SEG Segment Number

```
100 'BASDS: display the BASIC data segment add
    ress
110 '
120 DEF SEG=0:X=PEEK(&H510)+PEEK(&H511)*256
130 PRINT "BASIC's data segment begins at ";HE
    X$(X);":0000 or decimal"X*16
```

43

The first 4K of memory in the BASIC workspace is used to store information needed by the BASIC interpreter during the course of its work. This area contains many interesting bits of information as shown in Table 1-2. You can undoubtedly find other important data in this area by observing changes in this area while running programs or direct BASIC commands.

Table 1-2. Interpreter Work Areas

Offset	Length	Contents
02Ch	2	Offset of stack end
02Eh	2	Line number of line being executed
030h	2	Offset of program text
04Eh	1	Character color in graphics modes, default=3
05Ch	1	Number of lines before scrolling screen
06Ah	1	Keyboard buffer contents (0=none, 1=some)
1F7h	256	Keyboard buffer
30Ah	2	Offset of string space start
32Fh	2	Offset of string space end
347h	2	Line number of last error
350h	2	DEF SEG segment override
356h	2	Offset of program text end
358h	2	Offset of scalar variables
35Ah	2	Offset of array variables
35Ch	2	Offset of free space
464h	1	FEh if program protected
4F1h	11	Last file name
650h		Key titles
702h	2	Segment number of BASIC PSP
F79h	2	Random number seed

A PSP segment number is included in this area at location 702–3h. By referencing that segment and looking into the formatted parameter areas, you can obtain runtime parameters from the BASIC start-up line. If this line was entered to start BASIC—"BASIC ABC DEF XYZ"—then program ABC would be run, with DEF and XYZ left in the parameter areas for the ABC program to act upon as desired.

The various pointers contained in the interpreter work area divide up the BASIC workspace into partitions for data storage, as illustrated in Figure 1-13. This diagram is an amplification of that found in the 2.0 or PCjr BASIC manual on page I-2 or the DOS 3.0 BASIC manual on page B-29.

Figure 1-13. BASIC Workspace

DOS 2.10
24K-

*   ENVIRONMENT for BASIC
*P BASIC Extensions Disk=12K, Advanced=22K
Start of BASIC 64K workspace: (/M or CLEAR may be used to size) DS:0   4K interpreter work area
Communications (/C) buffers 180h default size
RS-232 routines 5E0h default size
File (/F) control blocks 234h default size
File (/S) random buffers 80h default size
DS:30–31>   BASIC program text
DS:358–9>   Scalars, toward FFFF
DS:35A–B>   Arrays, toward FFFF
DS:35C–D>   Free space
DS:32F–0>   Strings, toward 0000 DS:30A–B>
DS:2C–D>   Stack 200h bytes (/M or CLEAR may be used to size)
Unused and available

← redirected
INT 0,4,9,B,
1B,1C,
23,24

*   = Storage chain block, 10h bytes
P   = Program segment prefix, 100h bytes

If we can determine the DEF SEG value, which is the start
of the BASIC workspace, we can also determine the address
for the end of the workspace. This is a very useful thing to
know, since it tells us where we can BLOAD or POKE machine
language subroutines without destroying any of BASIC's data.

If the default DEF SEG number is now known to be contained in variable X by PEEKing the value from absolute locations 510–511h, then HI.SEG=X+&h1000 gives us the segment number that is just beyond the BASIC 64K workspace and HI.ADDR=HI.SEG * 16 yields the address of the first byte beyond BASIC. If you have shortened the workspace size with CLEAR or BASIC start-up options, simply adjust 1000h by the appropriate number of segments.

The next thing that should be done is to determine if there is enough memory installed to store our machine language routine (or routines) above the BASIC workspace. If not, we can resize BASIC to provide room for the routine. Absolute location 413–4h contains the number of Kbytes of usable memory. So DEF SEG=0:MEM.SIZE=PEEK(&h413)+256* PEEK(&h414) gives us the amount of memory available. If HI.ADDR plus the size of our routine exceeds MEM.SIZE, then we need to resize BASIC. Otherwise, our routine will fit above BASIC.

To resize BASIC to make room for the routines, simply calculate the override value for the 65,535-byte default workspace size by subtracting the length of the routines from 65,535 and use CLEAR n, where n is the recalculated workspace size in bytes (*not* segments).

Program Statement Storage

Your program is reduced in size by *tokenizing* the BASIC keywords in the text. Tokens are one- or two-byte shorthand codes for the BASIC keywords and are categorized by the version of BASIC that they are implemented in. Tokenized BASIC text is stored in the BASIC workspace, and the beginning of the program is pointed to by offset 30–31h in the interpreter work area. The program lines are stored in the format shown in Figure 1-14. This format is common to Microsoft BASIC implementations on various computers. A list of the BASIC tokens is presented in the Appendices. You can use the list to find the token for a keyword or the keyword for a token.

BASIC Variable Storage

Program variables are stored after the text of the program and are partitioned into types of data. First come the scalar (non-array) variables, the first of which is pointed to by DS:358h. Next is the area pointed to by DS:35Ah where array variables

Figure 1-14. BASIC Line Storage Format

NL	NM	LL	LM	.... tokens and text	0

NL   Offset of next line, LSB
NM   Offset to next line, MSB
LL   Line number, LSB
LM   Line number, MSB
0   end of line marker

If NL and NM both contain zeros, then that is end of program with no BASIC text on that line.

are saved. The entire contents of this area must be pushed upward whenever another scalar variable is added to the variable pool below it.

From the bottom of the stack area, the string variables are saved, but the scalar variable pool holds a pointer to the actual string contents. This string pointer can also point to the string in the program text, saving space in the string variable pool if the string has not been modified by the program. The string variable pool has two pointers, DS:30Ah which points to the highest address used in the pool and DS:32Fh which points to the lowest address. Remember that the string variables grow downward into the free area while the scalar and arrays grow upward into it. The free area is pointed to by DS:35Ch for the low address and DS:32Fh for the upper boundary.

The BASIC manual contains a general description of the variable storage format on page I-4, but some additional facts will prove useful. The common 4- to 42-byte header used for all variables is shown in Figure 1-15. We see that 1-character variable names save no storage in the variable pool compared with 2-character names. Variable names are unique up to 40 characters.

Integer variables (type 2, type declaration %) are stored in LSB/MSB format. The high-order bit is used to denote a negative value, in which case the number has been complemented (FFFFh = −1, FFFE= −2, etc). The range of integer variables is −32,768 to 32,767.

Figure 1-15. Standard Variable Header

0	1	2	3	4		4+Lr

Ty	N1	N2	Lr	remainder of variable name	Value

Ty   Type code of variable, length of data field
       2 integer
       3 string
       4 single precision
       8 double precision
N1   First character of variable name
       Type declaration characters (% $ #) are not stored as part of
       the variable name
N2   Second character of variable name
Lr   Length of remainder of name or zero
       Remainder of name is stored with the high-order bit of each
       byte turned on.
       The value for the variable begins at offset 4+Lr

String variables (type 3, type declaration $) contain a one-byte length code followed by a two-byte offset to the string in the string pool or BASIC program.

Single-precision variables (type 4, type declaration !) use three bytes (24 bits) to contain the exponent with right-to-left significance. The third byte high-order bit is the sign of the mantissa, 0 signifying positive. The fourth byte contains the binary exponent (the number of digits to the left of the binary point before a 1 is found) with the high-order bit turned on.

Double-precision variables (type 8, type declaration #) extend the single-precision variable's three-byte mantissa to seven bytes (56 bits). The eighth byte has the same format as the single-precision fourth byte.

Array variables use the standard variable header, but after any remaining characters in the name are the fields shown in Figure 1-16 followed by the data in the array.

The size of each element in the array is indicated by the type code in the variable header. The arrangement of the data values within the variable descriptor is rather interesting. Consider the example array G(1,1,2). First, be aware that Dnz, Dny, and Dnx will appear as 3,2,2 since dimensions include a zero numbered element. The elements would be in the following order: G(0,0,0), G(1,0,0), G(0,1,0), G(1,1,0), G(0,0,1), G(1,0,1), G(0,1,1), G(1,1,1), G(0,0,2), G(1,0,2), G(0,1,2), and G(1,1,2).

Strings are stored in the string variable pool with no intervening control information. For example, K$="abcde"+" " :K1$="fgh"+"i" is stored as "fghiabcde" in the string pool. The strings would be located in the string pool since the program has modified them. The string pool is built downward from the top, so the strings are in reverse order from their definition sequence.

Figure 1-16. Array Dimension Headers

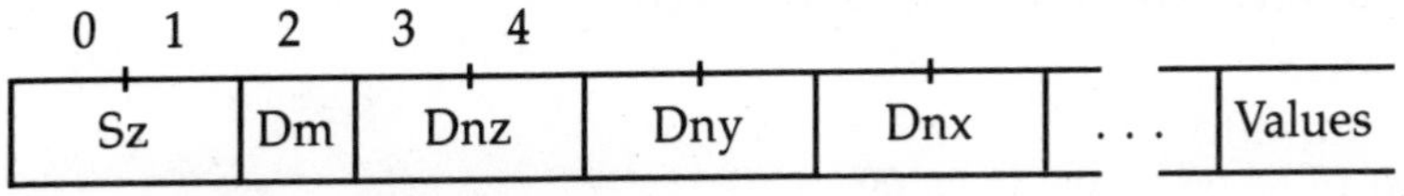

```
   0   1   2    3     4
 +----+---+-----+------+------+-----+--------+
 | Sz |Dm | Dnz | Dny  | Dnx  | ... | Values |
 +----+---+-----+------+------+-----+--------+
```

Sz Number of bytes in array
Dm Number of dimensions
Dnz Size of last dimension
Dny Size of next-to-last dimension
Dnx Size of second-from-last dimension

Protected Programs

BASIC provides a protection feature that allows a program to be saved in protected mode which prevents examination or modifications to the program. The BASIC manual states that there is no way to unprotect a protected program. POKE is not allowed from the immediate mode when a protected program is in memory. However, we will see how a program can protect or unprotect itself if desired (such as when the correct password has been entered) and how you can unprotect any BASIC program. The key to protection is the byte at DS:464h and the first byte of a BASIC program saved on disk.

When a protected BASIC program is saved, the text of the program is enciphered so that simply changing the one-byte indicator at the start of the file is not enough to unprotect or protect the BASIC program. The first byte of the BASIC created file is FFh for normal program text, FEh for a protected program, or FDh for BLOAD files. Programs saved with the ASCII option and data files do not have a leading byte that describes the file format.

The BLOAD command is the key to unprotecting. By using BLOAD, we can overlay the byte at DS:464h that indicates that the program is protected. Then we can list, change, and save the program as if it were never protected.

First, we must create a key file that will unlock a protected program. We'll use DEBUG to do this, as shown in Figure 1-17. The entered byte meanings are as follows: FDh indicates a BLOAD file, 66 66 is a dummy segment number, 64 04 is the offset of location 464h, 01 00 is the one-byte length of the following data, 00 is the new value to be placed in DS:464h that indicates the program is not protected, and 1A is the standard BASIC end-of-file marker. This is the format of all BLOAD files.

Figure 1-17. Creating SESAME.BLD

```
A>DEBUG
-n sesame.bld
-e 100 fd 66 66 64 04 01 00 00 1a
-rcx
:9
-w
-q
```

To use our newly created key, enter BASIC and load a protected file but do not run it. See what happens when you try to list it. Enter the command

BLOAD "sesame.bld",&h464

and the program is now unprotected. Try listing it now.

You may want your program to decide to unprotect or protect itself dynamically by setting DS:464h to FFh for protection or 00 to unprotect itself.

Issuing DOS Commands from BASIC

You can rename BASIC/BASICA.COM on the PCjr and run them to gain access to the BASIC SHELL command. Or you can use those programs under DEBUG on the PCjr without restriction. The PCjr cartridge will not allow return from a SHELL command, so we are stuck with using a disk version of BASIC to use SHELL on the PCjr. In all cases you still need the BASIC cartridge since Cassette BASIC in ROM checks for it when DOS is running. Of course, using a noncartridge version of BASIC on the PCjr excludes the fine PCjr enhancements to BASIC for video and sound.

On either the PC or PCjr, DOS 2.0/2.10 contains a version of SHELL that has a rather severe bug in the way it tramples on what it assumes to be offset 30–31h of the PSP, but which is really in the interpreter work area in BASIC. You can circumvent this pre-DOS 3.0 SHELL problem by saving and restoring this pointer to the beginning of the BASIC program text. The sample routine in Program 1-12 allows SHELL to be used successfully in DOS 2.0/2.10 BASIC or BASICA (*not* Cartridge BASIC).

The SHELL command causes a COPY of COMMAND.COM to be executed, so you may use SHELL to process batch file commands, use external and internal DOS commands, and perform redirection and piping. Many restrictions apply to the use of the SHELL command. You should be prepared to reset your screen mode and clear the screen when BASIC is re-entered. Interrupt vectors that are critical to your work should be saved and restored. Modifications to the following device ports could prove fatal: 8259, 8253, 8237, 8255, and 8250. Open files (including redirected standard input/output) should not be modified by any action during the SHELL session. Do not use the /M option when starting BASIC. You should not invoke terminate-but-stay-resident types of programs. BASIC cannot be started in a SHELL session.

Program 1-12. Issuing DOS Commands from BASIC

```
100 'MEMSHELL; Call for DOS functions from BAS
    IC
110 ' PCjr will receive a "Can't continue afte
    r SHELL" message
120 ' You may run BASIC(A) under DEBUG or rena
    me BASIC(A)
130 '
140  PRINT "Enter DOS command for SHELL
150 INPUT SHELL.CMD$ ' just press enter if you
     wish to stay in DOS
160 ' unit you enter the command EXIT.
170 ' Save data from BASIC's non-PSP
180 DEF SEG:X=PEEK(&H30):Y=PEEK(&H31)    'offset
     to pgm
190 SHELL SHELL.CMD$
200 ' Restore data to BASIC's non-PSP
210 DEF SEG:POKE &H30,X:POKE &H31,Y   'offset t
    o pgm
220 PRINT"Back in BASIC"
230 END
```

DOS 2.0/2.10 SS:SP Sequence Errors

The order in which the stack segment (SS) and stack pointer (SP) are set is significant to the PCjr and to 8088's that were released without an interlocking mechanism. SS should be set first, then SP. Any interrupt that occurs between the setting of SP and then SS would cause the wrong stack segment to be used, creating a real mess that usually means a power-on sequence to clear it. Using CLI to turn off interrupts helps, but an NMI from the PCjr keyboard (such as the Break key) can't be masked off, and it's a pain to have to remember to CLI/STI around SS:SP settings.

DOS 2.0 and 2.10 were released with some SS:SP settings in the wrong order. You can fix these errors. First, *make sure that this is not the only disk that contains the system files and be sure you have a duplicate copy of any important files saved on another disk.* If you make a mistake, you can create another copy of DOS from an unaltered disk by using FORMAT /S. Now, change the attribute byte for the file IBMDOS.COM with the commands:

A>DEBUG
- **l 100 0 5 1**   load the directory
- **d 120 1c**   show IBMDOS.COM and attribute
- **e 12B 20**   nonsystem, non-read-only, nonhidden file
- **w 100 0 5 1**   write the directory back
- **q**

Now, DEBUG IBMDOS.COM and unassemble the following areas for eight bytes each: 3AC, CD1, 1522, 311D, 325F, 409B. Change the order that SS and SP are set, being careful of the sequence used in the last instruction group. Write the file back to disk with the W command. You can now set the file attribute back to 27h by using the same process as you used to set it to 20h.

I/O Port Address Space

Besides the memory address space, there is another separate address space within the PC that is used for communications with I/O devices. The I/O port address space contains 1024 bytes (1K) and is accessed with the special IN and OUT Assembler instructions (INP and OUT in BASIC programs, and I and O in DEBUG).

I/O ports cannot necessarily be written to even if they can be read, or read even if they can be written to. The expected contents of the bits in the port, as well as the ability to read or write, are determined solely by the device connected to the port.

The I/O port address space is summarized in Figure 1-18. Those areas that are not used or reserved could be used by another vendor's equipment or future IBM products. See the Port Map Appendix for more detailed information about the port address space contents.

SRVCCALL: BIOS/DOS Interrupt/Function Service Routine

Functional compatibility in future releases of DOS or on new IBM computers is aided by utilizing the provided interrupts and DOS function calls. Also, BASIC is limited to a set of services that do not currently allow for the full range of capabilities provided in the interrupts and function calls. For example, the amount of used/available space on any attached disk is readily available from DOS, but no function supports this request for the BASIC programmer. The same is true of many other handy and available DOS and BIOS services.

An obvious solution to the problem is to provide a machine language subroutine for BASIC programs that allows the BASIC programmer to call interrupts and DOS functions, passing and receiving the standard register and flag parameters. Additionally, the returned parameters from one call must be available for later passing to another call. Program 1-13 is a demonstration program that shows the use of a SRVCCALL machine language routine that provides those features. The machine language module is BLOADed at the end of the BASIC workspace, then called to pass and return DOS/BIOS parameters.

Some interrupts and DOS functions just don't make any sense to use from a BASIC program since BASIC provides the equivalent function, and others can be downright ridiculous. DOS function 27h (terminate but stay resident) is an example. Even though you will have a tool to call any of the interrupts or functions, choose wisely those that you use.

The demonstration BASIC program illustrates the use of the subroutine in seven different calls for BIOS/DOS services, including the use of ASCIIZ strings and pointers to parameter areas (be sure to delete line 210 if you don't have a printer connected). Only 12 BASIC lines (Program 1-14) are needed to provide the SRVCCALL facility.

53

Figure 1-18. Allocation of PC I/O Port Address Space

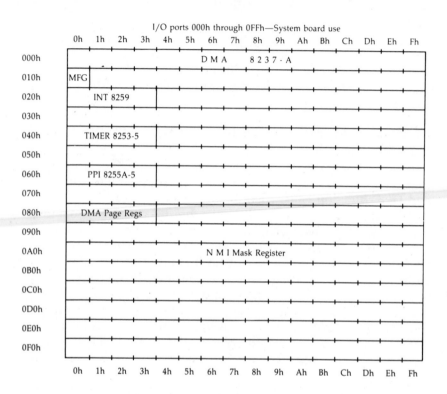

I/O ports 000h through 0FFh—System board use

I/O ports 100h through 1FFh—System board and I/O channel use
Restricted to output-only use, unused in PC

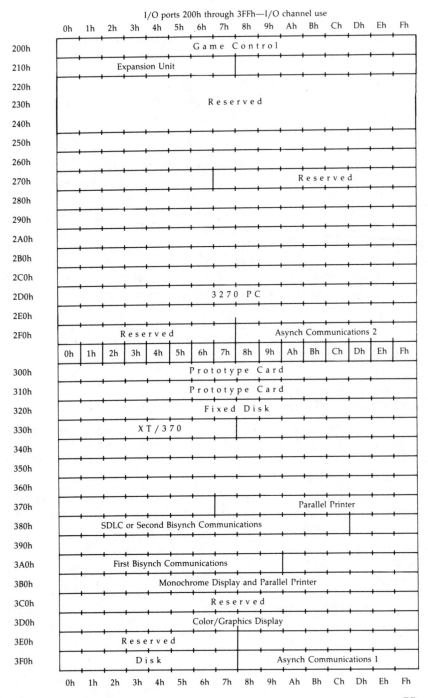

I/O ports 200h through 3FFh—I/O channel use

	0h	1h	2h	3h	4h	5h	6h	7h	8h	9h	Ah	Bh	Ch	Dh	Eh	Fh
200h									Game Control							
210h		Expansion Unit														
220h																
230h								Reserved								
240h																
250h																
260h																
270h										Reserved						
280h																
290h																
2A0h																
2B0h																
2C0h																
2D0h							3270 PC									
2E0h																
2F0h		Reserved							Asynch Communications 2							

	0h	1h	2h	3h	4h	5h	6h	7h	8h	9h	Ah	Bh	Ch	Dh	Eh	Fh
300h					Prototype Card											
310h					Prototype Card											
320h					Fixed Disk											
330h			XT / 370													
340h																
350h																
360h																
370h											Parallel Printer					
380h		SDLC or Second Bisynch Communications														
390h																
3A0h		First Bisynch Communications														
3B0h		Monochrome Display and Parallel Printer														
3C0h					Reserved											
3D0h					Color/Graphics Display											
3E0h		Reserved														
3F0h		Disk							Asynch Communications 1							

0h	1h	2h	3h	4h	5h	6h	7h	8h	9h	Ah	Bh	Ch	Dh	Eh	Fh

The use of an integer array to pass parameters between BASIC and the machine language routine would minimize the instructions in both the BASIC and machine language routines. For the BASIC program, the subscript could be a variable name to make it clear which register is being used, that is, PARMS(CL). Instead, I've elected to use discrete variables for the sake of rapid understanding of the code in the machine language routine. Since the instruction lines are slight variations of the preceding group of lines, duplication and modification of the preceding lines will speed data entry.

I've also arbitrarily chosen to use the BLOAD technique for storing the machine language module since the other techniques of using a BASIC string, array, or POKEing beyond BASIC are illustrated elsewhere in this book.

To create the SRVCCALL machine language routine, enter either the source code shown in Program 1-15 (if you have an assembler) and save it using the filename SRVCCALL.ASM, or use DEBUG to enter the hex values at the indicated offset and save the module as SRVCCALL.COM.

Assembler owners should then use the following batch file to create the SRVCCALL.COM module (you must have ASM, EXE2BIN.EXE, and your source file on the same disk):

```
asm %1,,,;
link %1,,con,;
exe2bin %1.exe %1.com
```

Once you have the batch file created, assuming you called it CREATE.BAT, enter this command to create SRVCCALL.COM:

A>CREATE SRVCCALL

Now we'll use the .COM module to create the necessary .BLD (BLOAD) module using DEBUG. Simply move it down seven bytes, and add the .BLD header as follows:

```
DEBUG SRVCCALL.COM
-n SRVCCALL.BLD
-m 100 l a8 107
-e 100
    fd 00 00 00 00 a8 00
-rcx
:af
-w
-q
```

Program 1-13. SRVCCALL.BAS

For error-free program entry, be sure to use "The Automatic Proofreader," Appendix H.

```
HK 100 'SRVCCALL; Demonstrate DOS/BIOS interrupts
       /functions from BASIC
GG 110 '
BA 120 ' Display options: -1=yes, 0=no   Caption
       is global switch
DA 130 CAPTION=-1: BEEP.ON=-1: FLAG.DEF=-1
HM 140 '
CL 150 GOSUB 470      'install machine language mod
       ule
KD 160 ' --- perform demo routines ---
IJ 170 GOSUB 610
IG 180 GOSUB 710
PI 190 GOSUB 790
NK 200 GOSUB 870
CI 210 GOSUB 960      'delete this line if printer n
       ot connected
DF 220 GOSUB 1080
DG 230 GOSUB 1170
LD 240 END
HP 250 '
GG 260 ' --- CALL DOS/BIOS ---
EA 270 FLAGS%=FLAGS% AND &HCD1 'isolate pertinent
       flags
NK 280 IF CAPTION THEN PRINT"   DOS/BIOS call: IN
       T "HEX$(INTERRUPT%)"h, function"HEX$(AH%)"
       h"
KD 290 IF CAPTION THEN LOCATE ,4: PRINT"     sent
       FLAGS = "HEX$(FLAGS%)"h";
GG 300 '
FB 310 DEF SEG=SRVCCALL.SEG    'segment bloaded at
NG 320 CALL SRVCCALL.OFF(FLAGS%,INTERRUPT%,ES%,SI
       %,DI%,AH%,AL%,BH%,BL%,CH%,CL%,DH%,DL%)
HM 330 '
EL 340 FLAGS%=FLAGS% AND &HCD1 'isolate pertinent
        flags
KA 350 IF CAPTION THEN IF BEEP.ON THEN BEEP
NF 360 IF NOT CAPTION GOTO 450
FA 370 PRINT", returned FLAGS = "HEX$(FLAGS%)"h"
MJ 380 '--- flag interpretation ---
CA 390 IF NOT FLAG.DEF GOTO 450
AE 400 PRINT"        value: 8421 8421 8421"
PJ 410 PRINT"          F    OD   SZ A    C"
EE 420 PRINT"          L    VI   GR U    R"
GG 430 PRINT"          G    RR   NO X    Y"
HP 440 '
NI 450 RETURN
KE 460 '    LOAD MACHINE LANGUAGE ROUTINE
```

```
FN 470 CLS: PRINT "Installing SRVCCALL...";
BM 480 DEF SEG=0: BASWS=PEEK(&H510)+256*PEEK(&H51
       1) 'find end of basic workspace
EC 490 BASEND=BASWS+&H1000+2: SRVCCALL.SEG=BASEND
LJ 500 DEF SEG=SRVCCALL.SEG: SRVCCALL.OFF=0   'use
       offset 0 because of LEA
FI 510 BLOAD "SRVCCALL.BLD",SRVCCALL.OFF       'loa
       d srvccall after basic
FI 520 PRINT"completed.": GOSUB 540: RETURN
BC 530 '--- CLEAR REGISTER PARAMETERS ---
IC 540 DEF SEG: INTERRUPT%=&H21: FLAGS%=0
KO 550 AH%=0:AL%=0:BH%=0:BL%=0:CH%=0:CL%=0:DH%=0:
       DL%=0:ES%=0:SI%=0:DI%=0
CK 560 IF CAPTION THEN PRINT: PRINT"Regs zeroed."
NN 570 RETURN
II 580 '
QL 590 '  -*-*-*- DEMO ROUTINES -*-*-*-
HJ 600 '
DD 610 '  --- get disk free space ---
OP 620 '       DOS function 36
PG 630 '        returned: bx=free clusters, dx=total
       clusters
HF 640 '                 cx=bytes/sector, ax=sector
       s/cluster
EF 650 GOSUB 540 'clean up registers
GP 660 INTERRUPT%=&H21: AH%=&H36: DL%=0    ' dl=0
       signifies default drive
AG 670 GOSUB 270 'call assembler routine   '
LJ 680 IF AL%=&HFF AND AH%=&HFF THEN PRINT"DRIVE
       NUMBER"DL%"INVALID": GOTO 700
MA 690 PRINT(BH%*256+BL%)*(AH%*256+AL%)*(CH%*256+
       CL%)"available bytes on disk"
MB 700 RETURN
JG 710 '  --- Request vector address ---
FH 720 '       DOS function 35h
QM 730 '        returned: es:bx vector
EE 740 GOSUB 540 'clean up registers
GO 750 INTERRUPT%=&H21: AH%=&H35: AL%=&H10   ' get
       vector for INT10 video
FM 760 GOSUB 270 'call machine language routine
GN 770 PRINT "vector points to "HEX$(ES%)":"HEX$(
       BH%*256+BL%)
NB 780 RETURN
DK 790 '  --- Request DTA address ---
CF 800 '       DOS FUNCTION 2FH
FF 810 '        returned: es:bx DTA address
EB 820 GOSUB 540 'clean up registers
JO 830 INTERRUPT%=&H21: AH%=&H2F
FJ 840 GOSUB 270 'call machine language routine
```

```
NA 850 PRINT "DTA is at "HEX$(ES%)":"HEX$(BH%*256
       +BL%)
NO 860 RETURN
HD 870 ' --- Request timer value ---
BE 880 '      bios INT 1a, type 0 service
KG 890 '      returned: dx=low, cx=high, al=0 if n
       ot 24 hrs
PL 900 GOSUB 540: Y=CAPTION: FOR X=1 TO 7: IF X>1
       THEN CAPTION=0
EC 910 GOSUB 920: NEXT: CAPTION=Y: RETURN
HL 920 INTERRUPT%=&H1A: AH%=&H0   ' ah%=0 is timer
       read
AB 930 GOSUB 270 'call assembler routine    '
QL 940 PRINT "Timer=";CH%;CL%;DH%;DL%: IF AL% <>0
       THEN PRINT"OVER 24 HOURS"
NN 950 RETURN
NL 960 ' --- Request printer output ---
QO 970 '      DOS function 5
LI 980 '      returned: nothing
LN 990 GOSUB 540: Y=CAPTION: CAPTION=0 'turn off
       tracing captions
HL 1000 '
HI 1010 INTERRUPT%=&H21:AH%=&H5:TEXT$="DOS functi
       on 5. Now you can call BIOS/DOS from BASI
       C!!!"
JF 1020 FOR X=1 TO LEN(TEXT$): DL%=ASC(MID$(TEXT$
       ,X,1)): GOSUB 270: NEXT
HB 1030 DL%=13: GOSUB 270: DL%=10: GOSUB 270 'end
       with CR/LF
HH 1040 '
EL 1050 CAPTION=Y: RETURN
IN 1060 '
CP 1070 ' --- get country information ---
ID 1080 '
MB 1090 '      DOS function 38
FA 1100 '      returned: 24 bytes of info in 32 by
       te area
KL 1110 GOSUB 540 'clean up registers
LD 1120 INTERRUPT%=&H21:AH%=&H38:BACK$=SPACE$(32)
       +"" 'DATA RETURNED
KA 1130 BACK!=VARPTR(BACK$): DEF SEG: DH%=PEEK(BA
       CK!+2): DL%=PEEK(BACK!+1)
MD 1140 GOSUB 270 'call machine language routine
II 1150 PRINT "Country info= ";BACK$
JP 1160 RETURN
FD 1170 ' --- get file attribute byte ---
NB 1180 '      DOS function 43
BO 1190 '      returned: cl=attribute
KK 1200 GOSUB 540 'clean up registers
```

```
JP 1210 INTERRUPT%=&H21:AH%=&H43:FILE$="CoMmAnD.C
        oM"+CHR$(0) 'case not significant
KJ 1220 FILE!=VARPTR(FILE$): DEF SEG: DH%=PEEK(FI
        LE!+2): DL%=PEEK(FILE!+1)
FI 1230 GOSUB 270 'call assembler routine
OG 1240 PRINT FILE$;"attribute="HEX$(CL%)"h": IF
        (FLAGS% AND 2^0) THEN PRINT"ERROR CODE="A
        L%
JO 1250 RETURN
```

Program 1-14. Functional Subset of SRVCCALL.BAS Invocation

For error-free program entry, be sure to use "The Automatic Proofreader," Appendix H.

```
HM 10 GOSUB 470    'install machine language modul
       e
AE 20 GOSUB 270    'call machine language routine
       ,
FC 30    'Main body of program
LF 250 END
GG 260 ' --- CALL DOS/BIOS ---
EA 270 FLAGS%=FLAGS% AND &HCD1 'isolate pertinent
        flags
FB 310 DEF SEG=SRVCCALL.SEG    'segment bloaded at
MG 320 CALL SRVCCALL.OFF(FLAGS%,INTERRUPT%,ES%,SI
       %,DI%,AH%,AL%,BH%,BL%,CH%,CL%,DH%,DL%)
EL 340 FLAGS%=FLAGS% AND &HCD1 'isolate pertinent
        flags
IF 350 DEF SEG: RETURN
BK 470 DEF SEG=0: BASWS=PEEK(&H510)+256*PEEK(&H51
       1) 'find end of basic workspace
EA 480 BASEND=BASWS+&H1000+2: SRVCCALL.SEG=BASEND
MK 490 DEF SEG=SRVCCALL.SEG: SRVCCALL.OFF=0   'use
        offset 0 because of LEA
OH 500 BLOAD "srvccall.bld",SRVCCALL.OFF   'load s
       rvccall after basic
IP 510 DEF SEG: RETURN
```

Program 1-15. SRVCCALL.ASM

```
; *************************************************************
; *  SRVCCALL; BASIC callable routine to invoke BIOS/DOS interrupts  *
; *       and functions. DS, CS, SS, SP, and BP not alterable.       *
; *                                                                  *
; *     CALL SRVCCALL(FLAGS%,INTERRUPT%,ES%,SI%,DI%,AH%,             *
; *            AL%,BH%,BL%,CH%,CL%,DH%,DL%)                          *
; *       Because of LEA instruction, always bload at offset 0.     *
; *************************************************************
```

```
                        service_call segment
                        SRVCCALL proc far
                        public SRVCCALL
off   hex               assume cs:service_call
set   instruction

00   FA                 cli
01   55                 push bp              ; use bp as parm frame
                                             ; pointer
02   8B  EC             mov bp,sp            ; from current stack pointer
04   1E                 push ds              ; save basic segment registers
05   06                 push es
     ;     -------------- set desired registers for call ---------------
06   8B  76  1E         mov si,[bp+30]       ; point to flag argument
09   8B  04             mov ax,[si]
0B   50                 push ax
0C   9D                 popf                 ; set flags, no other
0D   8B  76  14         mov si,[bp+20]       ; point to ah argument
10   8A  24             mov ah,[si]          ; set ah
12   8B  76  12         mov si,[bp+18]       ; point to al argument
15   8A  04             mov al,[si]          ; set al
17   8B  76  10         mov si,[bp+16]       ; point to bh argument
1A   8A  3C             mov bh,[si]          ; set bh
1C   8B  76  0E         mov si,[bp+14]       ; point to bl argument
1F   8A  1C             mov bl,[si]          ; set bl
21   8B  76  0C         mov si,[bp+12]       ; point to ch argument
24   8A  2C             mov ch,[si]          ; set ch
26   8B  76  0A         mov si,[bp+10]       ; point to cl argument
29   8A  0C             mov cl,[si]          ; set cl
2B   8B  76  08         mov si,[bp+8]        ; point to dh argument
2E   8A  34             mov dh,[si]          ; set dh
30   8B  76  06         mov si,[bp+6]        ; point to dl argument
33   8A  14             mov dl,[si]          ; set dl
35   8B  76  16         mov si,[bp+22]       ; point to di argument
38   8B  3C             mov di,[si]          ; set di
3A   8B  76  1A         mov si,[bp+26]       ; point to es argument
3D   50                 push ax              ; save ax, use temporarily
3E   8B  04             mov ax,[si]          ; es arg in ax
40   8E  C0             mov es,ax            ; set es
42   58                 pop ax               ; restore ax
43   8B  76  18         mov si,[bp+24]       ; point to si argument
46   8B  34             mov si,[si]          ; set si
     ;     ----------- set interrupt number in instruction -----------
48   50                 push ax              ; save users reg
49   53                 push bx              ; save users reg
4A   8B  5E  1C         mov bx,[bp+28]       ; point to interrupt num
4D   8A  07             mov al,[bx]          ; interrupt num in al
4F   8D  1E  005B R     lea bx,intins        ; get runtime offset of int
                                             ; instruction
53   43                 inc bx               ; plus one for argument
```

```
54   2E: 88  07        mov cs:[bx],al         ; overlay int argument
57   5B                pop bx                 ; restore users reg
58   58                pop ax                 ; restore users reg
     ;        ------------- call interrupt or DOS function -------------
59   55                push bp                ; save bp to avoid bios bug
5A   FB                sti
5B                     intins:
5B   CD  00            int 0                  ; argument overlaid by
                                              ; intro%
5D   FA                cli
5E   5D                pop bp                 ; restore bp
     ;        ------------- set registers returned from call -------------
5F   56                push si                ; process later
60   9C                pushf                  ; process later
61   8B  76  14        mov si,[bp+20]         ; point to ah argument
64   88  24            mov [si],ah            ; pass ah back
66   8B  76  12        mov si,[bp+18]         ; point to al argument
69   88  04            mov [si],al            ; pass al back
6B   8B  76  10        mov si,[bp+16]         ; point to bh argument
6E   88  3C            mov [si],bh            ; pass bh back
70   8B  76  0E        mov si,[bp+14]         ; point to bl argument
73   88  1C            mov [si],bl            ; pass bl back
75   8B  76  0C        mov si,[bp+12]         ; point to ch argument
78   88  2C            mov [si],ch            ; pass ch back
7A   8B  76  0A        mov si,[bp+10]         ; point to cl argument
7D   88  0C            mov [si],cl            ; pass cl back
7F   8B  76  08        mov si,[bp+8]          ; point to dh argument
82   88  34            mov [si],dh            ; pass dh back
84   8B  76  06        mov si,[bp+6]          ; point to dl argument
87   88  14            mov [si],dl            ; pass dl back
89   58                pop ax                 ; restore returned flags
8A   8B  76  1E        mov si,[bp+30]         ; point to flags argument
8D   89  04            mov [si],ax            ; pass back flags
8F   58                pop ax                 ; restore returned si
90   8B  76  18        mov si,[bp+24]         ; point to si argument
93   89  04            mov [si],ax            ; pass si back
95   8C  C0            mov ax,es              ; returned es to ax
97   8B  76  1A        mov si,[bp+26]         ; point to es argument
9A   89  04            mov [si],ax            ; pass es back
9C   8B  76  16        mov si,[bp+22]         ; point to di argument
9F   89  3C            mov [si],di            ; pass di back
     ;        ---------------------- return to caller ----------------------
A1   07                pop es                 ; restore BASIC segment regs
A2   1F                pop ds
A3   5D                pop bp                 ; restore bp
A4   FB                sti
A5   CA  001A          ret 26                 ; 13 arguments
A8                     SRVCCALL endp
A8                     service_call ends
                       end
```

Memory Related Locations and References

Location shows PC2 values, then PCjr if they differ. The TRM page indicated is the beginning or most significant page as found in the XT *Technical Reference* manual (see the Introduction concerning the edition of manuals referenced in this book). Examine the context of the surrounding pages.

Memory Support References

Location : **8h**
Label : (INT 2)
Usage : Vector to memory parity error NMI handler (not PCjr)
FE2C3h
TRM pg : A-11, A-72

Location : **48h**
Label : (INT 12)
Usage : Vector to memory size determination routine
FF841H
TRM pg : A-71; PCjr: A-97

Location : **60h**
Label : (INT 18) BASIC-PTR
Usage : Vector to ROM-resident Cassette BASIC
F6000H; PCjr: FFFCBh if no cartridge, else E8177h
TRM pg : PCjr: A-109

Location : **64h**
Label : (INT 19) BOOT-PTR
Usage : Vector to bootstrap routine
FE6F2h
TRM pg : A-20; PCjr: A-62, A-26

Location : **410–411h**
Label : EQUIP-FLAG
Usage : Configuration switch memory size information
System board memory size, PC1 includes I/O channel memory
See Memory Map Appendix and ports 60–62h in Port Map Appendix
PCjr: set by ROM BIOS for compatibility
TRM pg : 1-10; PCjr: 2-31

Location : **413–414h**
Label   : MEMORY-SIZE
Usage   : Usable memory size in 1K blocks
            PC1: I/O channel memory from switches added to system board
            PC2: all available memory in 1K blocks
            PCjr (64 or 128K): 16 (for video) in 1K blocks
            See Memory Map Appendix and ports 60–62h in Port Map Appendix
TRM pg : A-9; PCjr: A-16

Location : **415–416h (not XT)**
Label   : TRUE-MEM
Usage   : Total memory including I/O channel in 1K blocks
            PC1: I/O channel memory in 1K blocks from switches
            PC2: not used
            PCjr: all available memory in 1K blocks
            See Memory Map Appendix and ports 60–62h in Port Map Appendix

Location : **510-511h**
Usage   : BASIC's storage area for workspace segment number

ROM BIOS Memory Support References

PC2 ROM BIOS

FE0AEh	Call for ROM checksum
FE165h	Determine memory size and check memory in first 32K
FE1DEh	Set first 32 interrupts to temporary routine
FE1EFh	Fill INT 10–1F
FE202h	Save configuration switches in equipment flag
FE3DEh	Set up INT 0–15
FE418h	Check expansion box
FE46Ah	Test memory above 32K
FE518h	Check for ROM in C80000–F40000h
FE53Bh	Check BASIC ROM
FE66Dh	INT 19 to bootstrap loader
FE66Fh	Subroutine to test RAM
FE6F2h	Bootstrap loader
FF841h	INT 12 memory size service
FF85Fh	NMI interrupt, parity check
FF8F2h	ROM checksum subroutine
FF953h	Checksum optional ROM and initialize
FFEF3h	Interrupt vector table

PCjr ROM BIOS

F0134h	Test BIOS/BASIC ROMs
F015Fh	Test 0–2K RAM and just below end (for video buffer)
F01EBh	Initialize INT 0–1F
F0250h	Simulate configuration switches
F0503h	Size memory, test or clear
F07E0h	Check for cartridges in C00000–F00000h
F0B18h	Bootstrap loader
F0B59h	Initialize or test memory
FE6F2h	INT 19 redirection to bootstrap loader
FEB51h	Checks ROM C0000–F00000h
FF841h	INT 12 memory size service
FFE71h	Checksum optional ROM and initialize
FFEF3h	Interrupt vector table

Additional Memory Information

Subject	TRM Page
Port address map	1-8
Configuration switches	1-10, G-4
System memory map	1-11
Memory expansion board	1-197
8088 interrupts 0–1Fh	2-4; PCjr: 5-7
BASIC and DOS reserved interrupts	2-7; PCjr: 5-14
BASIC and DOS reserved memory locations	2-8; PCjr: 5-15
BASIC workspace variables	2-8; PCjr: 5-16
Expansion ROM characteristics	2-10; PCjr: 5-18
Parity error routine	A-72
Fixed-disk ROM initialization	A-86
Fixed-disk INT 19 bootstrap	A-89
8088 registers	B-2
8088 operation codes	B-3
Memory segmentation	B-4
System board 64K	PCjr: 2-17
Cartridge characteristics	PCjr: 2-107
64K expansion	PCjr: 3-5
Memory compatibility with PC	PCjr: 4-12

BASIC Memory Support

Basic provides many statements that may be used for memory functions. Check your BASIC manual for the following statements: PEEK, POKE, BLOAD, BSAVE, DEF SEG, VARPTR, VARPTR$, OUT, INP, FREE, CLEAR, CALL, USR. See the BASIC manual, Appendix C, for details of machine language interfacing, and Appendix I for a BASIC memory map and variables format.

DOS Memory Support References

Subject	DOS Page 2.0	2.10	2.10 TRM
Invoking a second COMMAND.COM	10-9	1-11	–
SET ENVIRONMENT command	10-22	2-128	–
Configuration commands	9-3	4-3	–
DOS structure	B-1	–	1-3
DOS initialization	B-1	–	1-4
COMMAND.COM	B-3	–	1-5
FCB	B-5	–	1-6
DTA	B-6	–	1-7
Device drivers	14-1	–	3-4
DOS memory functions	D-43	–	5-41
DOS EXEC function	D-44	–	5-42
DOS memory map	E-1	–	6-3
DOS PSP	E-3	–	6-5
DOS FCB	E-10	–	6-5
Invoking COMMAND.COM from an application	F-1	–	7-3
Fixed-disk system initialization	G-2	–	8-4
Fixed-disk boot record	G-4	–	8-6
EXE file contents	H-1	–	9-3
DOS memory management	–	–	10-1

2
Keyboard

2
Keyboard

The IBM keyboard can be redefined by a program to suit the needs of the application. A program may redefine key meanings, create additional key combinations, display Shift key and insert mode status indicators, or extend the standard keyboard functions. A program may even allow you to redefine the meaning of a combination of keypresses and save your definitions for later use. Such features are powerful boosts to productivity. Customization of the keyboard can give the program its own attractive keyboard personality.

In this chapter we'll see how various types of powerful keyboard customization are done. You can use these techniques in your own programs or those that you wish to modify. We'll monitor the keyboard as it goes about its job and explore ways that you can control and extend its capabilities.

If the software you write is to be used on the PC, XT, and PCjr, then the similarities and differences between the keyboards of the PC/XT and the PCjr will interest you. We'll see ways that the PCjr keyboard is different from the PC and discover how you can take advantage of these unique PCjr features. The memory locations and sample programs that we explore generally apply to all the IBM PC family, and I'll note the differences between them as we go along.

IBM PC DOS and BIOS provide interrupts and functions for programs to use to request upward-compatible keyboard services. Even though the PCjr keyboard produces completely different scan codes from the PC and XT, the keyboard services have remained compatible. This is a real-life testimonial to the wisdom of using the provided service routines whenever possible. Fortunately, IBM took extreme care to insure compatibility of the PCjr keyboard to several levels beyond the provided service routines.

BASIC provides functions and statements that can be used to predictably invoke several of these provided lower-level keyboard services. Machine language programs can, of course, invoke these keyboard services directly, and BASIC programs calling machine language routines are an attractive hybrid. But before we discuss the available BIOS, DOS, and BASIC keyboard facilities, let's look at the memory locations used for keyboard management and see how those locations can be of use to us in our programs.

Keyboard Flags at 417h, 418h, and 488h

Probably the most frequently used keyboard memory locations are the keyboard status flag bytes located at 417h and 418h. The PCjr uses an additional flag byte at 488h. The keyboard status flag bytes can be used effectively in your programs. A typical use involves checking to see if the Alt key is being pressed while another key is also held down. This Alt combination can be used to signal a command. For instance, Alt-E could be interpreted by your program to indicate *exit*. The *Technical Reference* manual lists suggested key-combination usages that you may choose to follow or not. For the PC2, this table starts on page 2-18 (as discussed in the Introduction, page references refer to the XT manual), while the PCjr table begins on page 5-38. The Ctrl key is also excellently suited for this purpose, and the PCjr adds yet another handy shifting key in the Fn key.

Additional shift keys can be implemented by providing a front-end routine for the keyboard interrupt routine INT 9h. You can determine if multiple keys are being pressed, because break codes are generated when a key is released. The break code for any key is the scan code plus 80h. The generation of break codes gives us the welcome capability for every key on the keyboard to become a shift key. You can find a table of the scan codes and extended scan codes in your *Technical Reference* manual just before the ROM BIOS listing. In my XT *Technical Reference* manual, the table begins on page 2-11 and is titled "Keyboard Encoding and Usage." A diagram of the locations of the keys and their scan codes is presented on page 1-68, "Keyboard Diagram," followed by a hexadecimal chart. Similar documentation starts on page 5-21 of the PCjr *Technical Reference* manual.

While a custom shift key is being held down, any number of other keys can be pressed in series or together. The program would know that the shift key had not yet been released because the break scan code for the key had not been received.

Given the inclusion of a customized keyboard interrupt routine, the sequence in which the keys were pressed, and possibly even the release sequence, could provide an astounding number of combinations. Human considerations limit this dizzying assortment to a more reasonable two or, infrequently, three simultaneous keys.

The PCjr keyboard suppresses invalid key combinations and sends a 55h scan code instead, indicating a problem. The PCjr INT 48h KEY62_INT routine simply discards this phantom keypress scan code.

On both the PC and PCjr, ROM BIOS resident KB_INT (INT 9) ignores many combinations of keys that you would think could be used in your programs. For example, only two of the ten number keys across the top of the keyboard are recognized when Ctrl is held down at the same time. See the "Character Codes" table in the *Technical Reference* manual a few pages before the ROM BIOS listing. Any −1 value in the table indicates a key combination that INT 9 ignores. Your own INT 9 or a front-end to the provided routine can cause ignored or acted-upon key combinations to be passed on to requesting programs. Figure 2-1 is provided as a recap of the *Technical Reference* manual tables Alt and Ctrl columns.

Figure 2-1. Alt or Ctrl Shifted Keys Ignored
Ignored Alt shifts:
    All cursor numeric keypad keys, including − + . *
    Backspace, Enter, Tab, Esc, Insert, Delete, semicolon, comma
    [ ] ' ' . / \(these last 7 are *not* ignored on the PCjr)

Ignored Ctrl shifts:
    cursor/numeric keypad keys 2 5 8 0 . + −
    Tab, Insert, Delete
    1 3 4 5 7 8 9 0 = ; ' ' , . /

You can use the short routine shown in Program 2-1 to determine whether a particular combination of pressed keys is suppressed. INKEY$ returns a one-byte CHR$ value or a CHR$(0) followed with a byte containing the CHR$ of the *extended scan code* keypress. INKEY$ does not provide a method for determining which key(s) was used to generate the same ASCII codes. Only the scan code can differentiate between a Ctrl-H and a Backspace, the two asterisks on the keyboard, Ctrl-M and Enter, and so on.

Program 2-1. Display INKEY$ Returned ASCII or Extended Scan Code

```
100 'KBINKEY$: Show the BASIC INKEY$ returned
    data in hex
110 X$=INKEY$:IF X$="" GOTO 110
    'wait for a keypress
120 FOR X = 1 TO LEN(X$)  'possibly extended s
    can code
130   PRINT HEX$(ASC(MID$(X$,X,1)));" ";
    'show the ascii or
140 NEXT:PRINT:GOTO 110   ' zero and extended s
    can code
```

When designing Alt or Ctrl alternate shift key patterns for keys, keep in mind that not all keys cause an extended scan code (or even an ASCII character) when depressed in combination with the Alt or Ctrl key. This is caused by the provided keyboard interrupt routine (INT 9) in ROM BIOS. Again, your *Technical Reference* manual shows those combinations as −1 in the "Character Codes" table. For your quick reference, those keys that are ignored with Alt or Ctrl are listed in Figure 2-1. You will be pleased to notice that the function keys are not ignored. Shift, Alt, and Ctrl provide unique codes so that 40 function keys may be supported. Additional function keys may be supported by examining the keyboard shift status bytes ourselves.

The *Technical Reference* manual for your computer lists the possible values for locations 417h and 418h on the second page of the ROM BIOS. Look for KB_FLAG and KB_FLAG_1 at offsets 17 and 18 within segment 40. The eye-catcher "KEYBOARD DATA AREAS" precedes the machine language equate statements. Table 2-1 indicates the usage of each bit in these keyboard flags, if you don't have a *Technical Reference* manual handy.

The PCjr *Technical Reference* manual doesn't show that a possible value for location 417h is 10h if Fn-ScrLk is currently toggled on and a value of 80h if the Ins key has been toggled.

The PCjr also uses an additional flag byte at 488h for tracking the function key, repeat key timing, and vertical screen positioning available through the Ctrl-Alt-cursor keys. This byte is labeled KB_FLAG_2. You'll find the equate statements for the byte under "BIT ASSIGNMENTS FOR KB_FLAG_2" on the next page of the *Technical Reference*

Table 2-1. Shift Status Flag Bytes

KB_FLAG at 417H

Bit	Hex	Dec	Meaning
7	80	128	Insert mode on
6	40	64	Caps Lock on
5	20	32	Num Lock on
4	10	16	Scroll Lock on
3	08	8	Alt pressed
2	04	4	Ctrl pressed
1	02	2	Left Shift pressed
0	01	1	Right Shift pressed

KB_FLAG_1 at 418H

Bit	Hex	Dec	Meaning
7	80	128	Insert pressed
6	40	64	Caps Lock pressed
5	20	32	Num Lock pressed
4	10	16	Scroll Lock pressed
3	08	8	Ctrl-Num Lock (pause key) toggled
2	04	4	PCjr keyboard clicker active
1	02	2	PCjr Ctrl-Alt-Caps Lock held
0	01	1	

KB_FLAG_2 at 488H (PCjr only)

Bit	Hex	Dec	Meaning
7	80	128	Fn flag pressed
6	40	64	Fn key released
5	20	32	Fn next key pending
4	10	16	Fn key locked on
3	08	8	Typamatic off
2	04	4	Half rate typamatic
1	02	2	Initial typamatic delay increased
0	01	1	Put character out, typamatic delay has lapsed

manual. Program 2-2 tracks and reports the function key status flag bits in KB_FLAG_2. The keyboard clicker flag in KB_FLAG_1 is also included in the display for the PCjr.

The program displays the current keyboard Shift key status on the twenty-fifth line of the screen. Examine and tailor the BASIC program to your own needs. You may want to place a subset of the program in your own program as a subroutine. Notice that multiple PEEKs to the keyboard status bytes are used. This technique will detect an individual keypress more quickly than setting a variable from the result of one PEEK at the start of the main loop.

Program 2-2. Displaying Keyboard Status

For error-free program entry, be sure to use "The Automatic Proofreader," Appendix H.

```
LJ 100 'KBSTATUS; display status indicators for s
       hift keys
BO 110 '            Does not use conventions of DOS
           int 16h
HF 120 '25th line status indicators are: KB=iunlA
       CSkf
CB 130 'status indicator in caps if key being hel
       d down
BF 140 '         see comments below for meanings
GG 150 BIT0=1:BIT1=2:BIT2=4:BIT3=8:BIT4=16:BIT5=3
       2:BIT6=64:BIT7=128:BITALL=255
AD 160 DEF SEG=&HFFFF:IF PEEK(&HE)=&HFD THEN JR=1
        'determine if jr
GM 170 DEF SEG=0:KEY ON:KEY OFF  'clear 25th line
AH 180 :K$=INKEY$:IF K$=CHR$(27) THEN KEY ON:END
        'esc key exits
KN 190 KBSTAT$="             " '10 indicators
IP 200 IF PEEK(&H417) AND BIT7 THEN MID$(KBSTAT$,
       1,1)="i" 'insert
EI 210 IF PEEK(&H418) AND BIT7 THEN MID$(KBSTAT$,
       1,1)="I" 'insert held
QP 220 IF PEEK(&H417) AND BIT6 THEN MID$(KBSTAT$,
       2,1)="u" 'caps lock
PP 230 IF PEEK(&H418) AND BIT6 THEN MID$(KBSTAT$,
       2,1)="U" 'caps lock held
OK 240 IF PEEK(&H417) AND BIT5 THEN MID$(KBSTAT$,
       3,1)="n" 'num lock
BN 250 IF PEEK(&H418) AND BIT5 THEN MID$(KBSTAT$,
       3,1)="N" 'num lock held
EK 260 IF PEEK(&H417) AND BIT4 THEN MID$(KBSTAT$,
       4,1)="1" 'scroll lock
KE 270 IF PEEK(&H418) AND BIT4 THEN MID$(KBSTAT$,
       4,1)="L" 'scroll lock held
FE 280 IF PEEK(&H417) AND BIT3 THEN MID$(KBSTAT$,
       5,1)="A" 'alt
GE 290 IF PEEK(&H417) AND BIT2 THEN MID$(KBSTAT$,
       6,1)="C" 'ctrl
OG 300 IF (PEEK(&H417) AND BIT1) THEN IF (PEEK(&H
       417) AND BIT0) THEN MID$(KBSTAT$,7,1)="B":
       GOTO 340 'both shifts
GG 310 REM: IF (PEEK(&H417) AND BIT1) OR (PEEK(&H
       417) AND BIT0) THEN MID$(KBSTAT$,7,1)="S"'
       either shift key
PB 320 IF PEEK(&H417) AND BIT0 THEN MID$(KBSTAT$,
       7,1)="R" 'right shift
EF 330 IF PEEK(&H417) AND BIT1 THEN MID$(KBSTAT$,
       7,1)="L" 'left shift
```

```
EK 340 IF JR=0 GOTO 390
LN 350 IF PEEK(&H488) AND BIT5 THEN MID$(KBSTAT$,
       9,1)="F" 'Fn held
KM 360 IF PEEK(&H488) AND BIT6 THEN MID$(KBSTAT$,
       9,1)="f" 'Fn active
FH 370 IF PEEK(&H418) AND BIT2 THEN MID$(KBSTAT$,
       8,1)="k" 'click active
NP 380 IF PEEK(&H418) AND BIT1 THEN MID$(KBSTAT$,
       8,1)="K" 'click held
FD 390 LOCATE 25,1:COLOR 5:PRINT "KB:";:COLOR 2:P
       RINT KBSTAT$;:COLOR 7:GOTO 180
```

The keyboard status flag bytes can be set or reset by your program to cause the desired keyboard state. Simply POKE the desired value into the status byte to set the keyboard status you desire. Individual status flag bits can be set or reset by selecting the bit used to indicate the state desired and set it on with

POKE *byte*,PEEK*(byte)* OR BIT*n*

The flag bit can be turned off with

POKE *byte*,PEEK*(byte)* AND (255−BIT*n*)

To flip the setting of a flag bit to the opposite setting:

POKE *byte*,PEEK*(byte)* XOR BIT*n*

The PCjr Fn flags in 488h can be used in your programs to provide yet another unique shifting key. If 488h contains A0h, then a key was pressed while the Fn key was held. If 80h is in 488h, then the key was pressed after an Fn related key (a key with a green caption), and while Fn continued to be pressed. The program fragment shown in Program 2-3 can be used to experiment with the Fn flags in 488h. Obviously, green-captioned Pause, Echo, Break, and PrtSc keys pressed while Fn is held (or immediately after) may cause unwanted results. Green-captioned cursor and function keys are particularly well-suited for custom use; however, the BASIC ON KEY( ) statement provides trapping for green captioned keys.

Program 2-3. Experimenting with PCjr Fn Status Flag

```
10 'JR488H; Show PCjr KB_FLAG-2, ascii and hex
   for keypress
20 DEF SEG=0
30 X$=INKEY$:IF X$="" GOTO 30    'wait for a ke
   ypress
```

```
40 PRINT HEX$(PEEK(&H488))" ";   ' show PCjr kb
   _flag_2
50 PRINT X$" ";                  'show characte
   rs
60 FOR X = 1 TO LEN(X$)          'possibly exte
   nded scan code
70   PRINT HEX$(ASC(MID$(X$,X,1)));" ";   'show
   the ascii or
80 NEXT:PRINT:GOTO 30
```

Another technique for defining still more special-meaning keys involves using a unique key (such as Esc, a function key, or a duplicate key such as the numeric keypad + key) as a prefix that then causes the program to act upon the next key pressed as a special key. For example, Esc-S could mean SAVE or F10 Alt-X could mean that the user wants to extract a portion of data.

DOS service 16h can be used to obtain information about the current setting of KB_FLAG (but not KB_FLAG_1 or _2) and to set clicking and repeat key values for the PCjr. To follow IBM compatibility conventions, use the BASIC SRVCCALL routine to call service 16h.

The ROM BIOS routines that are responsible for maintaining the keyboard status flags can be inspected in the *Technical Reference* manual. The PC2 routine can be found on page A-28, labeled KB_INT. The PCjr manual has the equivalent routine on page A-45. A preceding routine used to convert the PCjr keyboard actions into PC-like actions is KEY62_INT (INT 48h), starting on page A-37. This routine shares the management of the status flags with the KB_INT routine.

Keyboard Buffer and Pointers 41E–43Dh, 41Ah, and 41Ch

Keypresses are buffered in the memory of the computer until the running program requests keyboard input. This keyboard buffer is maintained by ROM BIOS routines and normally occupies locations 41E–43Dh. All requests from programs, BIOS, or DOS for keyboard characters cause retrieval of keypresses from this buffer. The buffer is a *circular buffer* in that a pointer indicates the first entry that was placed in the buffer, and another pointer contains the address of the next available entry for buffering the next keypress. As keypresses are removed from the buffer in response to the program requesting keyboard input, the pointer to the next entry to be retrieved is advanced, making available the space used by the keypress just retrieved.

The head of the buffer (the next character to be retrieved) can be at any position within the buffer. When the head of the buffer is at the last position, the pointer simply wraps around from the end of the buffer to the beginning. That's why the term *circular buffer* is used. The address of the ASCII/scan code combination for the next key to be retrieved is maintained at location 41Ah and is called BUFFER_HEAD. The pointer to the next unused buffer location is called BUFFER_TAIL and is at 41Ch. If BUFFER_HEAD and BUFFER_TAIL contain the same address, the buffer is empty. If BUFFER_TAIL should point to the buffer location before BUFFER_HEAD, then the buffer is full. Figure 2-2 illustrates the pointer relationships during a full-buffer condition.

Figure 2-2. Schematic Diagram of a Full Keyboard Buffer

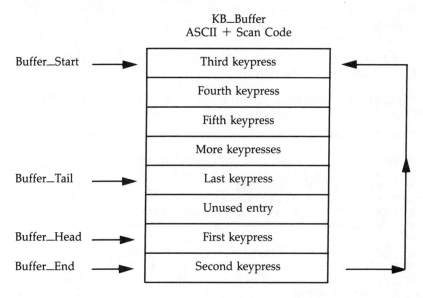

The keyboard buffer is normally large enough to hold 16 keys, each key needing two bytes to store its ASCII value and scan code. Since BUFFER_TAIL contains the same address as BUFFER_HEAD if the buffer is empty, the buffer is considered full when only one entry is left unused. Because of this, only

15 keypresses can be in the buffer at any time. We'll be enlarging this buffer shortly.

The *Technical Reference* manual shows the BUFFER_ prefixed labels on the second and third pages of the ROM BIOS listing. The management of these pointers is performed in the INT 9 routine, KB_INT. The PC2 routine can be found on page A-28, and the PCjr manual has the equivalent routine on page A-45.

The keyboard buffer can be logically emptied by setting BUFFER_HEAD to the same value as BUFFER_TAIL with DEF SEG=0:POKE &H41A,PEEK(&H41C). DOS INT 21 function Ch provides a service that clears the keyboard buffer.

Program 2-4 monitors the keyboard buffer contents and pointers in operation. As characters are entered, the BUFFER_TAIL pointer is shown being updated and the ASCII and scan codes for the new key are displayed along with its character representation. When the buffer becomes full, a flashing message will be displayed. You may want to use the program to experiment with the ROM BIOS KB_INT routine's logic. See how unique scan codes can differentiate between a Ctrl-H and a Backspace, the two asterisks on the keyboard, Ctrl-M and Enter, and so on.

Program 2-4. Monitoring the Keyboard Buffer and Pointers

For error-free program entry, be sure to use "The Automatic Proofreader," Appendix H.

```
JC 100 'KBBUFFER; display keyboard buffer content
       s and pointers
HH 105 '         Does not use compatibility servic
       e calls
66 110 '
CH 120 ' --- display header info ---
DP 130 SCREEN 0:WIDTH 80:CLS:DEF SEG=0:COLOR 2,0
PL 140 PRINT"----------- Keyboard Buffer Contents
       -----------"
EK 150 LOCATE 2,1:COLOR 5,0
OD 160 PRINT "Keyboard buffer at &H41E thru &H43D
PK 170 PRINT"Head = Tail indicates all have been
       processed"
CC 180 PRINT"Tail = head - 2 when buffer is full"
BN 190 BUFFHEAD=&H400+PEEK(&H41A)
MF 200 LOCATE 6,1:COLOR 5:PRINT"Current head at &
       H"HEX$(BUFFHEAD);
JD 210 ' --- display scale lines ---
6A 220 GOSUB 410:GOSUB 430:GOSUB 460
IM 230 ' --- time to update the screen ---
EK 240 BUFFTAIL=&H400+PEEK(&H41C)
```

78

```
JL 250 LOCATE 6,22:COLOR BUFFTAIL MOD 7+1
LH 260 PRINT"  Tail at &H"HEX$(BUFFTAIL);
ME 270 IF BUFFTAIL=BUFFHEAD-2 THEN COLOR 7+16:PRI
       NT" BUFFER FULL"
EK 280 Y=&H41E:Z=&H42D
IJ 290 R=10:GOSUB 340 'show the contents of the b
       uffer
EH 300 Y=&H42E:Z=&H43D
FP 310 R=17:GOSUB 340 'show the buffer contents
LP 320 GOTO 240     ' and back to top of loop
FG 330 ' --- show the address range of the buffer
       ---
JH 340 LOCATE R,1:COLOR 6,0:FOR X=Y TO Z STEP 2
JI 350 X$="      ":IF PEEK(X)>32 THEN X$="    "+CH
       R$(PEEK(X))+"   "
ID 360 PRINT X$;:NEXT:PRINT
OH 370 ' --- show the contents of the buffer, asc
       ii and scan code ---
PP 380 COLOR 4,0:FOR X=Y TO Z STEP 2
OB 390 PRINT " ";RIGHT$("0"+HEX$(PEEK(X)),2);"/";
       RIGHT$("0"+HEX$(PEEK(X+1)),2);:NEXT:PRINT:
       RETURN
JD 400 ' --- display scale lines ---
PP 410 R=12:GOSUB 420:R=19:GOSUB 420:RETURN
CH 420 LOCATE R,1:COLOR 3,0:FOR X=1 TO 8:PRINT "
       as/sc";:NEXT:RETURN
LM 430 R=9:Y=&H41E:GOSUB 440:R=16:GOSUB 440:RETUR
       N
KJ 440 LOCATE R,1:COLOR 2,0:FOR X=0 TO 14 STEP 2
OO 450 PRINT " &h"HEX$(Y+X);:NEXT:Y=Y+X:RETURN
OG 460 LOCATE 7,1:COLOR 3,0:PRINT "Watch buffer a
       s you enter characters":RETURN
```

DOS services are not provided for the direct inspection of the keyboard buffer contents. DOS services 1, 6, 7, 8, Ah, and Ch provide various combinations of waiting for a single character, reading it, echoing it to the screen, and checking for Ctrl-Break. Only the ASCII character or an extended scan code is provided by these services; scan codes are not normally made available. But your program can place a simulated keyboard entry directly in the keyboard buffer for later processing or for future INPUT or INKEY$ statements. Try the example listed in Program 2-5. When prompted for characters to place in the buffer, enter the statement FILES.

The ROM BIOS and DOS do not provide keyboard buffer plugging services.

79

ROM BIOS INT 16 can be used to determine if the keyboard buffer contains any keypresses, retrieve the ASCII and scan code representation of the key, and obtain the KB_FLAG status byte. To follow IBM compatibility conventions, use the BASIC SRVCCALL routine to call service 16h.

Program 2-5. Example of Plugging the Keyboard Buffer

For error-free program entry, be sure to use "The Automatic Proofreader," Appendix H.

```
JM 100 'KBPLUGER; Demonstrate plugging the keyboa
        rd buffer from keys entered
HK 110 '          Does not use compatibility servic
        e calls
GK 120 CLS : DEF SEG=0:PRINT"Enter characters (up
        to 14) for keyboard buffer."
QP 130 PRINT "Function keys may be used."
BC 140 INPUT K$ : IF K$="" THEN END  ' enter with
        out characters causes exit
GI 150 K$=LEFT$(K$,14)+CHR$(13)     ' limit to 14 c
        hars, add return
HM 160 DUBL=2*LEN(K$)  ' double length since asci
        i/scan code
BP 170 FOR X=1 TO DUBL STEP 2  ' fill every other
        byte with key
NE 180    Y=ASC(MID$(K$,(X+1)/2,1))  ' character
        for this buffer position
MG 190 POKE &H41D+X,Y  ' fill character buff
BE 200 NEXT : POKE &H41C,&H1E+DUBL  ' point tail
        ptr to word after last character
KO 210 POKE &H41A,&H1E  ' point head ptr to start
        of buffer
```

An extension of this technique is demonstrated by Program 2-6. Lines of text carefully placed on the screen are "entered" into the computer by positioning the cursor properly and placing a carriage return in the keyboard buffer. This method can be used to cause a runtime-determined set of commands to be issued and to allow programs to modify themselves or to create whole programs themselves.

If more lines than will fit on a screen are needed, the last line to be displayed for "entry" should be a statement that sets a variable to the number of the statement to put on the screen next and a GOTO statement to the line of the running program that will continue with further screen line formatting and simulated entry. (Line 390 will cause the program to delete itself. Be sure to save the program before running it.)

Program 2-6. Entering Screen Lines via the Keyboard Buffer

For error-free program entry, be sure to use "The Automatic Proofreader," Appendix H.

```
IL 100 'KBGENLNS; example of dynamic creation of
        program lines
IA 110 '           Does not use compatibility serv
        ices
NA 120 SCREEN 0:WIDTH 80  'so locates correctly
IB 130 CLS : DEF SEG=0
PM 140 ' --- program lines to be created, could b
        e built dynamically ---
OF 150 X$="995 'generated line ; when pgm done, t
        he next line will say ok and cursor placed
        on the beginning of next line. therefore
        2 crsr ups placed in the buffer move us to
        the last of the generated lines."
EE 160 PRINT X$
ID 170 PRINT:PRINT"996 'second generated line, pl
        aced after first, leaving blank line for '
        ok' prompt by basic"
QK 180 PRINT:PRINT"997 'third generated line"
KO 190 PRINT:PRINT"998 'last generated line, plac
        ed after third, leaving blank line for 'ok
        ' prompt by basic"
JK 200 ' --- locate the cursor for enter keys com
        ing ---
II 210 LOCATE INT((LEN(X$)/80))+2,1 'place ending
        cursor on last screen line of first gener
        ated line
DM 230 ' --- Update the buffer pointers to hold e
        nter keys ---
LH 240 POKE &H41A,&H1E   ' head ptr points to buf
        fer
IA 250 POKE &H41C,&H1E+18   ' tail ptr points to
        word after last character
GA 260 ' num of following pokes *2, can't excee
        d 30
QJ 270 ' --- Position the cursor ---
NJ 280 POKE &H41E,0:POKE &H41F,&H48 'crsr up twic
        e to get back to gened line,
PM 290 POKE &H420,0:POKE &H421,&H48 'above 'ok' p
        rompt
LJ 300 ' --- place enter keys in buffer ---
ND 310 POKE &H422,13            'enter the line
EI 320 POKE &H424,13   'down to 2nd generated line
NL 330 POKE &H426,13   'enter the 2nd line
BJ 340 POKE &H428,13   'down to 3rd generated line
BI 350 POKE &H42A,13   'enter the 3rd line
CA 360 POKE &H42C,13   'down to last line
DK 370 POKE &H42E,13   'enter the last line
```

81

```
EN 380 ' --- all done, clean up ---
CP 390 DELETE 100-400  ' only generated lines to
       be left at end
OK 400 END  ' end the program and process the buf
       fer
```

Keyboard Buffer Relocation 480h, 482h

In the PC1, the keyboard buffer location and length remain
constant. The ROM BIOS routines use absolute addresses for
the buffer location. The buffer is always located in the 32
bytes between 41Eh and 43Dh. This provides room for 15
keypresses, each made up of an ASCII byte and a scan code.
The newer PC models use the same locations for the keyboard
buffer by default, but the address and length of the keyboard
buffer can be changed. The XT, PC2, and PCjr contain pointers
at 480h and 482h that are used in ROM BIOS for the keyboard buffer starting and ending addresses, allowing a different location and length for the keyboard buffer. To see how
to relocate the keyboard buffer so that it can hold more
keypresses, look at the example in Program 2-7.

The location chosen to contain the new keyboard buffer is
used by MODE.COM, the intra-application communications
area, and part of the area is reserved by IBM. This location
may not be suitable in all instances.

DOS and ROM BIOS do not provide services for relocat-
ing the keyboard buffer.

If you need to put the keyboard buffer back to its original
position for buffer location sensitive programs, Program 2-8
will do this for you.

Program 2-7. Relocating the Keyboard Buffer

For error-free program entry, be sure to use "The Automatic Proofreader," Appendix H.

```
JJ 100 'KBBUFFMV; Create a 54 char buffer in segm
       ent 40
OC 105 ' Does not use compatibility service calls
HF 110 DEF SEG=0
HM 120 '--- change buffer pointers ---
DI 130 POKE &H480,&H90   'start
HI 140 POKE &H482,&HFE   'end
LC 150 POKE &H41A,&H90   'head
CM 160 POKE &H41C,&H90   'tail
CO 170 '--- show current pointers ---
JD 180 DEF SEG=0:CLS 'goto here to examine ptrs
CC 190 LOCATE 1,1
```

```
NF 200 PRINT"Buffer pointers"
PN 210 PRINT "start="HEX$(PEEK(&H480));
FJ 220 PRINT ", end="HEX$(PEEK(&H482))
HL 230 PRINT "head="HEX$(PEEK(&H41A));
HO 240 PRINT ", tail="HEX$(PEEK(&H41C))
HK 250 GOTO 190
```

Program 2-8. Restoring the Keyboard Buffer's Default Location

```
100 'KBBUFFBK; return keyboard buffer to origi
    nal position
110 DEF SEG=0
120 '--- restore default buffer pointers ---
130 POKE &H480,&H1E   'start
140 POKE &H482,&H3E   'end
150 POKE &H41A,&H1E   'head
160 POKE &H41C,&H1E   'tail, mark as empty
```

ANSI.SYS Escape Sequences

DOS 2.0 and 2.1 provide a tool that can be used to redefine keys to suit the user. A string of characters beginning with the escape character (1Bh, 27 decimal) can be used to specify user key redefinitions. These escape sequences do not correspond to any particular memory locations; they are simply written as messages to the standard output device. A provided DOS device driver, ANSI.SYS, intercepts and acts appropriately upon the escape sequences. These sequences are detailed in Chapter 13 of the DOS 2.0 manual and Chapter 2 of the DOS 2.10 *Technical Reference* manual. You can install the device driver with the following (remember, [F6] means press the F6 key):

A> COPY CON: CONFIG.SYS
DEVICE=ANSI.SYS
[F6]

   Programs that set the meanings of keys themselves may be confused by the user ANSI.SYS redefinition of keys, so be prepared to turn off your redefinitions before executing sensitive programs. BASIC manages to totally ignore the redefinitions.

   A typical problem in the use of ANSI.SYS escape sequences is the creation of the required escape code (1Bh) that must begin each sequence. The Esc key on the keyboard cannot be used to directly enter this character while in DOS because of the special meaning associated with that key. EDLIN also uses the escape key for its own purposes, but you can create the escape code by entering Ctrl-V and (letting up on the Ctrl key) the left square bracket. It looks strange, but follow this with the left square bracket required by ANSI.SYS and the remainder of the escape sequence. For example, the escape sequence to turn on high intensity would look like this in EDLIN: ^V[[1m.

Using EDLIN, DEBUG, or an editor program that allows the entry of the escape code (ASCII 27), such as the *Personal Editor, Professional Editor, VEDIT*, and so on, you can easily create the escape sequences in batch file ECHO, REM statements, or data files to TYPE or COPY to the standard output device (display).

The sample machine language program shown as Program 2-9 can be used to create ANSI.COM which allows the direct keyboard entry of the desired escape sequences. In addition, ANSI.COM will create the left square bracket character that must follow the leading escape character. For example, to set function key 10 for a DIR command, ANSI 0;68;'dir';13p can be entered at the keyboard or placed in a batch file. ANSI 44;37m will select white characters on a blue background and ANSI 2J will clear the screen.

To create ANSI.COM, you must first assemble Program 2-9. Next, LINK the .OBJ file to create an .EXE file. Use ANSI.EXE with EXE2BIN.EXE to create a .COM file with the following command:

EXE2BIN ANSI.EXE

If you don't have an assembler, ANSI.COM can also be created with DEBUG as follows (as you can see it is much easier to create ANSI.COM using DEBUG):

```
A> DEBUG ANSI.COM
File not found
- E 100 BB 80 00 02 1F BF 80 00 C7 05 1B 5B C6 47 01 24
- E 110 BA 80 00 B4 09 CD 21 CD 20
- R CX
CX 0000
:19
- W
- Q
```

Program 2-9. Escape Code Generator for ANSI.SYS Sequences

```
;ANSI; append escape code (1Bh) and [ on front of entered
;string and issue to standard output device.
;
;DOS 2.x CONFIG.SYS must contain "DEVICE=ANSI.SYS", and
;      both files must be on the booted disk.
;Note error in DOS 2.0 manual on page 13-11: semicolon should
;      not be placed between ending quote of string and
;      the lowercase letter p. Same error in DOS 2.1 manual on
;      page 2-11.
;

PARM_LEN    EQU        0080h
ESC_LBRK    EQU        5B1Bh                              ; escape, left
                                                          ; square bracket (reversed)

CODE        SEGMENT
            ASSUME     CS:CODE
ANSI        PROC       FAR
  ; determine end of string location
            MOV        BX,PARM_LEN                        ; PSP parm length address
            ADD        BL,[BX]                            ; add length to address
  ; place esc [ on front of string
            MOV        DI,PARM_LEN                        ; overlay parm length byte
                                                          ; and
            MOV        WORD PTR [DI],ESC_LBRK  ; leading space of string
  ; place dollar sign on end
            MOV        BYTE PTR [BX+1],'$'                ; dollar marks
                                                          ; end for INT 21 9
  ; write out the ANSI.SYS string and end
            MOV        DX,PARM_LEN                        ; starting address of
                                                          ; message
            MOV        AH,9                               ; message output wanted
            INT        21H                                ; call for DOS service
            INT        20H                                ; all done
ANSI        ENDP
CODE        ENDS
  ;
            END        ANSI
```

The repeated entry of ANSI for each escape sequence can be inefficient when there is a whole group of escape sequences to be issued. Let's create a file of the escape sequences we wish to issue and then type that file on demand. A batch file would simplify the process. Program 2-10 creates a data file with example escape sequences as well as a batch file, KEYSON.BAT, to cause the data file to be typed. Why not just include the escape sequences in the batch file? Because batch processing is slow compared with TYPE and COPY.

Program 2-11 creates the same type of data and batch file for turning off the redefined keys.

For more speed, a machine language program can be used to issue the desired escape sequences directly, as shown in Program 2-12.

Before you get too thrilled with escape sequences, I have to tell you that there is a limit of around 200 characters of key redefinitions that can be saved in ANSI.SYS before they start to overlay COMMAND.COM. So you may want to use something like PROKEY for the really involved key redefinitions.

Program 2-10. Creation of Key Definition File and Batch Command

For error-free program entry, be sure to use "The Automatic Proofreader," Appendix H.

```
HB 100 'KEYSON Create ansi.sys file to be typed t
       o set function keys 9-10,
BC 110 '          set mode co80, and white on blue s
       creen.
CN 120 'DOS 2.x CONFIG.SYS must contain "DEVICE=A
       NSI.SYS", and
CO 130 '          both files must be on the booted d
       isk."
IB 135 'NOTE ERROR in DOS 2.0 manual on page 13-1
       1: semi colon should
HH 136 '          NOT be placed between ending quote
       of string and
ML 137 '          the lowercase letter p. SAME ERROR
       in DOS 2.1 manual on
IB 138 '          page 2-11.
HM 140 '
MJ 150 ESC$=CHR$(27)
EK 160 OPEN "keyson" FOR OUTPUT AS #1
CL 170 PRINT#1,ESC$;"[0;67;'DIR A:';13p" 'f9
JG 180 PRINT#1,ESC$;"[0;68;'BASICA';13p" 'f10
CO 190 PRINT#1,ESC$;"[=3h"        'mode co80
EA 200 PRINT#1,ESC$;"[44m"         'blue background
OM 210 PRINT#1,ESC$;"[2J"         'cls
EO 220 PRINT#1,ESC$;"[30m"        'msg in black
DM 230 PRINT#1,"                         f9=DIR
       f10=BASIC"  'key usage
GL 240 PRINT#1,ESC$;"[37m"         'rest in white
FM 250 CLOSE 1
QI 260 OPEN "keyson.bat" FOR OUTPUT AS #1
MD 270 PRINT#1,"echo off"
HH 280 PRINT#1,"type keyson"
FE 290 CLOSE 1
LM 300 SYSTEM
```

Program 2-11. Creation of Key Reset File and Batch Command

For error-free program entry, be sure to use "The Automatic Proofreader," Appendix H.

```
EN 100 'KEYSOFF; Create ansi.sys file to be typed
       to unset keys 9-10.
CL 110 'DOS 2.x CONFIG.SYS must contain "DEVICE=A
       NSI.SYS", and
CM 120 '        both files must be on the booted d
       isk."
HK 130 '
LH 140 ESC$=CHR$(27)
OA 150 OPEN "keysoff" FOR OUTPUT AS #1
HB 160 PRINT#1,ESC$;"[0;67;0;67p"        'f9
MG 170 PRINT#1,ESC$;"[0;68;0;68p"        'f10
MM 180 PRINT#1,ESC$;"[40m"               'black back
       ground
MB 190 PRINT#1,ESC$;"[2J"                'cls
EC 200 CLOSE 1
OL 210 OPEN "keysoff.bat" FOR OUTPUT AS #1
MJ 220 PRINT#1,"echo off"
MF 230 PRINT#1,"type keysoff"
FK 240 CLOSE 1
LF 250 SYSTEM
```

Program 2-12. EXE Program to Issue Escape Sequence Series

```
;
;KEYSON; use ansi.sys to set function keys 9-10,
;       set mode co80, and white on blue screen.
;DOS 2.x CONFIG.SYS must contain "DEVICE=ANSI.SYS", and
;       both files must be on the booted disk.
;Note error in DOS 2.0 manual on page 13-11: semicolon should
;       not be placed between ending quote of string and
;       the lowercase letter p. Same error in DOS 2.1 manual on
;       page 2-11.
;
STACK    SEGMENT STACK
         DW        64 DUP (?)
STACK    ENDS
;
KEYS     SEGMENT PARA PUBLIC 'DATA'
KEYSEQ   DB        27,'[0;67;"DIR A:"      ;13p' ;f9
         DB        27,'[0;68;" BASICA"     ;13p' ;f10
         DB        27,'[=3h'               ;mode co80
         DB        27,'[44m'               ;blue background
         DB        27,'[2J'                ;cls
         DB        27,'[30m'               ;msg in black
```

```
                DB          '                         F9=DIR  F10=BASIC'
                DB          27,'[37m'                 ;rest in white
                DB          '$'
KEYS            ENDS
;
CODE            SEGMENT
                ASSUME      CS:CODE
KEYSON          PROC        FAR
                PUSH        DS
                SUB         AX,AX                      ; save return address
                PUSH        AX
;
                MOV         AX,KEYS
                MOV         DS,AX
                ASSUME      DS:KEYS
                MOV         DX,OFFSET KEYSEQ
                MOV         AH,9
                INT         21H
                RET
KEYSON          ENDP
CODE            ENDS
;
                END         KEYSON
```

Break and Reboot Keys

BASICA in DOS 2.0 and 2.10 allows the programmer to trap
up to five different combinations of Shift, Alt, Caps Lock,
Num Lock, and Ctrl with an accompanying key's scan code.
These traps can send the program off to a subroutine to do the
desired actions whenever the selected combination of keys are
pressed. Use the ON KEY( ) statement to trap function or
cursor keys. Program 2-13 demonstrates how the Break key
and the Ctrl-Alt-Del sequence (REBOOT) can be trapped and
disabled by a BASIC program. This trapping is done asyn-
chronously, as demonstrated by the trap subroutines sometimes being driven between the LOCATE 2,1 statement and
the following PRINT statement for the countdown value.

Program 2-13. Trapping Break and Reboot Keys in BASIC

For error-free program entry, be sure to use "The Automatic Proofreader," Appendix H.

```
LA 100 'BREAKNOT; use BASICA key statement to tra
       p Break and Ctrl-Alt-Del
66 110 '
MA 120 CLS:PRINT"Try to Break or Ctrl-Alt-Del"
IB 130 CTRL.BREAK$=CHR$(4)+CHR$(70)        ' Ctrl=4
       , 70=scan code for Break
EP 140 CTRL.ALT.DEL$=CHR$(12)+CHR$(83)     ' Ctrl+A
       lt=12, Del=83
```

88

```
IA 150 ' --- setup trap routines ---
BG 160 KEY 15, CTRL.BREAK$: KEY (15) ON: ON KEY (
       15) GOSUB 240 ' set trap routine
OG 170 KEY 16, CTRL.ALT.DEL$: KEY (16) ON: ON KEY
       (16) GOSUB 280
OE 180 ' --- try to use keys ---
AD 190 FOR X= 400 TO 0 STEP -1: LOCATE 2,1:PRINT
       "countdown"X:NEXT:
EM 200 PRINT"Break and Ctrl-Alt-Del now enabled"
LB 210 KEY (15) OFF:KEY (16) OFF ' reset the tra
       ps
FD 220 GOTO 220 ' give time to try keys
DK 230 ' --- Break trap routine ---
KP 240 BRK=BRK+1:LOCATE 10,1:PRINT"^C BREAK KEY T
       RAPPED"BRK
EP 250 '.... here you could perform any break act
       ion desired - depending ....
HP 260 '.... on program conditions, possibly wrap
       up the program quickly ...
NK 270 RETURN
BA 280 ' --- Ctrl-Alt-Del trap routine ---
JA 290 CAD=CAD+1:LOCATE 12,1:PRINT"!!! REBOOT TRA
       PPED !!!"CAD
MN 300 RETURN
```

Break Interrupt Vector at 6C–6Fh INT 1B

You may want to disable the Break key when your non-BASICA program is running so that the user must use a program-provided option to gracefully wrap things up. If we want to simply ignore the Break key, one way to do this in BASIC is to overlay the break interrupt vector at 6C–6Fh that BASIC has established. Use the address of the routine that the power-on routine places there before BASIC changed it. The routine is a "return to caller" IRET instruction. To be safe, we can save and restore the address that's currently in the vector, as Program 2-14 demonstrates. The statements in lines 150 and 190–220 overlay the BASIC established break vector. The pause function will still be available for the user to pace output, even though the Break key has no effect.

Program 2-14. Ignoring the Break Key in BASIC

For error-free program entry, be sure to use "The Automatic Proofreader," Appendix H.

```
JP 100 'BRKIGNOR; ignore BASIC's break vector, sa
       ving and restoring
BE 110 '         Does not use convention of DOS
       services 25 and 35
```

89

```
QN 120 PRINT "BRKIGNOR; disables Break while runn
       ing
OO 130 '--- Show and save current BASIC break int
       errupt vector ---
HE 140 DEFINT A-Z
IN 150 DEF SEG=0
HA 160 PRINT"BASIC's vector=";: GOSUB 300 'Show B
       ASIC's break vector
GM 170 FOR X=0 TO 3: POKE &H180+X,PEEK(&H6C+X): N
       EXT 'Save BASIC's break vector
CN 180 '--- Change break vector to do-nothing rou
       tine at 840h ---
PL 190 POKE &H6C,&H40
FE 200 POKE &H6D,&H1
DJ 210 POKE &H6E,&H70
GB 220 POKE &H6F,&H0
IB 230 '--- Restore and show current BASIC break
       interrupt vector ---
DE 240 PRINT"Ignore vector=";: GOSUB 300 'Show du
       mmy break vector
BG 250 PRINT"running, try to break... ": FOR X=1
       TO 9000: NEXT
JH 260 FOR X=0 TO 3: POKE &H6C+X,PEEK(&H180+X): N
       EXT 'Restore BASIC's break vector
PF 270 PRINT"BASIC's vector restored=";: GOSUB 30
       0 'Show BASIC's break vector
ML 280 END '
PM 290 '--- Subroutine to print current break vec
       tor contents ---
KJ 300 FOR X=0 TO 3: PRINT PEEK (&H6C+X);'show cu
       rrent break vector
OC 310    NEXT: PRINT: RETURN
```

DOS offers services 35 and 25 to retrieve and store interrupt vectors. To follow IBM compatibility conventions, use the BASIC SRVCCALL routine to save, modify, and restore the break interrupt vector. The DOS manual for DOS 2.0 discusses the use of services 25 and 35h in Appendix D. For DOS 2.10, see Chapter 5 of the DOS *Technical Reference* manual.

Sometimes the single IRET instruction in the dummy routine set by power-on may not return control to the BASIC program because of several levels of pending interrupts. You can read about this consideration on page 5-8 of the PCjr *Technical Reference* manual or page 2-5 of the XT manual. If this problem surfaces during testing, set the break vector to the address of a BASIC variable that contains enough IRET instructions, each composed of a CHR$(207).

Reboot Trapping Outside BASIC

The Ctrl-Alt-Del (REBOOT) sequence may be detected and by-passed by a short machine language front-end routine that you can place before the normal ROM BIOS resident keyboard INT 9 routine. The example Program 2-15 changes the INT 9 vector to point to the program and disallows the reboot sequence by turning off the Ctrl key when Alt and Del are being pressed. On the PCjr, other Ctrl-Alt sequences are used for key clicker start/stop, left/right screen adjustment, and the starting of diagnostic routines with Ctrl-Alt-Ins. The program carefully disables only the Delete and Insert keys while Ctrl-Alt is pressed. The routine then allows the normal INT 9 routine to do its keyboard interrupt processing. BOOTNOT.COM installs itself and stays resident, meaning that you must power-on or reboot (using the "secret" Ctrl-Alt–right Shift sequence with the Del or Ins keys) to rid it from the system.

To create the BOOTNOT.COM routine, enter the source code shown in Program 2-15 (if you have an assembler), and save it using the filename BOOTNOT.ASM. If you don't have an assembler, BOOTNOT.COM can also be created with DEBUG from the disassembly in Program 2-16.

Assembler owners should then use the following batch file (this is the same batch file used in Chapter 1 to create SRVCCALL.COM) to create the BOOTNOT.COM module (you must have ASM, EXE2BIN.EXE, and your source file on the same disk):

```
asm %1,,,;
link %1,,con,;
exe2bin %1.exe %1.com
```

Once you have the batch file created, assuming you called it CREATE.BAT, enter this command to create BOOTNOT.COM:

A>CREATE BOOTNOT

Program 2-15. Disabling Reboot via INT 9

```
;BOOTNOT; Example int 9 interception routine
;            to monitor shift status bits,
;            changing any Ctrl-Alt-Del to Alt-Del
;            so that machine cannot
;            be booted. Program stays resident,
;            power-on needed to remove.
;
;
;            Ctrl-Alt-Ins also disabled
;            (PCjr diagnostics), but other
```

```
;              PCjr Ctrl-Alt combinations
;              allowed: clicker, screen shift.
;
;              Authorized users may use
;              Ctrl-Alt–right Shift–Del
;              to reboot, or Ctrl-Alt–right
;              Shift–Ins for PCjr diagnostics.
;
cseg          segment para public 'code'
              org       100h
BOOTNOT  proc far
              assume cs:cseg,ds:cseg
;
              jmp install                    ; go install the new int 9 routine
;
oldint9   dd        0                 ; saved original int 9 vector
int9loc   equ       9h*4              ; location of int 9 vector
kb_flag   equ       417h              ; location of keyboard status flag
ctrl      equ       04                ; kb_flag with ctrl bit on
alt       equ       08                ; kb_flag with alt bit on
rshift    equ       01                ; kb_flag with right shift bit on
noctrl    equ       0ffh – ctrl       ; kb_flag with ctrl bit off
delete    equ       83                ; delete keyscan code
insert    equ       82                ; insert keyscan code
;
newint9:                              ; entry here on keyboard interrupt 9
          sti                         ; interrupts enabled
          push      es                ; save requisites
          push      di
          push      ax
          push      cx
          pushf
;
          mov       ax,0
          mov       es,ax             ; es is segment 0
          mov       di,kb_flag        ; kb_flag
          mov       ah,es:[di]        ; into ah
;
          test      ah,alt            ; Alt key down?
          jz        return            ; no, exit
          test      ah,ctrl           ; Ctrl key down?
          jz        return            ; no, exit
;
          in        al,60h            ; get the keypress from 8255
          cmp       al,delete         ; check for Del key pressed
          jne       pcjr              ; not delete, PCjr has other Ctrl-Alts
;
authtest:
          test      ah,rshift         ; right Shift down?
          jnz       authuser          ; yes, allow request
          jmp       inhibit           ; no, don't allow reboot
;
pcjr:
          cmp       al,insert         ; check for Ins key pressed
          jne       return            ; no, allow other PCjr combos
          jmp       authtest          ; yes, allow diagnostics if authorized
```

92

```
;
inhibit:
                and         ah,noctrl           ; turn off the ctrl flag
                mov         es:[di],ah          ; and put back KB_flag
                jmp         return
;
authuser:                                       ; authorized user requests,
                                                ; let it go through
;
return:                                         ; back to the normal int 9 routine
                popf
                pop         cx
                pop         ax
                pop         di
                pop         es
                jmp         cs:[oldint9]        ; goto the original int 9 routine
;
install:                                        ; installation of this new int 9
                mov         ax,0
                mov         es,ax
                mov         di,int9loc          ; save old int 9 vector
                mov         ax,es:[di]          ; int 9 ip
                mov         bx,es:[di+2]        ; int 9 cs
                mov         si,offset oldint9
                mov         [si],ax
                mov         [si+2],bx
;
                mov         ax,0
                mov         es,ax
                mov         bx,ds
;
                cli                             ; disable interrupts
; - - interrupts disabled - -
                mov         di,int9loc
                mov         ax,offset newint9
                mov         es:[di],ax          ; change int 9 vector ip
                mov         es:[di+2],bx        ; change int 9 vector cs
; - - - - - - - - - - - - -
                sti                             ; reenable interrupts
;
                mov         dx,offset install
                                                ; length of resident portion of program
                int         27h                 ; terminate, but stay resident
;
BOOTNOT         endp
cseg            ends
end             BOOTNOT
```

Program 2-16. Disassembly of BOOTNOT.COM

```
0100   EB47        JMP      0149
0102   90          NOP
0103   0000
0105   0000
0107   FB          STI
0108   06          PUSH     ES
0109   57          PUSH     DI
010A   50          PUSH     AX
010B   51          PUSH     CX
010C   9C          PUSHF
010D   B80000      MOV      AX,0000
0110   8EC0        MOV      ES,AX
0112   BF1704      MOV      DI,0417
0115   26          ES:
0116   8A25        MOV      AH,[DI]
0118   F6C408      TEST     AH,08
011B   7422        JZ       013F
011D   F6C404      TEST     AH,04
0120   741D        JZ       013F
0122   E460        IN       AL,60
0124   3C53        CMP      AL,53
0126   7508        JNZ      0130
0128   F6C401      TEST     AH,01
012B   7512        JNZ      013F
012D   EB07        JMP      0136
012F   90          NOP
0130   3C52        CMP      AL,52
0132   750B        JNZ      013F
0134   EBF2        JMP      0128
0136   80E4FB      AND      AH,FB
0139   26          ES:
013A   8825        MOV      [DI],AH
013C   EB01        JMP      013F
013E   90          NOP
013F   9D          POPF
0140   59          POP      CX
0141   58          POP      AX
0142   5F          POP      DI
0143   07          POP      ES
0144   2E          CS:
0145   FF2E0301    JMP      FAR [0103]
0149   B80000      MOV      AX,0000
014C   8EC0        MOV      ES,AX
014E   BF2400      MOV      DI,0024
```

```
0151    26          ES:
0152    8B05        MOV     AX,[DI]
0154    26          ES:
0155    8B5D02      MOV     BX,[DI+02]
0158    BE0301      MOV     SI,0103
015B    8904        MOV     [SI],AX
015D    895C02      MOV     [SI+02],BX
0160    B80000      MOV     AX,0000
0163    8EC0        MOV     ES,AX
0165    8CDB        MOV     BX,DS
0167    FA          CLI
0168    BF2400      MOV     DI,0024
016B    B80701      MOV     AX,0107
016E    26          ES:
016F    8905        MOV     [DI],AX
0171    26          ES:
0172    895D02      MOV     [DI+02],BX
0175    FB          STI
0176    BA4901      MOV     DX,0149
0179    CD27        INT     27
```

You'll notice in BOOTNOT.COM that the 8255 I/O port at address 60h can be retrieved by your own routine without destroying the contents of this port for the following normal interrupt routine. The provided INT 9 routine is long and somewhat complicated in its processing of scan code tables. To add a few instructions to the middle of INT 9, copy the INT 9 routine and tables to user memory, patch in a call to your revisions at the proper location, and point the INT 9 vector to your version of the routine. A disassembly of the provided INT 9 routine can be directed to a disk file with DEBUG, tailored and modified to suit your needs, an installation routine added, the resulting instructions assembled, and then saved as a program to be installed when desired.

An easier technique (although incompatible with other versions of ROM BIOS and highly discouraged by IBM) involves reproducing any foregoing INT 9 instructions into your own routine. Then perform the processing you desire and jump directly into the ROM BIOS at the instruction that you wish to resume in the provided INT 9 routine. PC-compatible machines may not handle this well.

Such manipulations are seldom needed because of the excellent support offered by the standard BIOS and DOS service routines. Generally, custom INT 9 routines are needed only when the provided routines would take some undesired action upon or ignore certain keypress combinations.

BIOS Keyboard I/O Interrupt at 58–5Ch INT 16

The ROM BIOS includes keyboard service routines reached by issuing INT 16 with the desired function code placed in the AH register. The INT 16 routines are labeled KEYBOARD_IO in the PC2 ROM BIOS at FE82Eh or in the PCjr at F13DDh. See *Technical Reference* manual, page A-24, or page A-43 in the PCjr manual for a listing of the routines.

INT 16 services can be called upon to inform us if there is one or more keypresses currently in the keyboard buffer, retrieve a keypress ASCII character and scan code from the buffer, or obtain the current Shift key status flag byte.

In BASIC, there is no way provided for determining the shift status of the keyboard beyond INKEY$, and only six keys at a time can be tested in the KEY(15–20) statement. And this facility is limited to BASICA asynchronous traps, so it's not particularly usable as a facility to extend key possibilities by the combination of Shift keys. INT 16, function 2 can provide this capability to our BASIC and machine language programs.

BASIC programs can use the INKEY$ statement to request the ASCII value of a keypress waiting in the keyboard buffer. INKEY$ will return with no data, the keypress character, or a zero followed by the extended code. It does not, however, provide a method for determining which of the few duplicated keys have been pressed, such as the asterisk on the 8 key and on the PrtSc key. We may want to use these duplicate keys for different purposes in our program, and we will need the scan code to differentiate which key was pressed. Also, INKEY$ won't help us determine whether the left or right Shift key was pressed, or if a combination of Shift and Ins, for example, were pressed together.

The BIOS keyboard I/O interrupt routine (INT 16) will provide this scan code information as well as wait for a keypress if needed, eliminating the IF X$="" test needed for INKEY$. The returned information is always two bytes (ASCII value, then scan code), with an ASCII value of 0 indicating that an extended code is present in the scan code byte. Break and Pause key combinations will be honored by BIOS and will not be passed on as data to the caller.

Program 2-17 demonstrates how to call various INT 16 functions from BASIC with SRVCCALL.

Program 2-17. SRVCCALL Routines to Call BIOS INT 16

```
' --- Request key availability status ---
'     bios INT 16, type 1 service
'     returned: zero flag=1 if none available
'     al%=ascii or 00, ah%=scan code
INTERRUPT%=&H16:AH%=&H1:AL%=0
'     Does not remove key from
'     buffer, but does return (in ax)
'     ASCII value of key.
GOSUB nnn 'call assembler routine
IF (FLAGS% AND 2^6) <> 0 GOTO 620
PRINT"keypress in buffer:"AL%"/"AH%:GOTO 630
620 PRINT"no keys in buffer":RETURN
630 ' Request ASCII and scan code of keypress
'     bios INT 16, type 0 service
'     returned: al%=ascii or 0
'     ah%=scan code or extended code
INTERRUPT%=&H16:AH%=&H0:AL%=0
' Unlike INKEY$, waits if needed
' and provides scan code besides
' ASCII value of key. BASIC's break
' routine is in effect.
GOSUB nnn 'call assembler routine
PRINT CHR$(AL%)"= scan code"AH%
' Request keyboard shift status
'     bios INT 16, type 2 service
'     returned: al%=kb_flag contents
'     (see location 417h)
INTERRUPT%=&H16:AH%=&H2:AL%=0
'     kb_flag_1 at 418h is not
'     provided by this function
'     See 417h in Appendix A of TRM
GOSUB nnn 'call assembler routine
PRINT "KB_FLAG = "HEX$(AL%)
RETURN
```

Two more BIOS INT 16 functions are provided on the PCjr: the ability to toggle on/off the keyboard clicker and typamatic key rate adjustment. Program 2-18 demonstrates the use of SRVCCALL to call these PCjr functions.

The appropriate PCjr settings could be made directly to KB_FLAG at 417h and KB_FLAG_2 at 488h with POKE statements. This is not recommended when such accessible services exist that provide a level of protection from future changes. However, the instructions in Program 2-19 could be used in place of the statements starting at 990 in Program 2-18 if direct change to the typamatic bits in KB_FLAG_2 is needed.

Program 2-18. SRVCCALL Routines to Call BIOS INT 16 PCjr Functions

```
' Request PCjr clicker on
'     bios INT 16, type 4 service
'     returned: nothing
INTERRUPT%=&H16:AH%=&H4:AL%=1
' al%=1 is clicker on
' al%=0 would turn off clicker
GOSUB nnn 'call assembler routine
PRINT "PCjr keyboard clicker now ON"
RETURN
' Request PCjr typamatic rate change
'     bios INT 16, type 3 service
'     returned: nothing
PRINT"-- Which PCjr typamatic adjustment? --"
PRINT"     0 - return to defaults      "
PRINT"     1 - increase initial delay  "
PRINT"     2 - half rate of repeat     "
PRINT"     3 - both 1 and 2 above      "
PRINT"     4 - typamatic function off "
990 INPUT X:IF X<0 OR X>4 GOTO 990
INTERRUPT%=&H16:AH%=&H3:AL%=X
' al% is 0 through 4
GOSUB nnn 'call assembler routine
PRINT "PCjr typamatic function now adjusted"
RETURN
```

Program 2-19. PCjr Modification of Typamatic Key Values

```
990 INPUT X:IF X<0 OR X>4 GOTO 990
X=X*2:DEF SEG=0
' change 0-4 to 0,2,4,6,8
Y=(PEEK(&H488) AND (&HFF-&HE))
' turn off bits 1-3
POKE &H488,(Y OR X)
' adjust KB_FLAG_2
PRINT "PCjr typamatic function now adjusted"
```

DOS Standard Input Interrupt Functions

DOS interrupt 21 offers standard input device (keyboard) services as summarized by Table 2-2. SRVCCALL can be used to invoke these services from BASIC. The number of the service is placed in AH%. In Table 2-2, the "Waits" column indicates that the service will wait until there is a keypress to return. The obtained character will be displayed on the screen if the "Echo" column indicates this. Most service functions check and act upon the Break key.

Detailed descriptions of the DOS INT 21 keyboard functions can be found starting on page D-17 of the DOS 2.0 manual or starting on page 5-17 of the DOS 2.10 *Technical Reference* manual.

Table 2-2. DOS INT 21 Keyboard Functions

AH	Service performed	Waits	Echo	Breaks
1	get character	yes	yes	yes
6	get character (or display character)	no	no	no
7	get character	yes	no	no
8	get character	yes	no	yes
A	buffered input	yes	yes	yes
B	any characters available	no	no	yes
C	clear buffer, call 1, 6, 7, 8, or A	no	no	yes

The examples below demonstrate the use of DOS INT 21 service function 1, and the combined services of function Ch calling function Ah.

```
' keyboard input with echo, break, wait
'      DOS INT 21, type 1 service
'      returned: ascii character in al%
INTERRUPT% = &H21:AH% = &H1:AL% = 0
GOSUB nnn 'call assembler routine
RETURN

' DOS buffered keyboard input
'      DOS INT 21, type A service
'      returned: second byte of buffer
'      contains character count
AL% = &HA:BUFFER$ = CHR$(&H80) + SPACE$(80) + " "
'      keyboard buffer
BUFF! = VARPTR(BUFFER$)
DH% = PEEK(BUFF! + 2)
DL% = PEEK(BUFF! + 1)
DEF SEG:GOSUB 1060
'call DOS int 21 function Ch
```

```
        PRINT "Received"ASC(MID$(BUFFER$,2,1))"characters"
        PRINT MID$(BUFFER$,3,80):RETURN
1060 '  keyboard clear and function 1, 6, 7, 8, or A
     '      DOS INT 21, type C service,
     '      then al% function
     '      returned: depends on al% function selected
        INTERRUPT%=&H21:AH%=&HC
     '      al% should be 1, 6, 7, 8, or Ah
        GOSUB nnn 'call assembler routine
        RETURN
```

8255A-5 PPI Ports A, B, and C at Ports 60–62h

The keyboard has no idea what the meaning of any particular key is; it simply views a key as one of 83 possible buttons (62 on the PCjr) that may be pressed and reports that occurrence to the system unit. The 8048 microprocessor in the keyboard (or 80C48 in the PCjr keyboard) reports when a key has been pressed and passes the scan code for the key along to be interpreted by the default INT_9 routine in ROM BIOS. The scan code comes into the computer over I/O port 60h, known as 8255 Port A (PA). In the PCjr, the scan code is placed into this port address by ROM BIOS routine INT 48 KEY62_INT to maintain PC compatibility.

The handshaking between the 8048 and INT 9 is complete when the 8048 receives an acknowledge signal. This acknowledgment of the reception of the scan code is sent on the output port at 61h (8255 PB) by turning on bit 7. Bit 6 of the same port allows clocking signals to be sent to the keyboard if it contains a 1 and turns off clocking (and effectively the keyboard) if a 0 is placed in that bit. In summary, the normal contents of the bits in port 61h are bit 6 = 1 (keyboard receiving clocking pulses) and bit 7 = 0 (not acknowledging).

Let's see how to turn off the PC and XT keyboards using the bits in port 61. If we turn on the acknowledge bit in 8255 port B (61h bit 7), then all scan codes from the keyboard will be regarded as received by the keyboard 8048 and no longer presented to the system unit. This, in effect, throws away all keyboard input. The BASIC statement needed to turn off the keyboard is

OUT &H61,&HCC

It turns on acknowledge bit (7). Now all keys are ignored—even Break and reboot.

This line will turn the keyboard on again:

OUT &H61,&H4C

It will turn off acknowledge bit (7).

The PCjr needn't acknowledge the reception of keyboard scan codes, and keyboard clocking isn't required. The PCjr's keyboard is connected directly to the Non-Maskable Interrupt (NMI) line of the 8088 processor and can only be preempted by a special timer that insures that the disk drive isn't left un-attended too long if it's currently active. On the PCjr, bit 6 of the 8255 port at 61h isn't needed for the keyboard (it's used for control of the sound chip), and bit 7 is reserved for future use. The PCjr does use bit 0 of port 62h (8255 PC) to sense that a scan code is inbound from the keyboard. This bit is used on the PC and XT to implement a loop in the power-on diagnostics for manufacturer testing purposes.

On the PCjr, bit 6 of port 62h (8255 PC) indicates that keyboard data is being serially received. Bit 7 contains a 0 if the keyboard cable is attached, indicating that the infrared link is not active. The PC and XT use these bits to flag I/O chan-nel checks (expansion slot card problems) and memory parity errors, respectively.

The PCjr keyboard can be turned off by simulating a Pause key before every real key pressed. This causes the real keypress to be thrown away, since it appears that this is a key pressed to end the pause function. Use this BASIC statement to simulate the Pause key (Fn-Echo is not ignored), thus effec-tively turning off the keyboard:

DEF SEG=0:POKE &H418,(PEEK(&H418) OR 8)

And this statement to turn it back on:

DEF SEG=0:POKE &H418,(PEEK(&H418) AND &HFF−&H8)

The power-on tests initialize ports 60–63h and then use them to do keyboard tests. These routines can be found at FE3A2h and FFA2Ah in the PC2 *Technical Reference* manual. The PCjr keyboard tests and initialization routines are unique because of the different keyboard implementation. The PCjr routines are at F04CCh and F0640h. The microprocessor in the keyboard of the PC, XT, and PCjr is programmed to self-test during the power-on sequence. If any keys are depressed, they are assumed to be stuck in the down position, error code 301 is displayed on the screen (ERROR B on the PCjr), and a shrill tone is produced to alert you of the condition.

Keyboard Interpret Interrupt INT 9 at FE987h PCjr:F1561h

For the keyboard input to be made available for use by programs, there must be a small flurry of activity in ROM BIOS INT 9 for each keypress. In order for INT 9 to be activated on the PC, a level-1 8259 interrupt (keyboard interrupt) is generated by the keyboard 8048. Only the timer interrupt at level 0 has more priority for the 8259. Bit 1 of the 8259 Interrupt Request Register (IRR) is set to keep track of the pending interrupt. If no other interrupt is being processed (the 8259 In Service Register has zeros in bits 0 and 1) and the Interrupt Mask Register allows the interrupt type, then the 8259 sends an interrupt to the 8088. If the 8088 is enabled for that interrupt, the 8259 is allowed to pass the interrupt type code, 9h for the keyboard, to the 8088 for processing. The 8088 pushes the CS:IP (code segment and offset) and flag register onto the stack and jumps using the INT 9h CS:IP vector contained in locations 24–27h. The 8259 sets on its ISR bit 1 to indicate that a keyboard interrupt is being processed and lower level interrupts must wait.

The INT 9 routine reads the scan code from port 60h and sends an acknowledge signal to the keyboard through bit 7 of port 61h. Bits 6 and 7 of port 61h are then set to their normal clock- and keyboard-enabled mode. The instructions that do this can be examined at label KB_INT in the ROM BIOS listing. Any shifting-key make or break scan code is detected, and the appropriate status flags are set or reset in 417h and 418h, KB_FLAG, and KB_FLAG1. Machine language equate statements for the bit meanings within these flag bytes can be found on the second page of the ROM BIOS listing. Shift keys that can be toggled (Caps Lock, Insert, Scroll Lock, and Num Lock) are processed specially so that typamatic repeating "make" scan codes are ignored, and only a "break" will allow a following "make." If this test wasn't there, it would be difficult to determine the state of a locking shift since it could bounce back and forth very rapidly.

After the Shift key flags are adjusted, the Pause key is acted upon if it was pressed. This sequence of processing means that a toggled Shift key such as Ins or Caps Lock is set even though the Pause key has been pressed. If the paused bit is on in 418h and a key other than the Num Lock key is pressed, then the key is discarded and the paused bit is reset. This discarding of the key that terminated the pause can be

102

used to throw away unwanted keypresses as shown above.

At label K29, a test is made for the Ctrl-Alt-Del keys, and a jump to the RESET routine is performed if that combination is found. Before the jump is made, 1234h is placed in location 472h to indicate that this is not the initial power-on sequence. This indicator will later allow the POST routines to bypass time-consuming tests.

If the Alt key is held while numeric keypad digits are used, the keys are accumulated into ALT_INPUT to form the ASCII character number. A space may be entered before, during, or after the numeric sequence and will be acted upon immediately without disturbing the accumulated ALT_INPUT value. ALT_INPUT is accumulated in location 419h. If the 0 key is the only ALT_INPUT value accumulated, the value is discarded as though it was not entered. Several methods could have been used to allow the entry of a ASCII code of zero, but this is not provided in the method chosen.

The Insert and Delete keys become zero and decimal point, respectively, while the keyboard is in Num Lock mode unless the Shift key is also pressed. The Shift keys can normally be used to temporarily toggle the Num Lock mode on or off, but the Shift keys will be ignored while the Alt key is depressed.

The routine at label K38 checks for the Break key combination of Ctrl–Scroll Lock. If found, the high-order bit in location 471h is set and an INT 1B is issued. When a program hasn't set this interrupt vector, nothing happens. If DOS is in control at the time, ^C will be displayed.

If the Shift and PrtSc keys are pressed, INT 5 is issued to cause the screen to be printed.

The balance of the interrupt routine is concerned with translating the scan code to ASCII and placement of the character in the keyboard buffer, calling the K4 routine to update the buffer pointers. A special test is performed to allow the Shift keys to provide lowercase letters when the keyboard is in Caps Lock mode. Extended scan codes are handled in the routine labeled K63, with the zero preceding the extended scan code being placed by routine K64.

The routine at K62 is called to sound the error tone when the keyboard buffer is full or scan code FFh is received, indicating a full buffer in the keyboard itself.

Once the scan code has been either acted upon, discarded as meaningless, or translated (to ASCII or an extended scan code) and placed in the buffer, 20h is sent out on port 20h to inform the 8259 that the End Of Interrupt processing (EOI) has occurred. The 8259 responds by resetting bit 1 of the ISR so that lower priority (higher numbered) interrupts can now be processed. An IRET instruction is issued by the keyboard interrupt routine and normal processing is resumed.

Keyboard-Related Locations and References

Locations show PC2 values, then PCjr if they differ. The *Technical Reference* manual page indicated is the beginning or most significant page from the XT manual. Examine the context of the surrounding pages.

Location: 24h
Label   : (INT 9)
Usage   : Vector to KB_INT FE987h; PCjr: F1561h
TRM pg : A-28; PCjr: A-45

Location: 58h
Label   : (INT 16)
Usage   : Vector to KEYBOARD_IO FE82Eh; PCjr: F13DDh
TRM pg : A-24; PCjr: A-43

Location: 6C–6Fh
Label   : (INT 1B)
Usage   : Break interrupt vector, during BASICA FAD34h; PCjr: EAC49h
TRM pg : 2-5; PCjr: 5-8

Location: PCjr: 120h
Label   : KEY62_PTR (INT 48)
Usage   : Vector to KEY62_INT routine; PCjr: F10C6h
TRM pg : PCjr: A-38

Location: PCjr: 124h
Label   : EXST (INT 49); PCjr: F109Dh
Usage   : Vector to nonkeyboard scan code table
TRM pg : 5-42

Location: 417–418h
Label   : KBD_FLAG, KBD_FLAG_1
Usage   : Keyboard toggle and Shift key status
TRM pg : A-3; PCjr: A-4
          The PCjr TRM doesn't show that 417h=10h if Fn-ScrLk is toggled and 80h if Ins is toggled.

Location: 419h
Label : ALT_INPUT
Usage : Accumulated Alt–numeric keypad entered ASCII value
TRM pg : A-3, A-31; PCjr: A-4, A-47

Location: 41Ah
Label : BUFFER_HEAD
Usage : Pointer to first character slot in circular keyboard buffer; 1Eh is first slot in buffer.
TRM pg : A-3; PCjr: A-4

Location: 41Ch
Label : BUFFER_TAIL
Usage : Pointer to next unused character slot in circular buffer
TRM pg : A-3; PCjr: A-4

Location: 41E–43Dh
Label : KB_BUFFER
Usage : Circular buffer for keyboard
TRM pg : A-3; PCjr: A-4

Location: 472h
Label : RESET_FLAG
Usage : 1234h indicates reboot in progress, not power-on sequence
TRM pg : A-4, A-30; PCjr: A-5, A-46

Location: 480h (not in PC1)
Label : BUFFER_START
Usage : Address of first byte of circular buffer in segment 40h, defaults to 1Eh
TRM pg : A-4, PCjr: A-5

Location: 482h
Label : BUFFER_END (not in PC1)
Usage : Address of last byte of circular buffer in segment 40, defaults to 3Eh
TRM pg : A-4; PCjr: A-5

Location: PCjr: 488h
Label : KB_FLAG2
Usage : PCjr additional flag byte for Fn and repeating keys
TRM pg : PCjr: A-5

Location: FE3A2h and FFA2Ah; PCjr: F04CCh and F0640h
Usage : Keyboard initialization and POST test routines
TRM pg : A-13, A-76; PCjr: A-16, A-18

Location: FAD34h; PCjr: EAC49h
Label : (INT_1B routine)
Usage : BASICA break routine

Location: **PCjr: F0F78h**
Label   : KBDNMI (8088 NMI routine)
Usage   : Keyboard read and deserialization
TRM pg : PCjr: A-35

Location: **PCjr: F04CFh**
Usage   : Initialize keyboard buffer parms during power-on
TRM pg : PCjr: A-16

Location: **FE3A2; PCjr: F0640h**
Label   : TST12; PCjr: Q43
Usage   : Test keyboard during power-on
TRM pg : A-13; PCjr: A-18

Location: **PCjr: F109Dh**
Label   : EXTAB (INT_49 table)
Usage   : Nonkeyboard scan code mapping table
TRM pg : PCjr: A-38

Location: **PCjr: F10C6h**
Label   : KEY62_INT (INT_48 routine)
Usage   : Converts 62-key scan code to 83-key scan code
TRM pg : PCjr: A-38

Location: **PCjr: F131Eh**
Label   : TPM
Usage   : Typamatic repeating key effector
TRM pg : PCjr: A-41

Location: **FE82Eh; PCjr: F13DDh**
Label   : KEYBOARD_IO (INT_16 routine)
Usage   : BIOS Services: status, read, available check. PCjr additions: typamatic and click adjustments
TRM pg : A-24; PCjr: A-43

Location: **FE987h; PCjr: F1561h**
Label   : KB_INT (INT_9 routine)
Usage   : BIOS keyboard interrupt interpretation routine
TRM pg : A-28; PCjr: A-45

Location: **FEB09h; PCjr: F1749h**
Label   : K38
Usage   : Break test. PCjr additions: F11CBh (INT_48 detects also)
TRM pg : A-24; PCjr: A-43

Location: **PCjr: F1937h**
Label   : NEW_INT_9
Usage   : Cassette BASIC examination for Ctrl-Esc or Esc key
TRM pg : PCjr: A-51

Location: **PCjr: FE01Bh**
Label   : REAL_VECTOR_SETUP
Usage   : Setup INT_9 vector at 24h after power-on sequence
TRM pg : PCjr: A-53

Location: **PCjr: FF068h**
Label   : KEY_SCAN_SAVE
Usage   : Save any keypresses during power-on sequence
TRM pg : PCjr: A-82

Location: **Ports 60–63h**
Label   : PORT_A ,_B, _C, CMD_PORT
Usage   : Keyboard I/O port usage
TRM pg : 1-8, 1-10; PCjr: 2-30, 2-36

Additional information about the keyboard and its interpretation may be found in the following:

Subject	TRM Page
Keyboard Encoding Section	2-11; PCjr: 5-21
Character codes table	
Extended codes table	
Shift states effects discussion	
Suggested keyboard key combination usage table	
DOS and BASIC special function keys tables	
Keyboard keys/scan code layout	1-65; PCjr: 5-22
Keypresses needed for CHR$(0) through CHR$(255)	C-1; PCjr: C-1
Keyboard connector	1-70; PCjr: 3-87
PCjr keyboard compatibility with PC	PCjr: 4-14, 5-25, 5-10
PCjr 8088 NMI usage	PCjr: 2-7, 2-15, A-35
PCjr infrared link cordless keyboard	PCjr: 2-97, 2-101
Keyboard schematics	D-12, D-14; PCjr: B-42 (IR link only)

BASIC provides several statements that may be used for keyboard functions. Check your BASIC manual for the following statements: INKEY$, INPUT, INPUT$, INPUT#, KEY, KEY(n), and ON KEY.

Subject	DOS page
ANSI.SYS device driver	DOS page: Chapter 13 of DOS 2.0, Chapter 2 of DOS 2.10
DOS INT 21 keyboard functions	D-17 of DOS 2.0, 5-17 of DOS 2.10

Keyboard Interrupts and Interrupt Functions

09 BIOS keyboard interrupt vector
16 BIOS keyboard functions
    00 read key
    01 get character status
    02 get shift status
    03 set typamatic rates (PCjr only)
    04 set keyboard clicker on/off (PCjr only)
21 DOS function request
    01 keyboard input (with wait, echo, break)
    06 direct console I/O (no wait, break, or echo); DL=FFh return
    input character
    07 direct console input (with wait, no echo or break)
    08 console input (with wait and break, no echo)
    0A buffered keyboard input (with wait and break)
    0B check standard input character availability
    0C clear keyboard buffer and do function 1, 6, 7, 8, or A
48 BIOS cordless keyboard 62 to 83 key translation (PCjr only)
49 BIOS nonkeyboard scan code translation (PCjr only)

3
Music and Sound

3
Music and Sound

The appropriate use of sound in your programs will make them more attractive, friendly, enjoyable, and entertaining. Besides programs that use sound to simulate existing or innovative musical instruments, game and educational software are obvious choices for sound effects and melodies. Sound is a powerful tool for establishing the setting and simulating activity. A catchy tune can provide a reward, while a rude blat can cajole the user to do better.

Business and management software can also be enhanced by appropriate audible signals, such as audio feedback of keypresses, calling attention to errors, alerting the user that a lengthy process has been completed, and even simulating speech output. The future promises highly complex and sophisticated voice recognition/response capabilities.

The PC and PCjr incorporate a small speaker that can be driven to achieve a broad tonal range. The PCjr also features an audio-out jack for attaching an external amplifier and sound system such as those incorporated in a monitor with an audio-in jack. The television attachment jack on the PCjr also includes sound-output signals. Combined with the sophisticated multivoice sound chip in the PCjr, your stereo and computer can make beautiful music together. You can even tape the music you create.

The speaker internal to the PC and PCjr may be driven by turning the 8255A-5 Programmable Peripheral Interface chip speaker control bit rapidly on and off, at the frequency of the desired tone, or by programming the 8253 Programmable Interval Timer chip to produce a given frequency automatically. BASIC employs the latter sound production technique. Machine language programs can mix these two methods to achieve the desired effects. Later example programs will demonstrate both of these speaker-driving methods.

The PCjr's complex sound generator chip is also supported by BASIC, with SOUND and BEEP statement parameters specifying whether the internal speaker or the sound chip is to be used. BASIC's support of sound production has a few minor flaws. To name some: Notes may not be double sharped or double flatted by including a second + or − after the first; a double dot after a note incorrectly increases the note length too much; notes may not be tied; and ML (legato) incorrectly ties all notes.

Again, machine language programs can program the sound chip directly. It's a shame that neither ROM BIOS nor DOS provides any sound support services to ease the machine language programmer's task in sound production. The variable length beep routine provided in ROM BIOS (XT *Technical Reference* manual, page A-76; PCjr manual, page A-107) cannot be employed since it ends with a near return.

You will want to design and collect your own generalized support routines and macro interfaces if you intend to use machine language frequently for producing sounds or music.

Let's explore the various ways that sound can be generated on the PC and PCjr.

Direct Method of Producing Sound: 8255 Port B at I/O Port 61h

The direct method of sound generation is the most flexible method, but it requires coding precise timing loops for both the pitch and the duration of the desired tones. When using this method, the programmer has the responsibility for, and the advantages of, absolute control over the audio environment.

The 8088 microprocessor is kept busy with these timing loops and little other program activity can take place concurrently. The other sound production methods discussed in this chapter provide sound creation facilities that are independent of the microprocessor, allowing simultaneous program activity.

Since the 8088 instruction set execution speed is generally used to determine and measure the amount of time elapsed in a direct-method timing loop, other implementations of the microprocessor (such as an IBM-compatible machine or superset microprocessors like the 8086, 80286, or 80188) may produce different sounds.

Architectural and component differences may also cause variations. This effect can be heard on the PCjr where the non-DMA memory-refresh method, the sharing of main memory for video buffers, and a different speaker component cause direct-method sounds to be almost halved in pitch. By placing the machine language sound generation routines above the first 128K (when expansion memory is added beyond the first 64K expansion), PC-like performance and sound-timing loop values can be used.

The direct method of sound generation can be pictured schematically as shown in Figure 3-1.

Each time port 61h, bit 1 is changed to a one, a click is produced at the speaker. When the clicks are generated rapidly enough, a pitch is heard.

Schematically again, the process may be thought of as depicted in Figure 3-2. A and C represent speaker clicks caused by the port 61h, bit 1 being turned on. B and D represent turning off the speaker by changing the contents of the bit to zero. A plus B compose a complete square wave cycle. When generated *N* times per second, a tone of *N* hertz is produced.

The A note above middle C (concert tuning A) on a piano may be produced by using a frequency of 440 hertz or 440 AB cycles per second. Table 3-1 shows the approximate integer frequencies required to generate four octaves of musical notes. Note that an octave begins at a C note and ends with the following B note.

Figure 3-1. Direct Method Sound Production Schematic

Port 61h

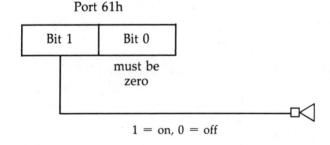

Figure 3-2. Direct Method Sound Production Schematic

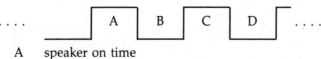

A speaker on time
B speaker off time
AB complete square wave cycle time:
  AB 500 times per second = tone of frequency 500 hertz

113

Table 3-1. Musical Notes and Associated Frequencies, Piano Key Arrangement

Note				Frequency (Hz)						
A		55	110	220	440	880	1760	3520	7040	14080	28160
A♯,B♭		58	117	233	466	932	1857	3714	7428	14856	29712
B		62	123	247	494	988	1976	3952	7904	15808	31616
C		65	131	262*	523	1046	2093	4186	8372	16744	
C♯,D♭		69	139	277	554	1109	2217	4434	8868	17736	
D	37	74	149	294	587	1175	2349	4698	9396	18792	
D♯,E♭	39	78	156	311	622	1245	2489	4978	9956	19912	
E	41	82	165	330	659	1319	2637	5274	10548	21096	
F	44	87	175	349	698	1397	2794	5588	11176	22352	
F♯,G♭	47	93	185	370	740	1480	2960	5920	11840	23680	
G	49	98	196	392	784	1568	3136	6272	12544	25088	
G♯,A♭	52	104	208	415	831	1661	3322	6644	13288	26576	

*middle C

Program 3-1 will create a .COM file that will generate an 800 hertz tone indefinitely using the direct method of sound production. Use Ctrl-Alt-Del to stop the example program. Later examples will build upon the groundwork of concepts presented in this example. On the PCjr, modify line 310 from 50 to 25 to produce the 800 hertz tone.

Line 310 loads a value into the CX register to be used in line 320 to count down an amount of time before the speaker state is reversed by the XOR instruction in line 280. In this way, the number of cycles per second is specified, based upon the 8088 execution speed for the LOOP instruction in the IBM PC.

The important concept in Program 3-1 is the method employed to cause a time delay between speaker clicks. Also, note the segregation of bit 1 of port 61h set up in lines 230–280. Destroying the contents of any other bits (other than turning off bit 0) can have disastrous effects since port 61h is used for keyboard, cassette, and parity error control. On the PCjr sound input, cassette, sound chip, and display controls share the bits in port 61h.

Since the 18.2 times per second timer tick interrupt routine (INT 8) has not been disabled in Program 3-1, you can hear a slight warble in the tone produced. This may be desirable in certain situations, but a purer tone can be obtained by disabling interrupts, as shown in Program 3-2. While interrupts are disabled, the time-of-day clock will not be updated. Program 3-2 also adds the capability to stop the generated tone when a key is pressed, eliminating the need to reboot the computer to exit from the program.

A tone of 800 hertz is produced by Program 3-2 also, so change line 440 from 50 to 25 for the PCjr. You may want to experiment with the CX value to hear other tone pitches. As always, you may leave out the comments and place multiple statements on a line to reduce the time needed to enter the program.

Notice that this second example used a machine language routine contained in a string, while the first example created a COM file program. The different implementations used are illustrative and are not a cause of any differing results. You may wish to refer to these examples in the future as implementation samples. Comments in the examples note the changes needed for the machine language routines when a different implementation is used.

Program 3-3 demonstrates a method for providing a parameterized called machine language subroutine that produces a chosen pitch for a specified duration. Moreover, it allows the caller to build these values into a table of sounds to be produced in succession as well as the means to overlay a previous sound table with the currently desired sound sequences. This third example also uses another implementation technique for called machine language routines. As before, PCjr frequency values should be about 0.45 times the PC values.

The duration of the desired tone in Program 3-3 calculates the value to be used in the DX register to count down the number of loops through the AB cycle. The value that the user specifies for duration is roughly equivalent to seconds on both the PC and PCjr. The resulting calculated DX value is the product of the frequency requested times the duration. As the frequency of AB increases, the DX value is decreased since more time is spent in loops for A and B.

Greater precision of the duration can be obtained by multiplying (or dividing) the DX result of line 360 by an additional precision factor such as DX=DX*1.13.

You may wish to implement the program as shown rather than implementing it as a COM file so that you can call it from your BASIC programs. The called machine language string technique does not allow enough room for an involved sound table. You can enhance the example program to suit your own needs as your experience in direct sound generation grows.

Variations in the volume of tones produced can be observed when an ascending or descending scale of tones is produced. The loudness of each tone is a factor of the frequency response of the speaker and its associated driving circuitry. No volume control mechanism is available.

Program 3-1. Sample Direct Method Speaker Control Program

For error-free program entry, be sure to use "The Automatic Proofreader," Appendix H.

```
NN 100 'BEEPDIR1; direct method of speaker contro
        l
66 105 ' This program creates a COM file from DAT
        A statements.
LA 110 ' Turn speaker data bit on and off at vari
        able rate
BM 120 ' determined by CX value. The higher the v
        alue of CX,
HE 130 ' the more delay between pulses and so the
        lower the tone.
OP 140 ' Notice the "warble" in the tone when the
        com program is run.
NG 150 ' USE CTRL-ALT-DEL TO GET OUT OF THE CREAT
        ED BEEPDIR1.COM PROGRAM !!
HA 160 '
AG 170 COMNAME$="beepdir1.com"
ON 180 OPEN COMNAME$ FOR OUTPUT AS #1
KB 190 READ X$: IF X$="/*" GOTO 210
GN 200 PRINT #1,CHR$(VAL("&H"+X$));:GOTO 190
IA 210 CLOSE #1:END
MD 220 ' REQUEST DIRECT CONTROL OF SPEAKER MODUL
        ATION
LL 230    DATA E4,61 :    IN      AL,61  ;GET 8255
        PORT B
GK 240    DATA 24,FE :    AND     AL,FE  ;DIRECT SP
        EAKER CONTROL VIA BIT 0 OFF
NN 250    DATA E6,61 :    OUT     61,AL  ;SET IT BA
        CK INTO PORT B
BF 260 ' -- MAIN LOOP --
OI 270 ' TOGGLE SPEAKER
NJ 280    DATA 34,2 :$LP XOR AL,2 ;REVERSE BIT ONE
        TO TOGGLE SPEAKER ON/OFF
HN 290    DATA E6,61 :    OUT     61,AL
QJ 300 ' DELAY A WHILE
EN 310    DATA B9,50,00 : MOV CX,50 ; ON PC:CX=1E+0
        9/(7140*FREQUENCY DESIRED)
BJ 320    DATA E2,FE :$HR LOOP    $HR         ;LOOP H
        ERE TILL CX=0
DM 330 ' KEEP ALTERNATING SPEAKER ON/OFF, NO EXI
        T!!
```

NK 340   DATA EB,F5 :   JMP $LP
KP 350 DATA /*

Program 3-2. Direct Method Speaker Control with Stop-On-Any-Key

For error-free program entry, be sure to use "The Automatic Proofreader," Appendix H.

```
OK 100 'BEEPDIR2; direct method of speaker contro
       l
KN 110 ' This program uses BASIC call to ml routi
       ne in a string.
GB 120 ' Enhancement of BEEPDIR1, adds eliminatio
       n of "warble"
DE 130 ' by disabling interrupts and periodically
       (DX loop value)
LC 140 ' checks for a keypress to stop the tone.
       You'll hear a
GN 150 ' slight click every time the keypress is
       checked for.
HA 160 '
6J 170 GOSUB 220
PJ 180 PRINT"Calling ML routine ....";:CALL ASMRO
       UT!:PRINT"back to BASIC."
MM 190 END
GF 200 '
LL 210 ' --- LOAD ML ROUTINE ---
PM 220 DEF SEG:PRINT "Installing ml routine ...."
       ;
EB 230 ASMROUT$=SPACE$(255) 'string for routine
EN 240 I=I+1:READ X$:IF X$="/*" GOTO 260   'read l
       oop
NL 250 MID$(ASMROUT$,I,1)=CHR$(VAL("&H"+X$)):GOTO
       240
EP 260 PRINT"completed."
OJ 270 ASMROUT!=VARPTR(ASMROUT$)
LC 280 ASMROUT!=PEEK(ASMROUT!+1)+(PEEK(ASMROUT!+2
       )*256)
NO 290 RETURN
BP 300 ' --- ML routine ---
DL 310 ' TURN OFF INTERRUPTS
GN 320   DATA FA : CLI ;ELIMINATES "WARBLE"
PC 330 ' HOW MANY CX LOOPS BETWEEN STOP CHECK
AG 340   DATA BA,0,9  : MOV  DX,1600   ;NOT TOO O
       FTEN
NK 350   ' REQUEST DIRECT CONTROL OF SPEAKER MODUL
       ATION
IA 360   DATA E4,61   : IN   AL,61      ;GET 8255
       PORT B
ND 370   DATA 24,FE   : AND  AL,FE ;DIRECT SPEAKE
       R CONTROL VIA BIT 0 OFF
```

117

```
JK 380   DATA E6,61    : OUT  61,AL ;SET IT BACK I
         NTO PORT B
CM 390   ' -- MAIN LOOP --
NM 400   ' TOGGLE SPEAKER
QN 410   DATA 34,2 : XOR AL,2 ;RVS BIT ONE TO TOGG
         .SPEAKER ON/OFF
NP 420   DATA E6,61    : OUT  61,AL
AA 430   ' DELAY A WHILE
QK 440   DATA B9,50,00 : MOV  CX,50   ;ON PC:CX=1E+
         09/(7140*FREQUENCY DESIRED)
HF 450   DATA E2,FE : LOOP 000F ;LOOP TILL CX=0
QI 460   ' --- END OF LOOP ---
KH 470   ' IF DX IS DOWN TO ZERO, CHECK FOR KEYPRE
         SS
CG 480   DATA 4A : DEC  DX ;SUBTRACT ONE FROM DX
PI 490   DATA 83,FA,0 :CMP DX,0 ;IS DX EXHAUSTED Y
         ET PRINT
BI 500   DATA 75,F1 : JNZ 00A ;NO, BACK TO TOP OF
         MAIN LOOP
JP 510   DATA B4,1     : MOV  AH,1 ;REQUEST KEYPRE
         SS STATUS
NC 520   DATA CD,16    : INT  16    ;FROM BIOS
IF 530   ' IF A KEY WAS PRESSED, WRAP IT UP
II 540   DATA 74,E1 : JZ 000 ;IF NOT PRESSED YET,
         KEEP ON
QJ 550   DATA FB : STI ;RE-ENABLE INTERRUPTS
PF 560   '  for a COM file version, use 'CD 20 00
         : INT 20' for the line below
NG 570   DATA CA,00,00 : RETF 000 ;RETURN TO BASIC
KH 580 DATA /*
```

Program 3-3. Direct Method Speaker Control with Sound Table

For error-free program entry, be sure to use "The Automatic Proofreader," Appendix H.

```
OH 100  'BEEPDIR3; Direct method of speaker contro
        l
DB 110  'Calls an ml routine placed in reserved ar
        ea above BASIC
.EC 120 'Demonstrates the use of variable pitch an
        d duration values.
CJ 130  'The values are calculated by the BASIC pr
        ogram and stored in
EG 140  'a table for the called machine language r
        outine to play.
PG 150  'Rests are created by setting the frequenc
        y beyond the
KP 160  'limit of hearing (>18,000Hz).
HC 170  '
```

118

```
BN 180 GOSUB 480 'load the ml routine, once only
NE 190 PRINT"Calculating sound values ...."
OF 200 SOUND.TABLE=&H30    'displacement of table-4
          within ml routine
LI 210 DURATION=1.7:FREQUENCY=40000!:GOSUB 350
LG 220 DURATION=.2:FREQUENCY=400:GOSUB 350
DK 230 DURATION=.6:FREQUENCY=600:GOSUB 350
PD 240 DURATION=.4:FREQUENCY=500:GOSUB 350
EM 250 DURATION=1.7:FREQUENCY=19200:GOSUB 350    'i
          naudible resting time
FP 260 DURATION=.1:FOR FREQUENCY=100 TO 5000 STEP
          200:GOSUB 350:NEXT
EG 270 DURATION=.1:FOR FREQUENCY=5000 TO 100 STEP
          -200:GOSUB 350:NEXT
DH 280 DURATION=.01:FOR FREQUENCY=100 TO 3000 STE
          P 100:GOSUB 350:NEXT
HI 290 DURATION=.01:FOR FREQUENCY=3000 TO 100 STE
          P -100:GOSUB 350:NEXT
DI 300 DURATION=.01:FOR FREQUENCY=100 TO 3000 STE
          P 100:GOSUB 350:NEXT
CI 310 SOUND.TABLE=SOUND.TABLE+4:FOR X=0 TO 3:POK
          E SOUND.TABLE+X,0:NEXT
PM 315    ' line above marks end of sound table ent
          ries
OP 320 PRINT"Calling ML routine ....";:CALL ASMRO
          UT!:PRINT"back to BASIC."
LC 330 END
BP 340 ' --- CALCULATE FREQUENCY AND DURATION and
          PLACE VALUES ---
GO 350 CX=1E+09/(7140*FREQUENCY)
MC 360 DX=DURATION*FREQUENCY
BE 370 IF INT(CX/256)>255 OR INT(DX/256)>255 GOTO
          450
NB 380 SOUND.TABLE=SOUND.TABLE+4
JH 390 POKE SOUND.TABLE+1,INT(DX/256)
FN 400 POKE SOUND.TABLE+0,DX MOD 256
KI 410 POKE SOUND.TABLE+3,INT(CX/256)
GF 420 POKE SOUND.TABLE+2,CX MOD 256
ED 430 PRINT"Note stored: "DURATION;FREQUENCY
MG 440 RETURN
DM 450 PRINT"Duration*frequency>32767, note bypas
          sed:"DURATION;FREQUENCY:RETURN
HD 460 '
MJ 470 ' --- LOAD ML ROUTINE ---
OA 480 DEF SEG=&H1800:I=0    'starting address for
          ml routine
QO 490 PRINT "Installing ml routine ....";
JK 500 READ X$:IF X$="/*" GOTO 520    'read loop
MC 510 POKE I,VAL("&H"+X$):I=I+1:GOTO 500
EK 520 PRINT"completed."
```

119

```
IH 530  ASMROUT!=0
MH 540  RETURN
CL 550  ' --- ML routine ---
DI 560    DATA 1E : PUSH   DS ;SAVE ORIGINAL DATA SE
          GMENT
IA 570    DATA 0E : PUSH   CS ;SET DS TO SAME AS CS
DC 580    DATA 1F  :       POP    DS          ;
MD 590    DATA FA : CLI ;TURN OFF INTERRUPTS
KK 600    DATA BE,30,0 : MOV SI,$TB ;START OF LENGT
          H/TONE TABLE ADDRESS-4
FN 610    'For COM file use "BE,30,1" instead of li
          ne above
MO 620    DATA 83,D6,4 :$TP ADC SI,+4 ;POINT TO NEX
          T ENTRY IN TABLE
EN 630    DATA 8B,14 : MOV DX,[SI] ;FIRST 2 BYTES I
          S DX VALUE (DURATION)
ME 640    DATA 83,FA,0 : CMP DX,+0 ;IF DX=0,
GE 650    DATA 74,1C : JZ $DN ;YES, WE'VE DONE THE
          TABLE SO EXIT
GD 660    DATA 8B,5C,2 : MOV BX,[SI+2] ;NEXT 2 BYTE
          S IS FREQUENCY LOOP COUNT
DM 670    DATA E4,61 : IN AL,61 ;GET 8255 PORT B
LB 680    DATA 24,FE : AND AL,FE ;DIRECT SPEAKER CO
          NTROL VIA BIT 0 OFF
CD 690    DATA C,2   :$OR OR AL,2  ;REVERSE BIT 1 T
          O TURN ON  SPEAKER
CM 700    DATA E6,61 : OUT 61,AL   ;SET IT BACK INT
          O PORT B
PJ 710    DATA 89,D9 : MOV CX,BX ;INITIALIZE THE FR
          EQUENCY COUNTER LOOP
AB 720    DATA E2,FE :$L1 LOOP   $L1 ;WAIT WHILE TON
          E PULSE IS HIGH
DG 730    DATA 24,FD : AND AL,FD ;TURN OFF BIT 1 TO
          TURN OFF SPEAKER
GI 740    DATA E6,61 : OUT 61,AL ;SET IT BACK INTO
          PORT B
PB 750    DATA 89,D9 : MOV CX,BX ;INITIALIZE THE FR
          EQUENCY COUNTER LOOP
CN 760    DATA E2,FE :$L2 LOOP   $L2 ;WAIT WHILE TON
          E PULSE IS LOW
KI 770    DATA 4A : DEC DX ;DURATION MINUS ONE
BC 780    DATA 75,ED : JNZ $OR   ;NOT ZERO YET, DO M
          ORE ON/OFF PULSES
AF 790    DATA EB,DA : JMP $TP ;ZERO, GET THE NEXT
          TABLE ENTRY
DO 800    DATA FB :$DN STI ;ALL DONE, ENABLE INTERR
          UPTS
ID 810    DATA 1F : POP DS ;ONLY NEEDED IF CALLING
          FROM BASIC
```

```
PJ 820 '    for a COM file version, use 'CD 20 00
           ; INT 20' for the line below
MB 830  DATA CA,00,00 : RETF 000 ;RETURN TO BASIC
6E 840  DATA 00,00 UNUSED FILLER
II 850 ' TONE LENGTH AND FREQUENCY TABLE STARTS A
          T ROUTINE+34 HEX ($TB BELOW)
EM 860 ' Table is made up of 4 byte entries;
BE 870 ' 2 bytes DX value; Duration of tone
BO 880 ' 2 bytes CX value; Frequency of tone,
PK 890 ' End of table indicated by DX = 00
HJ 895 ' :$TB  actual sound table starts here
HJ 900  DATA 04,03,c0,00 : SAMPLE TONE ONE
00 910  DATA DC,00,8C,00 : SAMPLE TONE TWO
MF 920  DATA 00,02,50,00 : SAMPLE TONE THREE
ON 930  DATA 00,00,00,00 : END OF TABLE ENTRIES
N6 940  DATA /*
```

Timer Method: 8255 Port B at 61h, 8253 Timer Ports at 42–43h

Sounds may be produced independently of the 8088 micro-processor (and memory refresh interruptions that occur every 72 system-clock cycles except on the PCjr) by using the 8253 Programmable Timer chip to modulate a 1.19 megahertz clock signal to the speaker. This timer method is used by the BASIC SOUND statement. That's how background music may be played while the user's BASIC program continues.

A schematic representation of the 8253 timer method of sound production is shown in Figure 3-3.

Figure 3-3. Timer Method Sound Production Schematic

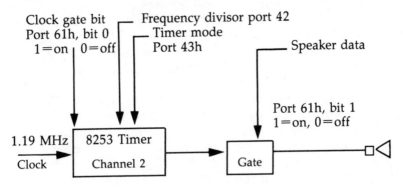

To produce sound using this method, an 8253 timer mode is used that causes it to produce a high output for half the desired time period and a low output for the other half. This generated AB square wave (described in the discussion of the direct method above) is directed to the speaker, based upon the gate status in port 61, bit 1. The 8253 automatically repeats the AB square wave of the desired time period. The number of AB cycles produced per second determines the pitch of the tone.

This tone pitch is indirectly specified by the programmer as a time period. The time period needed to produce a given tone is expressed in relationship to the 8253 input clock speed of 1,193,180 cycles per second (1.19 megahertz). This clock is derived from the 14.3178 megahertz crystal on the system board, as is the 8088 clock that runs at 4.77 megahertz.

For example, to produce a 1000 hertz tone at the speaker, the programmer causes the 8253 to be loaded with a frequency divisor of 1,193,180/1000 = 1193 (4A9h). The frequency divisor is the number that when multiplied by the desired frequency equals the 8253 input clock frequency. The higher the frequency desired, the lower the frequency divisor will be.

The 8253 (using square wave mode) decrements this frequency divisor in step with the input clock and switches from a high output to a low output when half the frequency divisor is exhausted. When it decrements to zero, the frequency divisor is automatically reloaded, and the process is repeated until some other frequency divisor is loaded, the input clock is gated off, or the mode port at 43h is changed.

Program 3-4 demonstrates the techniques needed to use the 8253 for sound production. The value of B6h sent to the 8253 mode port at 43h causes the 8253 to use channel 2. Using mode 3 (square wave generation) indicates that the frequency divisor will be loaded in LSB/MSB order and specifies that the divisor should be viewed as a binary number. The INTEL *Microprocessor and Peripheral Handbook* or other available chip data sheets should be consulted for information about the other possible meanings of this byte. The memory map in this book summarizes the meaning of each possible setting. The loop instruction is used only to waste time. Any other desired processing could be done while the tone is being sounded.

Once the speaker data gate has been turned off at the end of the sound production routine (as in lines 470–480 of Program 3-4), the square wave is still being continuously produced by the 8253 timer when the input clock is enabled. This production of the square wave does not affect the program or any other aspect of operation of the computer. At any time the speaker data gate may be turned on again and the tone will be heard on the speaker. By turning off the channel 2 input clock gate (which does *not* affect input clocking for other 8253 channels), the channel 2 timer function is suspended until the clock is once again enabled. This feature can be used to suspend music when the user presses a "freeze" key during a game.

Program 3-5 is a modified version of Program 3-4. It is modified to use the 8253 timer method of sound production. The slower execution speed of the PCjr requires that the duration value be halved to attain the same tone as on the PC.

Your BASIC manual includes a table for the SOUND statement that shows how to convert a tempo (quarter notes per minute) such as andante to clock ticks. Since a clock tick is about 55 milliseconds (0.055 seconds), you can easily determine the proper duration of a tone for the desired tempo.

The routine in lines 790–840 may be used in other programs where time, ranging from 1 to 65,535 milliseconds (65.535 seconds), needs to be wasted when other activity takes place, as in the direct method of sound production explored in the previous section.

The timer method and direct method of sound production can be used together to achieve a wide range of sound effects. You may further affect the channel 2 timer output by using port 61, bit 0 to enable and disable the timer clock input and/or port 61, bit 1 to turn the speaker on/off.

The contents of the decrementing frequency divisor inside timer channel 2 can be checked at any time to determine how much time has elapsed and, implicitly, remains. Simply put, the latch-value-of-channel-2 command (86h) to port 43h and the current value will be latched into port 42h.

Cassette tape write routines also use channel 2 of the 8253 timer chip, so avoid trying to do both sound and cassette I/O at the same time. Each 8253 channel has an input clock that operates at 1.19318 megahertz, giving a clock period of 838.1 nanoseconds. DMA memory refresh (except on the PCjr) uses channel 1 of the 8253 in mode 2 with a frequency divisor of 18 to create an interrupt every 15.12 microseconds. Channel 0 generates the time-of-day interrupt every 54.936 milliseconds, with the maximum divisor of 65,536 (0 in the frequency divisor). The clock frequency of 1.19318 megahertz divided by 65,536 equals 18.203 interrupts per second. The output of channel 0 is connected to the 8259 IRQ0 line, thereby signaling an INT 8 interrupt. It is possible to use 8253 channel 0 for your own timing purposes if disk I/O is not needed during that period and inaccuracy of the time-of-day clock is acceptable. The disk motor's timing is determined by BIOS using channel 0.

Program 3-4. Timer Method Sound with Stop-On-Any-Key

For error-free program entry, be sure to use "The Automatic Proofreader," Appendix H.

```
DO 100 'BEEPTIM1; timer method of sound productio
        n
NK 110 '   This program uses BASIC call to a ml ro
        utine in a string.
HH 120 '   Example of using 8253 timer method for
        sound production
CB 130 '   Load AX below (line 340) with 1,193,180
        /frequency
HM 140 '
EN 150 GOSUB 200
OF 160 PRINT"Calling ML routine ....";:CALL ASMRO
        UT!:PRINT"back to BASIC."
NI 170 END
HE 180 '
NK 190 ' --- LOAD ML ROUTINE ---
PI 200 DEF SEG:PRINT "Installing ml routine ...."
        ;
EN 210 ASMROUT$=SPACE$(255) 'string for routine
PB 220 I=I+1:READ X$:IF X$="/*" GOTO 240   'read 1
        oop
GF 230 MID$(ASMROUT$,I,1)=CHR$(VAL("&H"+X$)):GOTO
        220
EL 240 PRINT"completed."
NF 250 ASMROUT!=VARPTR(ASMROUT$)
LO 260 ASMROUT!=PEEK(ASMROUT!+1)+(PEEK(ASMROUT!+2
        )*256)
NK 270 RETURN
CO 280 ' --- ML routine ---
GE 290    DATA B0,B6   :    MOV   AL,B6  ;'10110110=
        8255 MODE BYTE
IF 300 '                              ;'1011=Chnl
        2:LSB then MSB
HH 310 '                              ;'  011=m
        ode3:square wave
```

124

```
LF 320 '                              ;          Ø=b
       inary divisor
BL 330  DATA E6,43   :    OUT   43,AL ;PUT 8255 M
        ODE
GC 340  DATA B8,A9,4 :    MOV   AX,4A9 ;1ØØØ HZ TO
        NE
KH 350  DATA E6,42   :    OUT   42,AL  ;PUT LSB
GF 360  DATA 88,EØ   :    MOV   AL,AH  ;MSB TO LSB
NE 37Ø  DATA E6,42   :    OUT   42,AL  ;PUT MSB
MC 38Ø  DATA E4,61   :    IN    AL,61  ;GET 8255 P
        ORT B
QJ 39Ø  DATA C,3 : OR AL,3 ;TURN ON SPEAKER DATA
        AND CHNL2 GATE
JJ 4ØØ  DATA E6,61   :    OUT   61,AL  ;REPLACE 82
        55 PORT B
MN 41Ø  DATA 31,C9   :    XOR   CX,CX  ;SET 65,536
        COUNT FOR LOOP
GK 42Ø  DATA E2,FE   :$LP LOOP $LP     ;WASTE SOME
        TIME
NO 43Ø  DATA B4,1 : MOV AH,1 ;REQUEST KEYPRESS ST
        ATUS
GD 44Ø  DATA CD,16 : INT 16 ; FROM BIOS
PF 45Ø  DATA 74,F8   :    JZ    $LP    ;NO KEYPRES
        S, KEEP ON RUNNING
MP 46Ø  DATA E4,61   :    IN    AL,61  ;GET 8255 P
        ORT B
JO 47Ø  DATA 24,FC   :    AND   AL,FC  ;TURN OFF S
        PEAKER DATA AND CHNL2 GATE
KJ 48Ø  DATA E6,61   :    OUT   61,AL  ;REPLACE 82
        55 PORT B
AG 49Ø  '  for a COM file version, use 'CD 2Ø ØØ :
        INT 2Ø' for the line below
NI 5ØØ  DATA CA,ØØ,ØØ : RETF ØØ ;RETURN TO BASIC
NM 51Ø  DATA /*
```

Program 3-5. Timer Method Sound with Sound Table

For error-free program entry, be sure to use "The Automatic Proofreader," Appendix H.

```
EL 1ØØ  'BEEPTIM2; Timer method of sound productio
        n
NL 11Ø  ' Calls a ml routine placed in reserved ar
        ea above BASIC
BD 12Ø  ' Demonstrates the use of variable pitch a
        nd duration values.
CF 13Ø  ' The values are calculated by the BASIC p
        rogram and stored in
GC 14Ø  ' a table for the called machine language
        routine to play.
IF 15Ø  ' Rests are created by setting the frequen
        cy beyond the
```

125

```
DF 160 ' limit of hearing (>18,000Hz).
HC 170 '
AH 180 GOSUB 480  'load the ml routine, once only
ME 190 PRINT"Calculating sound values ...."
LJ 200 SOUND.TABLE=&H38 'displacement of table mi
       nus 4 within ml routine
CA 210 CLOCK=1193180!   'frequency of 8253 clock
OO 220 DURATION=1.7:FREQUENCY=40000!:GOSUB 370
AE 230 DURATION=.2:FREQUENCY=400:GOSUB 370
II 240 DURATION=.6:FREQUENCY=600:GOSUB 370
EB 250 DURATION=.4:FREQUENCY=500:GOSUB 370
JA 260 DURATION=1.7:FREQUENCY=19200:GOSUB 370   'i
       naudible resting time
MH 270 DURATION=.1:FOR FREQUENCY=100 TO 5000 STEP
        200:GOSUB 370:NEXT
MA 280 DURATION=.1:FOR FREQUENCY=5000 TO 100 STEP
        -200:GOSUB 370:NEXT
LB 290 DURATION=.01:FOR FREQUENCY=100 TO 3000 STE
       P 100:GOSUB 370:NEXT
NB 300 DURATION=.01:FOR FREQUENCY=3000 TO 100 STE
       P -100:GOSUB 370:NEXT
YC 310 DURATION=.01:FOR FREQUENCY=100 TO 3000 STE
       P 100:GOSUB 370:NEXT
CK 320 SOUND.TABLE=SOUND.TABLE+4:FOR X=0 TO 3:POK
       E SOUND.TABLE+X,0:NEXT
OB 330 ' line above marks end of sound table ent
       ries
OD 340 PRINT"Calling ML routine ....";:CALL ASMRO
       UT!:PRINT"back to BASIC."
LG 350 END
BD 360 ' --- CALCULATE FREQUENCY AND DURATION and
        PLACE VALUES ---
AG 370 CX=CLOCK/FREQUENCY
CG 380 DX=DURATION*1000    'number of milliseconds
KH 390 ' DX=DX/2 'this line FOR PCjr ONLY: adjus
       t for slower execution
MC 400 SOUND.TABLE=SOUND.TABLE+4
JI 410 POKE SOUND.TABLE+1,INT(DX/256)
FB 420 POKE SOUND.TABLE+0,DX MOD 256
KM 430 POKE SOUND.TABLE+3,INT(CX/256)
HJ 440 POKE SOUND.TABLE+2,CX MOD 256
BH 450 PRINT"Note stored:"DURATION;FREQUENCY 'com
       ment out when tested
NK 460 RETURN
MJ 470 ' --- LOAD ML ROUTINE ---
OA 480 DEF SEG=&H1800:I=0  'starting address for
       ml routine
OO 490 PRINT "Installing ml routine ....";
JK 500 READ X$:IF X$="/*" GOTO 520  'read loop
MC 510 POKE I,VAL("&H"+X$):I=I+1:GOTO 500
EK 520 PRINT"completed."
```

```
IH 530 ASMROUT!=Ø
MH 540 RETURN
CL 550 ' --- ML routine ---
EF 560    DATA 1E   :  PUSH  DS ;SAVE ORIGINAL DATA
          SEGMENT
LJ 570    DATA ØE   :  PUSH  CS ;SET DS TO SAME AS
          CS
PO 580    DATA 1F   :  POP DS ;
CL 590 ' Set the next frequency from the sound ta
       ble into the timer
BC 600    DATA BE,38,Ø : MOV SI,$TB ;START OF LENGT
          H/TONE TABLE ADDRESS-4
GM 610 ' For COM file use "BE,38,1" instead of t
       he above line
MO 620    DATA 83,D6,4 :$TP ADC SI,+4 ;POINT TO NEX
          T ENTRY IN TABLE
CD 630    DATA 8B,14  :  MOV DX,[SI] ;FIRST 2 BYTES
          IS DX VALUE (DURATION)
MD 640    DATA 83,FA,Ø : CMP DX,+Ø  ;IF DX=Ø,
II 650    DATA 74,26 :$JZ DN 'YES, WE'VE DONE THE T
          ABLE SO EXIT
GD 660    DATA 8B,5C,2 : MOV BX,[SI+2] ;NEXT 2 BYTE
          S IS FREQUENCY LOOP COUNT
ML 670    DATA BØ,B6   :  MOV AL,B6; SET 8253 CHNL2,M
          ODE3,BINARY
CA 680    DATA E6,43   :  OUT 43,AL ;PUT TO 8253 MODE
          PORT
HA 690    DATA 89,D8   :  MOV AX,BX ;FREQUENCY DVISOR
IO 700    DATA E6,42   :  OUT 42,AL ; TO 8253,
DG 710    DATA 88,EØ   :  MOV AL,AH ; FIRST LSB
JI 720    DATA E6,42   :      OUT   42,AL   ; THEN MSB
LM 730 ' Set the 8255 speaker data and timer clo
       ck on
BE 740    DATA E4,61   :  IN AL,61 ;SAVE CURRENT CONT
          ENTS
GH 750    DATA 50 : PUSH  AX ; OF PORT 61H, 8255 PO
          RT B
CL 760    DATA C,3   :  OR AL,3 ;TURN ON SPEAKER DATA
CN 770    DATA E6,61   :  OUT  61,AL ; AND TIMER INPU
          T CLOCK
FN 780 ' Expend the required amount of time
KH 790    DATA 89,D1   :  MOV CX,DX ;LOOP FOR THE SPE
          CIFIED
GF 800    DATA 51   :  PUSH CX ; NUMBER OF MILLISECON
          DS.
JN 810    DATA B9,4,1 : MOV CX,104   ;EACH 104 LOOP
          TAKES ONE
EN 820    DATA E2,FE : LOOP   Ø12C ; MILLISECOND, TI
          MES THE NUMBER
LI 830    DATA 59   :  POP CX ; OF ITERATIONS SPECIF
          IED
```

```
HE 840    DATA E2,F7 : LOOP  Ø128  ; BY THE DURATIO
          N TABLE ENTRY.
EL 85Ø    ' Sound completed, time for another
JL 86Ø    DATA 58  : POP AX  ;REINSTATED THE SAVED
          8255 STATE
ED 87Ø    DATA E6,61  : OUT 61,AL ;AND GO GET THE N
          EXT
IK 88Ø    DATA EB,DØ  : JMP Ø106 ; SET OF TABLE ENT
          RIES.
LE 89Ø    ' All entries done, exit back to caller
GB 9ØØ    DATA 1F :$DN POP DS ;ONLY NEEDED IF CALLI
          NG FROM BASIC
PI 91Ø    '   for a COM file version, use 'CD 2Ø ØØ
          : INT 2Ø' for the line below
BE 92Ø    DATA CA,ØØ,ØØ : RETF ØØØ      ;RETURN TO BA
          SIC
PA 93Ø    DATA Ø,Ø UNUSED FILLER
JI 94Ø    '   TONE LENGTH AND FREQUENCY TABLE STARTS
          AT ROUTINE+3C HEX ($TB BELOW)
HB 95Ø    '    Table is made up of 4 byte entries;
BJ 96Ø    '       2 bytes DX value; Duration of tone
PG 97Ø    '       2 bytes CX value; Frequency of tone
          ;
JA 98Ø    '    End of table indicated by DX = ØØ
NL 99Ø    '           :$TB  actual sound table sta
          rts here
IB 1ØØØ   DATA Ø4,Ø3,CØ,ØØ : SAMPLE TONE ONE
BH 1Ø1Ø   DATA DC,ØØ,8C,ØØ : SAMPLE TONE TWO
QP 1Ø2Ø   DATA ØØ,Ø2,5Ø,ØØ : SAMPLE TONE THREE
EI 1Ø3Ø   DATA ØØ,ØØ,ØØ,ØØ : END OF TABLE ENTRIES
BC 1Ø4Ø   DATA /*
```

PCjr Complex Sound Generator Method: I/O Ports at C0h and 61h

The PCjr's sound subsystem includes a Motorola MC14529B sound multiplexor chip used to select a sound source to be directed to all the audio output connectors: television, composite video, direct-drive (RGB) monitor, and audio-out jack. Software selects the desired sound source by setting bits 5 and 6 of port 61h. Figure 3-4 illustrates the input and output connections attached to the sound multiplexor chip. Be sure to set only bits 5 and 6, because corrupting the other bits in this port can cause some bizarre things to happen to your PCjr.

The ROM BIOS initializes this port during the power-on sequence to select channel 2 of the 8253 timer as the default sound source.

Figure 3-4. PCjr Output Sound Source Selection

Port 61h, bits 5 and 6

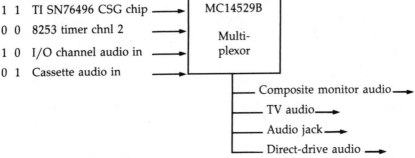

IBM refers to the sound chip used in the PCjr as the "Complex Sound Generator," although the manufacturer, Texas Instruments, titles it the "SN76496 Programmable Tone/Noise Generator." Throughout this section, we'll be referring to it simply as the sound chip.

You can request a data sheet for the sound chip from your local TI distributor from their Custom Logic Circuits library, document D2801 (November 1983). Unfortunately, application notes are not included, and the bulk of the information in the data sheet is concerned with operating conditions and electrical characteristics. The PCjr *Technical Reference* manual contains most of the meat from this data sheet and frequently quotes it.

The sound chip incorporates three programmable tone generators (voices) that can produce tones through the entire range of human hearing, a programmable noise generator, a separate attenuation control for each voice, and simultaneous mixed output. Separate volume controls allow a range of 2–28 decibel attenuation, as well as settings for full volume and no volume.

Unfortunately, the resolution of the frequency range (36.449 cycles) does not permit the same accuracy of tone that can be achieved with the direct or timer method of sound production.

Also, the *Technical Reference* manual is somewhat confusing in the method used to number the bits of the registers in the sound-system section. The bits are numbered in the reverse order from the rest of the manual, with the low-order bit labeled bit 7, downward to bit 0 for the high-order bit. This reversal obviously occurred when the TI data sheet information was blindly incorporated into the manual. We will remain consistent with the power-of-two method used elsewhere in the manual and will label the bits from low to high order as bits 0–7.

Figure 3-5 restates the command register data formats with conventional bit numbering.

Figure 3-5. PCjr Complex Sound Generator Command Formats

Frequency (double or single byte)

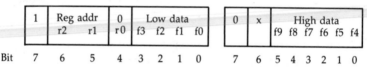

Bit 7 6 5 4 3 2 1 0   7 6 5 4 3 2 1 0

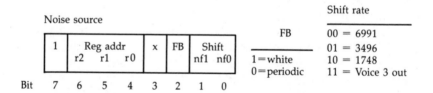

Bit 7 6 5 4 3 2 1 0

Attenuation

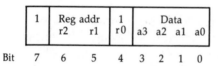

Bit 7 6 5 4 3 2 1 0

The meaning of zero when used as an attenuation value is not stated in the *Technical Reference* manual. Zero causes no attenuation (full volume), while the occurrence of all ones (Fh) turns the volume off (full attenuation).

Some early books about the PCjr have used the formula (1193180/32)/frequency, or 37287/frequency, to calculate the ten-bit frequency divisor. This is clearly incorrect and is based on the assumption that the input clock for the sound chip operates at 1.193180 megahertz, which is not the case. Use the formula in the *Technical Reference* manual, 3579540/(32*frequency), to obtain the correct frequency divisor. Since the resolution of the ten-bit frequency divisor is 36.449 cycles, some low notes may not be accurately pitched.

Again, no BIOS or DOS service routines are provided for the sound chip, but BASIC provides high-level language support. The SOUND statement ON/OFF parameter specifies whether the sound chip or the 8253 timer chip is used, with OFF causing the 8253 to be used. The BEEP statement selects whether or not the external audio connectors are used, with BEEP ON selecting external audio. BEEP ON and SOUND OFF signify that the 8253 is to be used with the external connections *and* the internal speaker. Table 3-2 shows the meanings of the possible combinations that the BEEP and SOUND statements may be given. Other BASIC statements that support sound production are PLAY, ON PLAY, and NOISE.

Table 3-2. PCjr BASIC SOUND and BEEP Settings

SOUND	BEEP	External Audio-out	Internal Speaker	Chip
ON	ON	X	–	CSG
ON	OFF	X	–	CSG
OFF	ON	X	X	8253 (default)
OFF	OFF	–	X	8253

The first example, Program 3-6, is an elementary program that saves the present value of the sound source selection bits from port 61h, sets each voice to a frequency, enables the sound chip for output, lets the sound occur for a length of time, and then disables the sound chip output.

The subroutines in this program could be used for general purposes in your own programs, but the BASIC SOUND statement does all this for you already. Our purpose here is to understand the mechanics of the sound chip.

You must be using a TV, monitor with audio input, or the audio-output jack on the PCjr to hear the sound output of this and the following program.

The second demonstration, Program 3-7, is a bit lengthy, but it will provide hours of enjoyment and will fire your imagination with marvelous ideas about how to experiment with the sound chip. Don't be surprised if you grab the attention of the whole household with this program. Because it is written entirely in BASIC, the amount of information displayed about the active state of the sound chip is minimized to allow fast response to user-controlled keystrokes.

When you start the program the first time, press the Enter key as the first command to set default frequencies and volumes. Now try this: Press the space bar to silence all voices and press 4 to select voice 4. Now press PgUp to turn the volume up full. Press cursor right twice to select voice 3 output for voice 4 input. Now press 3 to select voice 3. Notice the effect on voice 4 (the only one with volume on) as you vary the frequency of voice 3 by using the right and left cursor keys. Press Del to see what the same noise in white mode sounds like. Now press Ins to select periodic noise. Go back to voice 3 by pressing 3. Turn up the volume for voice 3 by pressing cursor up till a 3 volume appears next to the voice 3 indicator. Now you can hear how voices 3 and 4 change together as you press cursor right and left. Notice again the effect that pressing Del has on the noise generator.

Program 3-6. Sound Chip Fundamentals Example Program
For error-free program entry, be sure to use "The Automatic Proofreader," Appendix H.

```
BD 100 'Beepcsg1; CSG simple demonstration
EE 110 '          Set voice, freq, vol, and durat
        ion below.
OP 120 '          vol=0 is loudest, 15=off
HK 130 '
BE 140 FREQ.SELECT.BYTE.1=2^7 'High order bit val
        ue
EL 150 CSGPORT=&HC0:PORTB.8255=&H61
AE 160 OLD.8255=INP(&H61)  'Save old sound source
        byte
DB 170 DISABLE.BEEP.CASS=16
IO 180 ATTENUATION=2^4 'Bit indicating attenuatio
        n register
BH 190 SND.SOURCE=&H60   'CSG sound source
HD 200 VOICE=0:FREQ= 262:VOL=4:GOSUB 340 'Voice 1
        = middle C
FD 210 VOICE=1:FREQ= 330:VOL=0:GOSUB 340 'Voice 2
        = E above mid C
HM 220 VOICE=2:FREQ= 392:VOL=8:GOSUB 340 'Voice 3
        = G above mid C
OP 230 VOICE=3:FREQ=1200:VOL=15:GOSUB 340 'Noise
        voice off
```

```
CN 240 DURATION=3000   'An arbitrary duration
EL 250 GOSUB 290  'Let's hear them all now!
LH 260 END
NC 270 :
ON 280 'enable the CSG as the sound source for th
       e duration
NG 290 OUT PORTB.8255,SND.SOURCE+OLD.8255 'OR the
       sound source port
JI 300 FOR X=1 TO DURATION:NEXT 'Count down the d
       uration value
CL 310 OUT PORTB.8255,OLD.8255:RETURN  'Put back
       the old sound source
NJ 320 :
HE 330 'set the frequency and attenuation for the
       voice
JF 340 N=3579540!/(32*FREQ) 'Calculate the diviso
       r
CA 350 LSN=N MOD 2^4 'least sig nybble of divisor
NL 360 MSN=N/2^4  'most sig 6 bits of divisor
AA 370 VOICE=VOICE*2^5 'voice in bits 6-5
JD 380 OUT CSGPORT,FREQ.SELECT.BYTE.1+VOICE+ATTEN
       UATION+VOL
GD 390 OUT CSGPORT,FREQ.SELECT.BYTE.1+VOICE+LSN '
       freq least sig. nybble
LP 400 OUT CSGPORT,MSN:RETURN 'freq most sig. 6 b
       its
```

Program 3-7. Sound Chip Keyboard Controller Program

For error-free program entry, be sure to use "The Automatic Proofreader," Appendix H.

```
FE 10 'BEEPCSG2; Complex Sound Generator method o
       f sound production (PCjr)
DB 20 '          This program turns the PCjr keyb
       oard into a control panel
CN 30 '            for the complex sound generator.
       Directions are shown when
KF 40 '            the program is started.
PC 50 '            Use Fn-Break to end the program
       (may require several attempts)
NK 60 ' --- Instructions and Initialization ---
CD 70 CLS:PRINT"REAL-TIME COMPLEX SOUND GENERATOR
       PLAYER"
IE 80 PRINT" Voice selection: 1 2 3 4 keys, all f
       ollowing actions on last voice selected"
JA 90 PRINT"  space bar=silence all, enter key=mi
       d C/mid vol all"
JB 100 PRINT "  Cursor keys:  ^=up volume, v=dow
       n volume"
```

```
OE 110 PRINT "   Cursor keys:  <=down freq, >=up
         freq"
OK 120 PRINT " Home=low freq, End=high freq, PgUp
         =high vol, PgDn=low vol"
GG 130 PRINT " In voice 4: Ins=periodic noise, De
         l=white noise "
ED 140 LOCATE 18,1:PRINT " Voice,attenuation"
CP 150 DIM VOL(4),FREQ(4)
OK 160 FOR X=1 TO 3:FREQ(X)=262:VOL(X)=8:NEXT:VOL
         (4)=10  'setup initial values
FG 170 OUT &H61,INP(&H61) OR &H60 'TI76496 CSG is
         sound source
HA 180 ' --- Get a key, top of main program loop
         ---
AH 190 K$=INKEY$:IF K$="" GOTO 190          'wait fo
         r a key
EF 200 IF LEN(K$)=2 THEN K$=MID$(K$,2,1) 'elimina
         te lead 0 of extended scan code
JJ 210 '      because of above line, capital keys c
         an be used instead of cursor keys
LH 220 '      if the user desires. See the INSTR st
         atements below for details.
OP 230 ' --- Adjust frequency ---
EB 240 K=INSTR("GKMO",K$)    'freq lowest,lower,hi
         gher,highest
BK 250 IF K=0 GOTO 430    'not a freq adjustment
PL 260 IF VOICE=4 GOTO 350   'voice 4 gets one of
         four possible values
QO 270 ON K GOSUB 280,290,310,330:GOSUB 750:GOTO
         190
HL 280 FREQ(VOICE)=&H3FF:RETURN  'lowest frequenc
         y
HO 290 FREQ(VOICE)=FREQ(VOICE)+4:IF FREQ(VOICE)>&
         H3FF THEN FREQ(VOICE)=&H3FF 'lower
NN 300 RETURN
KC 310 FREQ(VOICE)=FREQ(VOICE)-4:IF FREQ(VOICE)<0
          THEN FREQ(VOICE)=10 'higher
MB 320 RETURN
QM 330 FREQ(VOICE)=10:RETURN 'highest frequency
JL 340 '
NG 350 ON K GOSUB 360,370,390,410:GOSUB 830:GOTO
         190  'select the proper voice 4 mode
LG 360 FREQ(4)=0:RETURN   'n/512
LH 370 FREQ(4)=FREQ(4)-1:IF FREQ(4)<0 THEN FREQ(4
         )=0  'freq lower
NN 380 RETURN
LG 390 FREQ(4)=FREQ(4)+1:IF FREQ(4)>4 THEN FREQ(4
         )=4  'freq higher
MO 400 RETURN
PO 410 FREQ(4)=3:RETURN   'use voice3 output
```

134

```
HE 420 ' --- Adjust attenuation 0=loudest, 14=sof
       test, 15=off ---
GC 430 K=INSTR("IHPQ",K$)   'vol highest,higher,lo
       wer,lowest
JF 440 IF K=0 GOTO 530
EJ 450 ON K GOSUB 460,470,490,510:GOSUB 800:GOTO
       190
OO 460 VOL(VOICE)=0:RETURN    'no attenuation, lo
       udest
JG 470 VOL(VOICE)=VOL(VOICE)-1:IF VOL(VOICE)<0 TH
       EN VOL(VOICE)=0
OD 480    RETURN 'less attenuation, more volume
OO 490 VOL(VOICE)=VOL(VOICE)+1:IF VOL(VOICE)>15 T
       HEN VOL(VOICE)=15
CH 500    RETURN 'more attenuation, less volume
DJ 510 VOL(VOICE)=15:RETURN    'full attenuation,
       no volume
BG 520 ' --- Select voice by number ---
JA 530 K=INSTR("1234",K$)
OO 540 IF K=0 GOTO 570
CB 550 VOICE=VAL(K$):GOSUB 800:GOSUB 860:GOTO 190
OD 560 ' --- Adjust noise type, periodic or white
       ---
OF 570 K=INSTR("RS",K$)
LP 580 IF K=0 GOTO 630
DJ 590 ON K GOSUB 600,610:GOSUB 830:GOTO 190
MG 600 NOISETYPE=0:RETURN
NH 610 NOISETYPE=1:RETURN
GI 620 ' --- Center or silence voices ---
NO 630 K=INSTR(CHR$(13)+CHR$(32),K$)   'center all
        voices at mid vol/mid c
LO 640 IF K=0 GOTO 190  'or silence all voices
HJ 650 ON K GOTO 660,680
FN 660 FOR X=1 TO 3:VOL(X)=8:FREQ(X)=252:NEXT
       'set voices to vol 8, mid c
DB 670  FREQ(4)=1:VOL(4)=15:GOSUB 700:GOTO 190
       'and voice 4 vol off, first freq
PD 680 FOR X=1 TO 4:VOL(X)=15:NEXT:GOSUB 740:GOTO
       190  'Silence all voices
EP 690 ' --- Set frequency and/or volume for voic
       es ---
KD 700 GOSUB 720:GOSUB 740:RETURN  'Set all freq
       and vol
HM 710 '
CL 720 V=VOICE:FOR VOICE=1 TO 4:GOSUB 750:NEXT:VO
       ICE=V:RETURN 'Set all freq
HA 730 '
DB 740 V=VOICE:FOR VOICE=1 TO 4:GOSUB 800:NEXT:VO
       ICE=V:RETURN 'Set all vol
```

```
NC 750 ' --- Set frequency for voice ---
LN 760 V1=FREQ(VOICE) MOD 16:V2=INT(FREQ(VOICE)/1
       6)
GA 770 OUT &HC0,&H80+((VOICE-1)*32)+V1
LB 780 OUT &HC0,V2
ND 790 RETURN
DM 800 '   --- Set volume for voice ---
MO 810 OUT &HC0,&H80+((VOICE-1)*32)+&H10+VOL(VOIC
       E)
NO 820 GOSUB 860:RETURN
OL 830   'Set noise type
DM 840 OUT &HC0,&HE0+NOISETYPE*4+FREQ(4):RETURN
KK 850 ' --- Show current voice and volumes ---
NB 860 FOR X=1 TO 4:LOCATE 18+X,1:PRINT" ";:NEXT
HD 870 LOCATE 18+VOICE,1:PRINT"*";VOICE;HEX$(VOL(
       VOICE));
NC 880 RETURN
```

When controlling the sound chip from a machine language program, you'll soon discover that timing loops, the 8253 timer, or INT 1Ch (the user timer tick interrupt vector at 70h) is needed to control the duration of the sounds being produced. This can get somewhat complicated when notes from multiple voices are to be timed concurrently. You'll want to minimize the path length of any routine that times note durations to prevent the distortion of the time resolution. But still the routine must at least signal the silencing of a particular note when its time is up and begin the next note unless the end of the melody has been reached.

If 18.2 times per second (55 milliseconds) is not a fine enough resolution for your purposes, then you must consider either the 8253 timer channel 2, timing loops, or changing the frequency of timer ticks. When changing the timer tick frequency, you'll want to front end the INT 8h routine (by changing the vector at 20h to point to your own routine) and pass control to the normal routine (if necessary for disk motor timing control) only every 55 milliseconds. Some factor of 65,536 will probably prove best for modification of the timer tick frequency to be loaded into port 40h. BASIC uses this method for sound timings. BASIC replaces the system timer tick interrupt routine vector to intercept the 8253 timer 0 interrupt. It also causes the interrupt to occur four times as often (72.8 per second) by replacing the 8253 channel 0 counter. Its interrupt handler routine then branches to the normal timer tick interrupt routine once every four 8253 channel 0 interrupts.

Sound-Related Locations and References

"Location," below, shows PC2 values, then PCjr if they differ. The *Technical Reference* manual page numbers are for the XT manual and indicate the beginning or most significant page. Examine the context of the surrounding pages as well.

Location: Port 61h
Label : 8255 port B
Usage : Speaker data enable bit 1, timer speaker gate bit 0; additionally, PCjr: disable internal speaker bit 4, sound source multiplexor bits 5–6
TRM pg : 1-10, 1-20; PCjr: 2-30, 2-32, 2-82

Location: Ports 42–43h
Label : 8253 timer channel 2 counter
Usage : Output frequency divisor
TRM pg : 1-20; PCjr: 2-85

Location: PCjr Port C0h
Usage : Sound chip command port
TRM pg : PCjr: 2-87

Basic provides several statements that may be used for sound functions. Check your BASIC manual for the following statements: BEEP, PLAY, ON PLAY, and SOUND.

Sound-related schematic diagrams may be found on the following pages of the TRMs:

	PC2	PCjr
8253 timer	D-9	B-11
8255 PIA	D-10	B-11
Speaker	D-9	B-11
		B-12, B-14 sound chip, multiplexor

4
Video

4
Video

Since the monitor image is the primary machine/human interface, the characteristics of the images that a program displays are usually the major criteria on which a program is judged. These characteristics include the appropriate use of color or monochrome attributes; the aesthetics of the format and design of the images displayed; the speed and smoothness with which the screen is updated; the use of graphics characters or screens; and the general impression of a rational, attractive, organized, easy-to-comprehend set of information.

As expected, diagrams and tables can have more visual impact than straight text. Also, indications that processing is taking place are appreciated—no one should have to wonder if the machine has locked up or is just busy processing information. A suggestion of humor in your displays, if not overdone, adds a friendly touch. Most of all, video displays should give a feeling of visual excitement.

In this chapter we'll concentrate on the memory and I/O ports used by the video display adapters and we'll see how programs can use them to do interesting and useful things. The discussion will touch on video hardware, DOS service routines, and BASIC language support of video only when relevant to programming the display adapters.

DOS and BASIC support of the graphics capabilities of the PC and PCjr are impressively powerful and complete. Many excellent references thoroughly cover those services. There are also several good books that describe the BASIC graphics commands and provide example programs.

Although the theory and details of video presentation electronics used in monitors and televisions are fascinating subjects, they are beyond the purpose and scope of this book. Technical intricacies are best left to expert references on those subjects. We'll be discovering how the various types of display devices (RGB monitor, composite monitor, monochrome monitor, and television) differ in capabilities and support.

The PCjr and 3270/PC have demonstrated that using the provided service routines for video is extremely important in maintaining compatibility with future machines and operating systems. IBM has stated that the direct manipulation of display adapter ports and memory should be avoided.

Then why do many commercial-quality software programs (including many marketed by IBM and even IBM-logo programs) ignore this admonition? For the sake of adequate performance and control. For example, BIOS INT 10, function Eh (write TTY character to current cursor position) may seem to be a fast and straightforward task for the BIOS to do. In actuality, up to four other INT 10 functions may be called, each saving and restoring registers whether they matter or not. When faced with the choice of this level of overhead or simply placing the character directly into the video display memory where it will eventually be placed by the service routine, the diversion from standard service routines is understandable.

While there is no easy solution to this dilemma, many programmers have taken the approach of replacing the interrupt vectors for less-efficient ROM service routines to point to their own optimized routines that use the same parameters. If a compatibility conflict should surface in the future, the vector overlay to the programmer's routine is simply omitted, causing the program to use the system-provided routine until an improved, and compatible, routine can be designed. IBM is coming to understand these trade-offs and is attempting to quietly accommodate both the DOS/BIOS-support-service method and the direct-video-memory-manipulation method for future compatibility's sake.

In any case, there is much to learn about how monochrome and color/graphics adapters function on the PC, how to use them, how the PCjr is different, and how to use the extended capabilities of the PCjr.

Adapter Components
The diagram in Figure 4-1 is not meant to be a comprehensive diagram of the display adapter's internal workings, but it does show the conceptual relationships of the components.

Notice that the character generator is used only for text modes, and that the PC can directly access the display buffer through the system bus address lines.

The monochrome display adapter has fast static RAM and an 8088 adapter switch circuitry onboard to prevent simultaneous access to the display buffer. The color/graphics display adapter does not, which causes glitches or snow. You'll learn more about avoiding these glitches later in this chapter. The PCjr incorporates the components of the color display adapter on the motherboard of the system rather than on a separate option card. Although the architecture of this built-in (integrated) adapter appears similar to the PC, there are major differences, including the location of the display buffer (main RAM), raster generation (done with a Video Gate Array, VGA), 8088/6845 access to the display buffer (controlled by the VGA), the character generator ROM (2K rather than 8K, since no monochrome characters are included), port usage, color palettes, and additional video modes. Figure 4-2 shows the overall architecture of the PCjr integrated display adapter.

Figure 4-1. Conceptual Architecture of Display Adapter

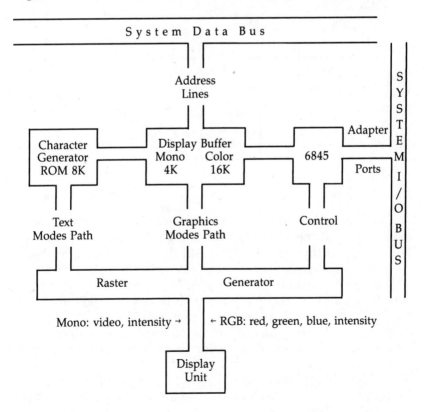

Figure 4-2. Conceptual Architecture of PCjr Integrated Display Adapter

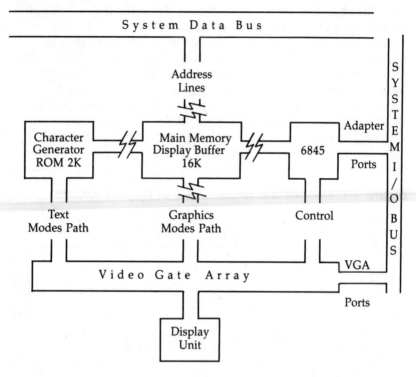

In Figure 4-2, the unconnected lines to the display buffer 2 indicate that the VGA, by way of a CRT/processor page register, controls the part of main RAM that will be used as the display buffer. Since the PCjr display buffer can start on any 16K boundary within the first 128K of memory (64K on an unexpanded PCjr), compatibility with the PC's B800h and B000h display buffer addresses is maintained by diverting any reference to those areas of memory to the display buffer that is selected in the processor portion of the CRT/processor page register.

The CRT portion of the page register determines the buffer to be used to generate the monitor display screen, while the 6845 registers determine which page within the buffer is to be displayed on the screen.

Since the main RAM of the machine is also used for a display buffer, 8088 and 6845 access to the memory must be arbitrated somehow. The VGA causes the 8088 to wait whenever the 6845 needs access to the video display memory. A happy outcome is that glitches never appear.

When the 64K display expansion is added to the PCjr, all the even-addressed bytes are located in the first 64K of RAM and the odd-addressed bytes are in the 64K expansion. With this interleaving technique, the memory access load is now shared between the 64K memory chips, rather than all being borne by one of them.

Because of the 8088 "wait-states" created by the VGA when the 6845 is accessing RAM, you can expect programs that run in the first 128K to run slower than on a PC, only 50 to 75% as fast. Memory refresh is eliminated on the PCjr since the 6845 reading of the display buffer causes the whole of memory to be refreshed automatically.

When expanding the PCjr above 128K, the additional memory must be supported by its own memory refresh scheme. Also, the vendor of the memory must supply software that repositions the PCjr default video-display memory so that it doesn't sit right in the middle of RAM at its normal position of 112K to 128K. Otherwise, the advantage of having additional memory would be negated by a hole in memory at 112K for the display memory. IBM's approach in the PCJRMEM.COM module is to relocate the display buffer at the lowest address available and allow the user to choose the amount of memory to be reserved for additional video pages. We'll discuss the concept of video pages in detail later in this chapter.

On the PCjr, the 4-color, high-resolution graphics mode (640 × 200) and the 16-color, medium-resolution graphics mode (320 × 200) require installation of the 64K display/memory enhancement, since two 16K buffers are used to support these modes. When these modes are used, the CRT/processor page register points to the first (lower addressed) of two consecutive 16K buffers.

Monochrome/Color Comparison

Table 4-1 describes the viewing requirements satisfied by the different monitors. Prices of monitors will erode as time goes on, particularly RGB and color composite monitors. Since the

IBM monochrome monitor gives the clearest 80-column text, you might consider it for intensive word processing tasks. Although 80 columns and color are obtainable on televisions, they are usually unsatisfactorily blurry. Color composite monitors may be marginally acceptable for color, depending on the quality of the monitor.

The IBM term *all-points addressable* refers to the ability to generate graphics displays on the color/graphics adapter attached monitor by setting picture elements (PELs) individually. This section will use the term *graphics* for the all-points-addressable display modes on the color adapter. *Text* will be used for the nongraphics display modes that are available on both monochrome and color adapters.

In the graphics display modes, characters may be displayed on the graphics screen. We'll call these *graphics characters*. The term *monochrome* will refer to the IBM monochrome monitor mode (unavailable on the PCjr), and *black and white* (b/w), to color-capable modes with the color burst signal disabled. So the available display modes with both monochrome and color adapters are monochrome text, b/w or color text, and b/w or color graphics with graphics characters.

Table 4-1. Viewing Requirements Satisfied by Monitor Types

Monitor Type	Color	Graphics	80 Columns	Starting Price
IBM monochrome	no	no	yes	$300
B/W television	no	yes*	no	100
Color television	no	yes*	no	250
B/W composite	no†	yes	yes	75
Color composite	maybe	yes*	no	200
RGB	yes	yes	yes	400

* Usually limited to medium resolution
† Shows as shades of gray, green, or amber

Determining and Switching Monitors

Since the PC doesn't include a display adapter as standard equipment (the PCjr does), many possible combinations of display devices may be attached to the computer. It is our program's responsibility to determine exactly the display environment. A program will need to do slightly different things depending on the display being used. Of course, there may be more than one monitor type attached. We may want

Table 4-2. Monochrome and RGB Monitor Characteristics

Do not attempt swapping monitors or adapters; permanent damage to monitors and/or adapters could result!

Characteristics	Monochrome†	RGB Color‡
PEEK(&h410) AND &H30	= &H30	<> &H30
Buffer address	&HB000	&HB800
		&HB800 or &HB000 on PCjr
Buffer size	&H1000 (4K)	&H4000 (16K)
		16K or 32K on PCjr
Pages in buffer	1	1–4
		half to four on PCjr, multiple buffers may be used
Buffer memory	static/no parity	dynamic/no parity
		PCjr: dynamic, no parity
6845 start ports	&H3B4	&H3D4
		&H3D4–5, &H3DA, &h3DF on PCjr
Band width	16.257 MHz	14.30 Mhz
Horz sweep rate	18.432 KHz	15.75 KHz
Vert sweep rate	50 Hz	60 Hz
Horz PELs	720	640
Vert PELs	350	200
Character box size	9 × 14	8 × 8
Character size (+ descenders)	7 × 9*	7 × 7 or 5 × 7 no 5 × 7 on PCjr
Characters in char ROM	256	text characters: 256 graphics characters: 128 in ROM, 128 in RAM 256 in ROM on PCjr
8088 access	when not refreshing	at any time
		PCjr: when not refreshing
Data rate	1.8 Mbytes/sec	1.5 Mbytes/sec
Light pen usable	no	yes

* Eighth dot of character propagated into ninth dot for B0h–DFh characters for nonbroken form design characters.

† Monochrome—High band width and nonstandard sweep rates require a special monitor.

‡ Color RGB—Intensity signal ignored by some monitors, causing only eight colors to be available.

our programs to use the monitor type best suited for the program or ask the user which monitor is preferred. Refer to Table 4-2.

On the PC, presence of a color adapter card doesn't always mean that an RGB monitor is available. Any type display might be in use. The same is true of the PCjr. Your well-designed and attractive color menu would appear in shades of gray on a b/w television or composite monitor. Because of this, you may want the user to select the monitor type and number of columns, regardless of the environment detected by the program.

The routines listed below do several useful things, such as determining the monitor in use at boot time and the adapters available, switching monitors within BASIC, and creating DOS commands to switch monitors. All these routines work correctly on the PCjr except for Programs 4-5 and 4-6, which produce a strange 39-column screen that doesn't wrap around to the next line, and Program 4-1, since the PCjr has no configuration switches to interrogate.

Program 4-1. Which Monitor Used at Boot Time

For error-free program entry, be sure to use "The Automatic Proofreader," Appendix H.

```
KO 10 ' read monitor configuration switches
JO 20 '
EC 30 'Read and store monitor captions
MC 40 FOR X=0 TO 3: READ MONITORS$(X): NEXT
JB 50 '
QJ 60 'Obtain monitor type switch info
BL 70 OUT &H61,&H84    'Set port for switch read
EH 80 MONITOR=(INP(&H60) AND &H30) / 16 'separate
       monitor type, shift to 0-3
PB 90 OUT &H61,&H40    'Set port for keyboard activ
       ity
GE 100 '
OF 110 ' Display the configuration found
OK 120 CLS: PRINT"Monitor configuration switches
       set for:"
QO 130 PRINT MONITORS$(MONITOR)
LC 140 END
HO 150 '
PE 160 ' Monitor type Captions
CA 170    DATA "FUTURE DISPLAY ADAPTER
MH 180    DATA "COLOR ADAPTER (40x25)
DF 190    DATA "COLOR ADAPTER (80x25)
CL 200    DATA "MONOCHROME ADAPTER (80x25)
```

148

Program 4-2. Which Monitors Available

For error-free program entry, be sure to use "The Automatic Proofreader," Appendix H.

```
LL 10 ' determine monitors available
FN 15 'Checks for the presence of a 6845 controll
       er at each adapter location
JO 20 '
LF 30 DEF SEG=&HFFFF: IF PEEK(&HE)=&HFD THEN PRINT
       "PCjr COLOR AVAILABLE":END
DJ 40 IF INP(&H3B5) <> &HFF THEN PRINT"MONO AVAIL
       ABLE" ELSE PRINT"MONO MISSING"
IO 50 IF INP(&H3D5) <> &HFF THEN PRINT"COLOR AVAI
       LABLE" ELSE PRINT"COLOR MISSING"
DI 60 END
```

Program 4-3. Which Monitor Is Active

For error-free program entry, be sure to use "The Automatic Proofreader," Appendix H.

```
EN 10 ' determine active monitor
KA 20 PRINT"The active monitor is ";
OA 21 'or change lines 10 and 20
CG 22 '  10 'Current video is       MONO       COLOR
PH 23 '  20 DEF SEG=0: IF PEEK(&H449) = 7 THEN POR
       T=&H3B8 ELSE PORT=&H3D8
OH 30 '--- direct BASIC ---
CF 40 DEF SEG=0:IF (PEEK(&H410) AND &H30) = &H30
       THEN PRINT"mono" ELSE PRINT"color"
CH 50 END
AA 60 ' --- BASIC using SRVCCALL ---
EO 70 INTERRUPT%=&H11:AH%=&H0:AL%=0
NI 80 GOSUB 220 'call ml routine
NJ 90 IF (AL% AND &H30) = &H30 THEN PRINT"mono" E
       LSE PRINT"color"
HO 100 ' --- direct machine language ---
AD 110 REM xor ax,ax
LP 120 REM mov ds,ax
CD 130 REM mov al,[410] ;equip flag
EG 140 REM and al,30
NE 150 REM cmp al,30
NM 160 REM jne color
NF 170 ' ---- BIOS machine language ---
BN 180 REM int 11 ; get config
FA 190 REM and al,30
NL 200 REM cmp al,30
ND 210 REM jne color
```

Program 4-4. Switching Monitors

For error-free program entry, be sure to use "The Automatic Proofreader," Appendix H.

```
MM 100 ' switch to color monitor while in BASIC
GG 110 '
HG 120 ' --- set equipment flag ---
EM 130 DEF SEG=0:POKE &H410,(PEEK(&H410) AND &HCF
       ) OR &H10
NG 140 ' --- call int 10 to set mode 80x25 color
       ---
DB 150 DEF SEG
PH 160 ASMROUT$=CHR$(&HB8)+CHR$(&H3)+CHR$(&H0)    '
       mov ax,0003
ED 170 ASMROUT$=ASMROUT$+CHR$(&HCD)+CHR$(&H10)    '
       int 10
IJ 180 ASMROUT$=ASMROUT$+CHR$(&HCA)+CHR$(&H0)+CHR
       $(&H0)    'retf
OM 190 ASMROUT!=VARPTR(ASMROUT$)
KC 200 ASMROUT!=PEEK(ASMROUT!+1)+(PEEK(ASMROUT!+2
       )*256)
LM 210 CALL ASMROUT!
MI 220 '--- start with clean screen and make curs
       or visible ---
GN 230 CLS:LOCATE ,,1,6,7
```

Program 4-5. Create COLORMON.COM for DOS and BASIC Color Use

For error-free program entry, be sure to use "The Automatic Proofreader," Appendix H.

```
IC 100 ' create colormon.com for DOS and BASIC co
       lor use
GG 110 '
JE 120 OPEN "colormon.com" FOR OUTPUT AS #1
PA 130 READ X$:IF X$="/*" GOTO 150
HE 140 PRINT #1,CHR$(VAL("&H"+X$));:GOTO 130
AF 150 CLOSE #1:SYSTEM
BO 160 ' --- switch to color routine ---
BF 180 DATA 1E  : PUSH DS
IH 190 DATA 50  : PUSH AX
NL 200 DATA 31,C0  : XOR  AX,AX
HK 210 DATA 8E,D8  : MOV DS,AX
HH 220 DATA A1,10,04 : MOV AL,[410]
CN 230 DATA 24,CF  : AND AL,CF
QJ 240 DATA 0C,20  : OR   AL,20
EF 250 DATA A3,10,04  : MOV [410],AL
DO 260 DATA B8,03,00  : MOV AX,3
MN 270 DATA CD,10  : INT 10
DB 280 DATA 58  : POP AX
II 290 DATA 1F  : POP DS
LL 300 DATA CD,20  : INT 20  ;EXIT
JH 310 DATA /*
```

150

Program 4-6. Switch to Monochrome Monitor While in BASIC

For error-free program entry, be sure to use "The Automatic Proofreader," Appendix H.

```
6I 100 ' switch to mono monitor while in BASIC
6G 110 '
H6 120 ' --- set equipment flag ---
OK 130 DEF SEG=0:POKE &H410,PEEK(&H410) OR &H30
NO 140 ' --- call int 10 to set mode monochrome 8
       0x25 ---
DB 150 DEF SEG
GP 160 ASMROUT$=CHR$(&HB8)+CHR$(&H7)+CHR$(&H0)     '
       mov ax,0007
ED 170 ASMROUT$=ASMROUT$+CHR$(&HCD)+CHR$(&H10)     '
       int 10
IJ 180 ASMROUT$=ASMROUT$+CHR$(&HCA)+CHR$(&H0)+CHR
       $(&H0)   'retf
OH 190 ASMROUT!=VARPTR(ASMROUT$)
KC 200 ASMROUT!=PEEK(ASMROUT!+1)+(PEEK(ASMROUT!+2
       )*256)
LH 210 CALL ASMROUT!
MI 220 '--- start with clean screen and make curs
       or visible ---
LE 230 CLS:LOCATE ,,1,12,13
```

Use this line to ascertain if a PCjr is enhanced with the 64K display/memory option:

DEF SEG=0: IF PEEK(&h416)*256+PEEK(&h415) > 64 THEN 128K.JR$="YES"

Video Modes

Because of the variety of available screen modes, widths, color sets, and corresponding memory requirements, the possible video modes and associated BASIC SCREEN statement parameters can be confusing.

The contents of the CRT_MODE byte at location 449h corresponds to the mode value specified to the ROM BIOS set-mode service (INT 10, AH=0) and returned from the read-mode service (INT 10, AH=15h). This screen mode indicator is saved here by the ROM BIOS after it uses it as an index to load the 6845 registers with the proper values. These values are from the tables in ROM that are pointed to by the vector at 74h (INT 1D) and listed in the XT *Technical Reference* manual on page A-48 (PCjr TRM, page A-82). The CRT_MODE byte is the definitive description of a mode. Each display mode has a unique value in this byte.

Table 4-3 summarizes the available video modes and their characteristics.

Table 4-3. Summary of Available Video Mode Characteristics

449h ROM BIOS CRT Mode	Display Screen Characteristics	BASIC Screen/ Width/Burst	465h 6845 PC	Mode PCjr	44Ch Page Length	462h Buffer Pages
00	40×25 b/w text	0/40/off	2Ch	Ch	2048*	8
01	40×25 16-col text	0/40/on	28h	8h	2048*	8
02	80×25 b/w text	0/80/off	2Dh	Dh	4096*	4
03	80×25 16-color text	0/80/on	29h	9h	4096*	4
04	320×200 4-col graphics	1,2,3,4/0/on	2Ah	Ah	16384*	1
05	320×200 b/w graphics	1,2,3,4/40/off	2Eh	Eh	16384*	1
06	640 × 200 b/w graphics	1,2,3,4/80/off	1Eh	Eh	16384*	1
07	80×25 monochrome text	any/any/any	29h	n/a	‡	
08	PCjr 160×200 16-col graphics	3/20/on	n/a	1Ah	16384*	1
09	PCjr 320×200 16-col graphics	5,6/40/on	n/a	1Bh	32768*†	
10	PCjr 640×200 4-col graphics	5,6/80/on	n/a	Bh	32768*†	

* The PCjr may have up to eight display buffers of 16K, each segmented into screen pages of the appropriate length.

† Requires PCjr 64K display/memory enhancement.

‡ Contains 16384 in error; should be 4096.

n/a Not applicable

152

The mode number stored in 449h is the video mode as it's known to ROM BIOS, while the mode stored in location 465h is the number that is actually loaded into the PC video adapter port at 3B8h (monochrome), 3D8h (color), or the PCjr's VGA register 0. You can read about this register in the PC *Technical Reference* manual starting on page 1-141; for the PCjr see pages 2-64 and 2-67 (as discussed in the Introduction, all page references are for the XT manual).

In addition, the PCjr has a bit in the 8255 port 61h (bit 2) that must be set to indicate whether a text or graphics mode is in effect. The bit may be thought of as a selection switch that causes the character generator output to go to the VGA (text, if the bit is 1) or the display buffer contents to be directed to the VGA (graphics, if the bit is zero). This is described in the PCjr *Technical Reference* manual on page 2-31.

Figure 4-3 illustrates the memory available for screen buffers. The PCjr allows all of its base 128K (assuming the 64K display/memory enhancement has been added) to be used for multiple 16K display buffers, but the first two, 0K–31K, should not be used since DOS and the application program reside in this area.

By default the PCjr display buffer is sized at 16K and located at the top of the base memory. BASIC allocates additional display memory (with the CLEAR statement) from the top of the base memory downward (toward lower memory addresses). While the PCjr CRT/processor page register is used to determine the 16K display buffer and the 6845 registers are used to select the display page, BASIC's SCREEN statement parameters, VPAGE and APAGE, refer to the page number from the beginning of the current 16K video buffer and change the 6845 registers appropriately. No mechanism is included within BASIC to change the CRT/processor page register.

You can tell when a graphics screen mode is in effect because the cursor changes from a flashing underline to a nonflashing solid block. An application program can, of course, change the cursor shape.

The color graphics/adapter has several advantages over the monochrome adapter for text. It has capabilities for 80- or 40-column line widths; selectable foreground, background, and border colors; and up to eight pages of text (more on the PCjr) that may be prebuilt for later instantaneous display.

Figure 4-3. Location and Size of Display Buffers

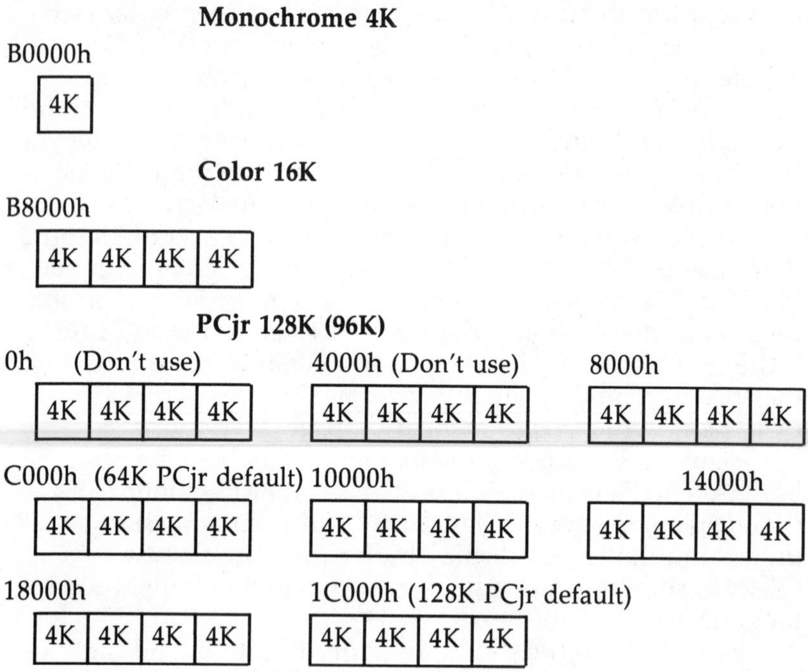

Monochrome 4K

B0000h

4K

Color 16K

B8000h

4K	4K	4K	4K

PCjr 128K (96K)

0h (Don't use)	4000h (Don't use)	8000h

4K	4K	4K	4K		4K	4K	4K	4K		4K	4K	4K	4K

C000h (64K PCjr default) 10000h   14000h

4K	4K	4K	4K		4K	4K	4K	4K		4K	4K	4K	4K

18000h   1C000h (128K PCjr default)

4K	4K	4K	4K		4K	4K	4K	4K

You'll notice by looking at the 6845 initialization tables in the *Technical Reference* manual that the 6845 registers are initialized with the same values for modes 0–1, 2–3, and 4–6. The difference between these is that the color burst signal is enabled or not via the fourth port on the adapter (3B8h for monochrome or 3D8h for color), and the contents of the CRT_MODE_SET byte at 465h is different. The value stored in location 465h for each mode is shown in Table 4-3. In 640 × 200 b/w graphics mode (6), the overscan register port at 3D9h and the CRT_PALETTE byte at 466h are also set differently from the 320 × 200 modes (4–5).

Memory locations 449h through 466h constitute an area in which BIOS records the current settings of various CRT-related values. Many of the 6845 control register ports are write-only; this area has been provided so that you can obtain the current values for the display adapter. Because the settings always reflect the active display adapter, the information here is especially valuable. This chapter will explore the area in detail, and we'll revisit the whole area later in the book.

The BASIC DRAW statement, M subparameter (Move absolute or relative), suffers from poor documentation in the BASIC manuals. BASIC 1.1 doesn't make it clear that variables may be used. BASIC 2.0 explains this but then offers an incorrect example of M+X1;,-=X2; which should actually be M+=X1;,-=X2;. Line 30 of the "Shooting Star" example in the BASIC manual should read STAR$= and not STAR$+.

Video Characters

The display adapters include 8K (2K on the PCjr) of ROM-resident PEL (picture element) maps for the characters that may be displayed on the screen. Actually, both the monochrome and color display adapters include the same character sets in ROM, but each adapter uses different sections. The PCjr doesn't include any monochrome characters in its character-set ROM. These character-generator ROMs are used only to produce the text-mode characters. ROM BIOS resident PEL maps are used to draw the characters when a graphics mode is in effect.

The 8K ROM used in the PC display adapters is the MK36000 chip. The PCjr uses a 2K MCM68A316E, which is compatible with 2716 and 2732 EPROMs. The PC 8K ROM contains a monochrome character set in locations 0–4095, a color single-dot set in locations 4096–6143, and the color text default double-dot character set in locations 6144–8191. We'll have more to say about the single-dot character set in a moment.

The ASCII character number placed in the display adapter memory to select the text character which displays in that position should be translated to row-by-row dots. The translation of the ASCII character to row-by-row dots is processed from the character ROM by a shift register on the display adapter or the VGA in the PCjr. This is done 50 or 60 times a second for each character on the screen so that the image won't fade from view.

The monochrome characters are each displayed in a 9 × 14 cell on the display screen, with capital letters occupying a 7 × 9 grid in the top center, descenders reaching down to the eleventh line, and the underline-style cursor using the twelfth and thirteenth rows. That leaves the fourteenth row blank for use as a line separation. Special circuitry on the monochrome adapter causes the eighth column of dots to be propagated into the ninth for characters B0–DFh so that form design characters do not have a gap between them. Vertical lines are two dots wide so as to achieve the most pleasing aspect ratio to horizontal lines. The monochrome monitor's sharp 720 × 350 resolution makes it an excellent choice for word processing and data entry functions. The monochrome text display cell is shown in Figure 4-4.

The color adapter text characters are each displayed in an 8 × 8 cell on the display screen, with capital letters occupying a 7 × 7 grid in the top left, descenders using the eighth line, and the underline-style cursor using the seventh and eighth lines. The bottoms of descenders will touch the tops of capital letters on the row beneath them. Form design characters B0–DFh are each 8 PELs wide or high so that they form continuous touching lines. The color display has a resolution of 640 × 200 and is a bit fuzzy for word processing. Monitors with a smaller dot pitch, such as 0.31 mm, improve the sharpness somewhat. The color text display cell is shown in Figure 4-5.

Figure 4-4. Monochrome Adapter Character Cell

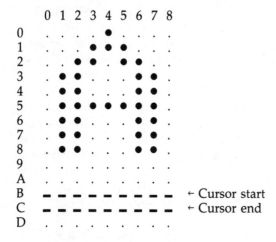

Figure 4-5. Color/Graphics Adapter Character Cell

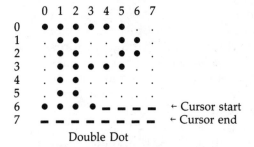

Double Dot

When using a text mode screen, all 256 characters, CHR$(0) through CHR$(255), are available for your use through direct keyboard entry, Alt-numeric keypad entry, or CHR$(n) statements. To display these characters as their assigned symbols (for example, Bh is a male symbol and Ch is a female symbol), the ASCII number of the character must be placed in screen memory when the screen is in text mode. When certain characters are included in PRINT statements or entered with Alt-keypad, they are acted upon by the ROM BIOS and cause control functions to occur rather than a character to be displayed. These characters are listed in Table 4-4.

Table 4-4. Control Characters

Decimal	Hex	Control Action
7	7	Beep
9	9	Tab
10	A	Linefeed
11	B	Home
12	C	Form feed/clear screen
13	D	Carriage return
28	1C	Cursor right
29	1D	Cursor left
30	1E	Cursor up
31	1F	Cursor down

Program 4-7 will produce a text character chart on the screen and label the characters in both decimal and hexadecimal order. Because the ASCII code for characters is POKEd into the screen memory, the control characters discussed above are displayed rather than acted upon. The program is set to use the color monitor, but you can change the DEF SEG statement in line 200 to support the monochrome monitor if you wish.

The PC ROM BIOS includes the necessary graphics PEL maps to produce the graphics dot-by-dot drawn characters 0–127 (0–7Fh). You can see these maps starting at address FFA6Eh on page A-77 of the *Technical Reference* manual. Each byte corresponds to the bit values needed to make up the on/off PELs in one character row. Additional characters 128–255 (80–FFh) may be created by the user. The vector at 7CH is then set by the user (in the offset LSB/MSB, then segment LSB/MSB format) to point to these PEL maps, allowing the additional 128 graphics characters to be customized to the user's needs. The default setting of the vector at 7Ch causes characters above 128 (7Fh) to be garbage.

The PCjr includes the PEL maps for graphics characters 128–255 (7F–FFh) in the ROM BIOS as well as characters 0–127 (0–7Fh). You can see the low-numbered set starting at address FFA6Eh (the same as the PC) in the ROM BIOS listing in Appendix A of the *Technical Reference* manual. The high-numbered set begins at address FE05Eh. The PCjr uses a vector at 110H to point to the low-numbered set of graphics characters (this vector is unused in the PC), and the vector at 7Ch (as in the PC) as a pointer to the high-numbered set. The user can change both of these vectors to implement a whole new set of graphics characters PEL maps—meaning that all 255 graphics characters may be substituted for characters more to the user's liking or copied from ROM BIOS and altered.

Program 4-8 can be used to display and optionally print with Ctrl-PrtSc the PEL maps for all graphics characters. The program will also map characters 128–255 if the vector at 7Ch is filled in.

The PEL maps created by Program 4-8 can be used to determine the correct decimal or hexadecimal values for on/off combinations needed to make up rows of your own characters. Simply code the PEL map for each row of a character in a separate DATA statement, POKE them into a free area of memory above BASIC, then point the appropriate vector (7Ch or 110h) to the start of the PEL maps that you have placed into memory. You may want to save to disk the PEL maps you have just built in memory. This image will be much faster to install than a byte-by-byte POKE program. Use the PCjr-to-PC character-copying program presented later in this chapter as a model, pointing the DEF SEG to your constructed graphics PEL maps.

Program 4-9 will produce the same type of character chart for the graphics text characters. Because the ASCII character code for certain control characters (9–13 and 28–31) would create havoc with the display, they are omitted from the display. You can hear the effect of CHR$(7) as it is displayed. If you have set the vector at 7Ch for a 128–255 character set, those characters will also be displayed; otherwise, you will see garbage for characters 128–255.

Program 4-7. Text Characters Display

For error-free program entry, be sure to use "The Automatic Proofreader," Appendix H.

```
JG 100 'Videoct; display text characters in decim
       al and hex
GG 110 '
BN 120 SCREEN 0:WIDTH 80:KEY OFF:CLS
NJ 130 COLOR 0,7:PRINT "          Characters 0-
       255 : CHR$(n) values in decimal
EN 140 PRINT " Hundreds ----------------->  1 1 1
        1 1 1 1 1 1 2 2 2 2 2 2"
PL 150 PRINT "  Tens -> 0 1 2 3 4 5 6 7 8 9 0 1 2
        3 4 5 6 7 8 9 0 1 2 3 4 5"
HN 160 PRINT "  Units    ----------------------
       -----------------------------";
JB 170 Y=0:FOR X=5 TO 5+(9*2) STEP 2:LOCATE X,3:P
       RINT Y;"---";:Y=Y+1:NEXT
HE 180 '
KI 190 COLOR 7,0:X=0:Y=0:Z=0
NC 200 DEF SEG=&HB800+((4*160)/16)+((12*2)/16) 's
       kip 4 rows, indent 12
EM 210 FOR Z=0 TO 9
EO 220   FOR X = 0 TO 25
EB 230   Y=Y+4:A=(X*10)+Z:IF A>255 GOTO 240 ELSE PO
       KE Y,A
JI 240 NEXT:Y=Y+216:NEXT
PA 250 FOR Z=0 TO 0:FOR X=0 TO 0:NEXT:NEXT
GG 260 LOCATE 25,1:PRINT"Press enter for hex tabl
       e or Esc to end.";
HD 270 '
KM 280 K$=INKEY$:IF K$="" GOTO 280
GP 290 IF K$=CHR$(27) GOTO 460
GJ 300 CLS:COLOR 0,7
JK 310 PRINT " Characters 0-255 : CHR$(n) values
       in Hex"
OC 320 PRINT "    MSB-> 0 1 2 3 4 5 6 7 8 9 A B C
       D E F"
```

159

```
IO 330 PRINT "  LSB   ---------------------------
       ------";
CG 340 Y=0
CH 350 FOR X=4 TO 4+(15):LOCATE X,3:PRINT " ";HEX
       $(Y);" ---";:Y=Y+1:NEXT
HC 360 '
JG 370 COLOR 7,0:X=0:Y=0:Z=0
KK 380 DEF SEG=&HB800+((3*160)/16)+((12*2)/16) 's
       kip 3 rows, indent 12
FC 390 FOR Z=0 TO 15
CO 400 FOR X = 0 TO 15
LG 410 Y=Y+4:A=(X*16)+Z:POKE Y,A
GK 420 NEXT:Y=Y+96:NEXT
MO 430 LOCATE 25,1:PRINT"Press enter for decimal
       table or Esc to end.";
GI 440 K$=INKEY$:IF K$="" GOTO 440
BN 450 IF K$<>CHR$(27) GOTO 120
JJ 460 KEY ON: LOCATE 23,1:END
```

Program 4-8. Display Graphics Characters PEL Maps

For error-free program entry, be sure to use "The Automatic Proofreader," Appendix H.

```
AC 10 'VIDEOGC; map all graphics characters in 8x
      8 pel map
JI 20 '   128-255 will also be mapped if 7C-7Fh in
      terrupt > 0
JP 30 '
OM 40 DEFINTG=A-Z:SCREEN 0:WIDTH 80:KEY OFF:CLS
JB 50 '
II 55 DEF SEG=0:LAST.128.OFF=PEEK(&H7C)+PEEK(&H7D
      )*256:LAST.128.SEG#=PEEK(&H7E)+PEEK(&H7F)*2
      56
JO 60 FIRST.128.SEG#=&HF000:FIRST.128.OFF=&HFA6E
      ' PC ONLY
NA 70 ' FIRST.128.SEG#=PEEK(&H112)+PEEK(&H113)*25
      6:FIRST.128.OFF=PEEK(&H110)+PEEK(&H111)*256
      '    PCJR ONLY
ID 80 CHAR.SEG#=FIRST.128.SEG#:OFFSET=FIRST.128.O
      FF:SET=0:GOSUB 130
IH 90 IF LAST.128.SEG#=0 THEN CLS:PRINT"NO TABLE
      FOR GRAPHICS CHARACTERS 128-255":END
HJ 95 IF LAST.128.SEG#=61440! THEN IF LAST.128.OF
      F=0 THEN CLS:PRINT"NO TABLE FOR GRAPHICS CH
      ARACTERS 128-255":END
EP 100 CHAR.SEG#=LAST.128.SEG#:OFFSET=LAST.128.OF
       F:SET=1:GOSUB 130
LM 110 END
HI 120 '
MN 130 DEF SEG=CHAR.SEG#
```

160

```
CC 140 FOR BEGIN=OFFSET TO OFFSET+(8*127) STEP 8
MJ 150 CHRNUM=(SET*128)+(BEGIN-OFFSET)/8
BJ 160 CLS
IA 170 PRINT"PEL MAP OF CHR$("MID$(STR$(CHRNUM),2
       ,3)")  / CHR$(&h"HEX$(CHRNUM)")"
KH 180 PRINT"starting at "HEX$(CHAR.SEG#)":"HEX$(
       BEGIN)"h"
JC 190 PRINT
LM 200 PRINT"7 6 5 4 3 2 1 0 decimal  hex"
MN 210 PRINT"- - - - - - - - "
HF 220 FOR X=0 TO 7 : Z=PEEK(BEGIN+X):FOR Y = 7 T
       O 0 STEP -1
DI 230 W=Z AND (2^Y) : IF W THEN PRINT"O ";:GOTO
       250
FL 240 PRINT". ";
OE 250 NEXT Y: PRINT"  "Z;:LOCATE ,26:PRINT HEX$
       (Z)"h": NEXT X:PRINT
QN 260 ' FOR X= 1 TO 1500:NEXT  'enable this line
        to allow break at character
GA 270 NEXT:RETURN
```

Program 4-9. Graphics Characters

For error-free program entry, be sure to use "The Automatic Proofreader," Appendix H.

```
BG 100 'Videocg; display all graphics text charac
       ters
IF 110 ' 128-255 will be garbage if vector at 7Ch
        hasn't been set by user.
HI 120 '
CL 130 SCREEN 1:WIDTH 80:KEY OFF:CLS
CP 140 PRINT "            Characters 0-255 : CHR$
       (n) values in decimal    "
EP 150 PRINT " Hundreds ----------------->  1 1 1
        1 1 1 1 1 1 2 2 2 2 2 2"
PN 160 PRINT " Tens -> 0 1 2 3 4 5 6 7 8 9 0 1 2
       3 4 5 6 7 8 9 0 1 2 3 4 5"
HP 170 PRINT " Units  -------------------------
       --------------------------";
JD 180 Y=0:FOR X=5 TO 5+(9*2) STEP 2:LOCATE X,3:P
       RINT Y;"---";:Y=Y+1:NEXT
HG 190 '
EK 200 FOR Z=0 TO 9
DA 210 FOR X = 0 TO 25
CJ 220 A=(X*10)+Z:IF A>255 GOTO 260
PF 230 IF (A>8 AND A<14) GOTO 260
HG 240 IF (A>27 AND A<32) GOTO 260
EF 250 LOCATE (Z*2)+5,(X*2)+11:PRINT CHR$(A);
FL 260 NEXT:NEXT
PE 270 FOR Z=0 TO 0:FOR X=0 TO 0:NEXT:NEXT
```

161

```
HK 280 LOCATE 25,1:PRINT"Press enter for hex tabl
       e or Esc to end.";
HH 290 '
MK 300 K$=INKEY$:IF K$="" GOTO 300
KO 310 IF K$=CHR$(27) GOTO 490
AD 320 CLS
JO 330 PRINT " Characters 0-255 : CHR$(n) values
       in Hex"
OG 340 PRINT "      MSB-> 0 1 2 3 4 5 6 7 8 9 A B C
        D E F"
IC 350 PRINT "  LSB        ------------------------
       ------";
DK 360 Y=0
DL 370 FOR X=4 TO 4+(15):LOCATE X,3:PRINT " ";HEX
       $(Y);" ---";:Y=Y+1:NEXT
HG 380 '
FC 390 FOR Z=0 TO 15
CO 400 FOR X = 0 TO 15
CP 410 A=(X*16)+Z:LOCATE Z+4,(X*2)+11
BA 420 IF (A>8 AND A<14) GOTO 450
JC 430 IF (A>27 AND A<32) GOTO 450
HF 440 PRINT CHR$(A);
FL 450 NEXT:NEXT
ME 460 LOCATE 25,1:PRINT"Press enter for decimal
       table or Esc to end.";
MI 470 K$=INKEY$:IF K$="" GOTO 470
DO 480 IF K$<>CHR$(27) GOTO 130
JP 490 KEY ON: LOCATE 23,1:END
```

Supplemental Characters

The PCjr includes the PEL maps for graphics characters
128–255, but the PC doesn't. Why not borrow them from the
PCjr, save them on disk, and load them into the PC whenever
these extended graphics text characters are desired? Program
4-10 does just that.

Now that you've created the file of characters from a
loaner PCjr, simply run Program 4-11 to load them into your
PC anytime you need them. If you load the characters at the
suggested segment which is above BASIC (unless you have
expanded your PCjr above 128K), the characters will be available for your use even after exiting BASIC.

Program 4-10. Program to Save PCjr Graphics Characters 128–255

```
10 'VIDEOGG; create bloadable graphics charact
   ers 128-256 from PCJR
20 '
```

162

```
 Ø DEFINTG=A-Z
4Ø '
5Ø INPUT "File name for chars 128-256 (.bld wi
   ll be added to name) ",FILE$
6Ø FILE$=FILE$+".BLD"
7Ø DEF SEG=Ø:LAST.128.OFF=PEEK(&H7C)+PEEK(&H7D
   )*256:LAST.128.SEG#=PEEK(&H7E)+PEEK(&H7F)*2
   56
8Ø DEF SEG=LAST.128.SEG#:BSAVE FILE$,LAST.128.
   OFF,1Ø24
9Ø PRINT"GRAPHIC characters 128-255 have been
   saved from PCJR to file "FILE$
```

Program 4-11. Program to Load PCjr Graphics Characters 128–255 into a PC

For error-free program entry, be sure to use "The Automatic Proofreader," Appendix H.

```
PK 1Ø 'VIDEOGP; load bloadable graphics character
      s 128-256 from PCJR
JO 2Ø '
BJ 3Ø DEFINTG=A-Z
MA 4Ø '  Prompt for filename, segment, offset
ED 5Ø INPUT "File name of chars 128-256 (.bld wil
      l be added to name)";FILE$
HI 6Ø FILE$=FILE$+".BLD"
PJ 7Ø INPUT "Segment to bload 1Ø24-byte character
       maps (in hex) suggestion:17ØØ";SEG$
FC 8Ø INPUT "offset to bload 1Ø24-byte character
      maps (in hex) suggestion : Ø";OFFSET$
CL 9Ø SEG#=VAL("&h"+SEG$):OFFSET=VAL("&h"+OFFSET$
      )
JF 1ØØ ' Set up extended graphics characters vect
       or
HF 11Ø DEF SEG=Ø
PI 12Ø POKE &H7F,VAL("&h"+MID$(RIGHT$("ØØØØ"+SEG$
       ,4),1,2))
ED 13Ø POKE &H7E,VAL("&h"+MID$(RIGHT$("ØØØØ"+SEG$
       ,4),3,2))
LI 14Ø POKE &H7D,VAL("&h"+MID$(RIGHT$("ØØØØ"+OFFS
       ET$,4),1,2))
BJ 15Ø POKE &H7C,VAL("&h"+MID$(RIGHT$("ØØØØ"+OFFS
       ET$,4),3,2))
DB 16Ø DEF SEG=SEG#:BLOAD FILE$,OFFSET
CB 17Ø ' Show the extended graphics characters
QM 18Ø SCREEN 1:WIDTH 8Ø
MI 19Ø PRINT"GRAPHIC characters 128-255 have been
        loaded from PCJR file "FILE$
JI 2ØØ PRINT"Vector 7C-7Fh has been set to point
       at this table, so"
```

163

```
BM 21Ø PRINT"GRAPHIC characters 128-255 are now u
    sable:"
BD 22Ø FOR X=128 TO 255:PRINT X"="CHR$(X)"    ";:N
    EXT
```

Unfortunately, some programs that you run after loading the characters and exiting BASIC may overlay the character set that you've loaded. Instead of loading the characters above BASIC, you could load them into a page of the color display adapter that you don't intend to use, but any change in screen mode or width will destroy the characters loaded there. The safest alternative is to create a .COM file that installs the character set and terminates but stays resident using DOS interrupt 27. That will make the character set logically a part of DOS. This is fairly simple and can be accomplished by using DEBUG on a PCjr that has a disk drive.

Do the following to create a resident COM module:

A> DEBUG	
-m f000:e05e L400 1700:0	(move the 128–255 character set to RAM)
-n char128.com	(name the COM module)
-f 16fe:0 L20 90	(put 20h bytes of NOPs in front of the set)
-a 16fe:0	(start assembling instructions)
-mov ax,0	(zero the AX register)
-push ax	(move the zero to...)
-pop ds	(the data segment register)
-mov [7e],cs	(save the segment of this set in the vector)
-mov ax,120	(the set begins 120h into the module)
-mov [7c],ax	(save the offset in the vector)
-mov dx,521	(tell DOS how long the set is, plus this code)
-int 27	(terminate but stay resident)
-	(press the Enter key to end assembly)
-rcs	(display the current CS register)
-16ee	(adjust for save beginning at CS+100)
-rcx	(display the CX register)
-520	(the length of this code and character set)
-rbx	(should zero this to prevent...)
-0	(an overly long disk file)
-w	(write the finished module to disk)
-q	(exit DEBUG)

After this is completed, you can install the character set permanently anytime you wish just by issuing the command CHAR128 at any DOS prompt.

If a PCjr is not available to you, you may use the DEBUG ENTER command to create the character set at 1700:0h from

164

Program 4-12. When you have finished entering the data, use the above procedure (minus the DEBUG MOVE command) to create the module. There are 1024 bytes of data to enter, so first pursue any opportunity to borrow a few moments of PCjr time.

Program 4-12. PCjr Graphics Characters 128–255

```
1700:0000 78 CC
1700:0002 C0 CC 78 18 0C 78 00 CC-00 CC CC CC 7E 00 1C 00
1700:0012 78 CC FC C0 78 00 7E C3-3C 06 3E 66 3F 00 CC 00
1700:0022 78 0C 7C CC 7E 00 E0 00-78 0C 7C CC 7E 00 30 30
1700:0032 78 0C 7C CC 7E 00 00 00-78 C0 C0 78 0C 38 7E C3
1700:0042 3C 66 7E 60 3C 00 CC 00-78 CC FC C0 78 00 E0 00
1700:0052 78 CC FC C0 78 00 CC 00-70 30 30 30 78 00 7C C6
1700:0062 38 18 18 18 3C 00 E0 00-70 30 30 30 78 00 C6 38
1700:0072 6C C6 FE C6 C6 00 30 30-00 78 CC FC CC 00 1C 00
1700:0082 FC 60 78 60 FC 00 00 00-7F 0C 7F CC 7F 00 3E 6C
1700:0092 CC FE CC CC CE 00 78 CC-00 78 CC CC 78 00 00 CC
1700:00a2 00 78 CC CC 78 00 00 E0-00 78 CC CC 78 00 78 CC
1700:00b2 00 CC CC CC 7E 00 00 E0-00 CC CC CC 7E 00 00 CC
1700:00c2 00 CC CC 7C 0C F8 C3 18-3C 66 66 3C 18 00 CC 00
1700:00d2 CC CC CC CC 78 00 18 18-7E C0 C0 7E 18 18 38 6C
1700:00e2 64 F0 60 E6 FC 00 CC CC-78 FC 30 FC 30 30 F8 CC
1700:00f2 CC FA C6 CF C6 C7 0E 1B-18 3C 18 18 D8 70 1C 00
1700:0102 78 0C 7C CC 7E 00 38 00-70 30 30 30 78 00 00 1C
1700:0112 00 78 CC CC 78 00 00 1C-00 CC CC CC 7E 00 00 F8
1700:0122 00 F8 CC CC CC 00 FC 00-CC EC FC DC CC 00 3C 6C
1700:0132 6C 3E 00 7E 00 00 38 6C-6C 38 00 7C 00 00 30 00
1700:0142 30 60 C0 CC 78 00 00 00-00 FC C0 C0 00 00 00 00
1700:0152 00 FC 0C 0C 00 00 C3 C6-CC DE 33 66 CC 0F C3 C6
1700:0162 CC DB 37 6F CF 03 18 18-00 18 18 18 18 00 00 33
1700:0172 66 CC 66 33 00 00 00 CC-66 33 66 CC 00 00 22 88
1700:0182 22 88 22 88 22 88 55 AA-55 AA 55 AA 55 AA DB 77
1700:0192 DB EE DB 77 DB EE 18 18-18 18 18 18 18 18 18 18
1700:01a2 18 18 F8 18 18 18 18 18-F8 18 F8 18 18 18 36 36
1700:01b2 36 36 F6 36 36 36 00 00-00 00 FE 36 36 36 00 00
1700:01c2 F8 18 F8 18 18 18 36 36-F6 06 F6 36 36 36 36 36
1700:01d2 36 36 36 36 36 36 00 00-FE 06 F6 36 36 36 36 36
1700:01e2 F6 06 FE 00 00 00 36 36-36 36 FE 00 00 00 18 18
1700:01f2 F8 18 F8 00 00 00 00 00-00 F8 18 18 18 18 18 18
1700:0202 18 18 1F 00 00 00 18 18-18 18 FF 00 00 00 00 00
1700:0212 00 00 FF 18 18 18 18 18-18 18 1F 18 18 18 00 00
1700:0222 00 00 FF 00 00 00 18 18-18 18 FF 18 18 18 18 18
1700:0232 1F 18 1F 18 18 18 36 36-36 36 37 36 36 36 36 36
1700:0242 37 30 3F 00 00 00 00 00-3F 30 37 36 36 36 36 36
1700:0252 F7 00 FF 00 00 00 00 00-FF 00 F7 36 36 36 36 36
1700:0262 37 30 37 36 36 36 00 00-FF 00 FF 00 00 00 36 36
1700:0272 F7 00 F7 36 36 36 18 18-FF 00 FF 00 00 00 36 36
1700:0282 36 36 FF 00 00 00 00 00-FF 00 FF 18 18 18 00 00
```

```
1700:0292  00  00  FF  36  36  36  36  36–36  36  3F  00  00  00  18  18
1700:02a2  1F  18  1F  00  00  00  00  00–1F  18  1F  18  18  18  00  00
1700:02b2  00  00  3F  36  36  36  36  36–36  36  FF  36  36  36  18  18
1700:02c2  FF  18  FF  18  18  18  18  18–18  18  F8  00  00  00  00  00
1700:02d2  00  00  1F  18  18  18  FF  FF–FF  FF  FF  FF  FF  FF  00  00
1700:02e2  00  00  FF  FF  FF  FF  F0  F0–F0  F0  F0  F0  F0  F0  0F  0F
1700:02f2  0F  0F  0F  0F  0F  0F  FF  FF–FF  FF  00  00  00  00  00  00
1700:0302  76  DC  C8  DC  76  00  00  78–CC  F8  CC  F8  C0  C0  00  FC
1700:0312  CC  C0  C0  C0  C0  00  00  FE–6C  6C  6C  6C  6C  00  FC  CC
1700:0322  60  30  60  CC  FC  00  00  00–7E  D8  D8  D8  70  00  00  66
1700:0332  66  66  66  7C  60  C0  00  76–DC  18  18  18  00  FC  30
1700:0342  78  CC  CC  78  30  FC  38  6C–C6  FE  C6  6C  38  00  38  6C
1700:0352  C6  C6  6C  6C  EE  00  1C  30–18  7C  CC  CC  78  00  00  00
1700:0362  7E  DB  DB  7E  00  00  06  0C–7E  DB  DB  7E  60  C0  38  60
1700:0372  C0  F8  C0  60  38  00  78  CC–CC  CC  CC  CC  CC  00  00  FC
1700:0382  00  FC  00  FC  00  00  30  30–FC  30  30  00  FC  00  60  30
1700:0392  18  30  60  00  FC  00  18  30–60  30  18  00  FC  00  0E  1B
1700:03a2  1B  18  18  18  18  18  18  18–18  18  18  D8  D8  70  30  30
1700:03b2  00  FC  00  30  30  00  00  76–DC  00  76  DC  00  00  38  6C
1700:03c2  6C  38  00  00  00  00  00  00–00  18  18  00  00  00  00  00
1700:03d2  00  00  18  00  00  00  0F  0C–0C  0C  EC  6C  3C  1C  78  6C
1700:03e2  6C  6C  6C  00  00  00  70  18–30  60  78  00  00  00  00  00
1700:03f2  3C  3C  3C  3C  00  00  00  00–00  00  00  00  00  00
```

Many times you will want to draw boxes or diagrams on the screen. Figure 4-6 shows the decimal character codes you will need. Since all the characters are above 127 (7Fh), you will need to use the monochrome monitor, a PCjr, or load the 128–255 character set as described above. The Alt keypad (Num Lock, then Alt and number keys on the PCjr) can be used to enter the character numbers directly or for use within PRINT statements. CHR$ may also be used in PRINT statements.

Printing Screen Characters

Since the Epson printer sold by IBM doesn't have the full screen text character set available in its ROM, you won't be able to print an exact image of a nicely designed nongraphics text screen on your printer. Non-IBM Epson printers support even fewer of the IBM text characters. And both styles of printers use many of the ASCII characters as control characters for the printer. Try the following line to see the effect that each character has, compared with the display that Program 4-7 produces:

FOR X=0 TO 255: LPRINT X;CHR$(X):NEXT

Figure 4-6. Border Drawing Text Mode ASCII Characters CHR$(n)

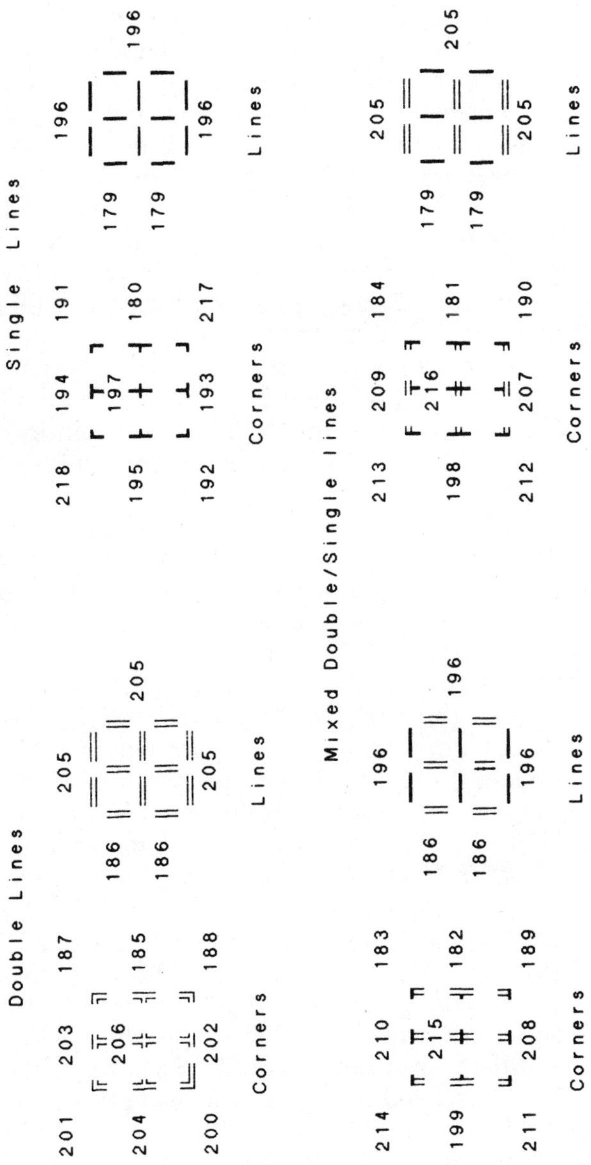

167

You may want to save the listing as a reference guide to show what effects the different ASCII characters have on the printer. Because of the effect of the various ASCII printer control characters, you'll get very strange results when using Shift-PrtSc if you have placed any of them in a display buffer. Additionally, many of the form design characters will print as only approximations of their screen images. What can we do to produce a more faithful representation of the screen image?

We know that when the GRAPHICS module has been loaded and the screen is in a graphics mode, it will be printed sideways on the paper. This is done by using the bit-image graphics capabilities of the printer to bitmap the screen image using the graphics text character set held in ROM/RAM. We've also seen how to extend the graphics character set with the text characters 128–255. These techniques enable us to print a fairly good representation of a graphics text screen.

If the screen is not in a graphics mode or if the GRAPH-ICS module is not resident, the PC reverts to printing the screen as ASCII characters, which causes the confusing mess we've already seen.

To prove that the GRAPHICS method works, use the CHAR128 program that you've created as described above, cause the GRAPHICS module to be loaded in DOS, run Program 4-9, and press Shift-PrtSc to print either the decimal or hexadecimal character set. This chart will prove handy in the future, so save it as a reference guide.

To reproduce the nongraphics mode text character set (such as monochrome) on the printer, we would need to intercept the characters going to the printer and cause bit-image graphics to be used to produce those characters as well as the characters that do not have a true representation in the printer character ROM (such as 128–159 and the double form design characters).

Perhaps a nice addition would be some method of specifying which printer ASCII control codes should be passed on to the printer. Carriage return (Dh) and linefeed (Ah) would definitely be needed to be passed through, but backspace, DC1–DC4, shift-in, shift-out, and ESC could be elected to be printed as the associated text character or sent as control characters.

A program that did this would probably replace the INT 17 vector with its own address and perform the needed printer special processing. This could be accomplished by converting a printer control code coming into INT 17 to the appropriate escape code sequence needed to produce the bit-image map of the text character. Several versions of this type of program are available from user groups or (for a small license fee) from several private software companies. Of course, you will learn the most by undertaking the task yourself—if you have the time, curiosity, and need. Such a program is far too lengthy to publish here. One version is 2688 bytes long, although a significant portion is taken up by the needed bit-image tables.

The PC or PCjr screen will be printed in response to the user pressing the Shift and PrtSc keys, or Fn-PrtSc on the PCjr. This feature is available in BASIC as well as DOS and most application programs. You may want to allow your BASIC program to print screen images automatically, as initiated by the program. Program 4-13 shows a method that can do this.

You may also want to disable the capacity to print screen images either for a period of time or permanently (even after returning to DOS). The next example, Program 4-14, shows how the vector for INT 05 can be saved, overlaid to point to a do-nothing IRET instruction, and later restored to allow screen printing to be performed.

Program 4-13. Causing the Screen to Be Printed in BASIC

```
100 'VIDEOPS; cause screen to be printed in ba
    sic program
110 '
120 DEF SEG=&HFFFF          'in an area above b
    asic
130 FOR X=0 TO 2: READ N:POKE X,N:NEXT 'build
    assembler routine
140 PRTSC=0:CALL PRTSC      'call the routine
150 '
160 DATA &hCD,&h05,&hCB  : 'INT5, RETF routine
```

Program 4-14. Disabling/Enabling PrtSc Feature in BASIC

```
100 'VIDEODEP; Disable PrtSc, then re-enable
110 '
120 DEF SEG=0
130 FOR X=0 TO 3:POKE &H180+X,PEEK(&H14+X):NEX
    T 'save int5 in user int60
140 FOR X=0 TO 3:POKE &H14+X,PEEK(&H4+X):NEXT
    'copy int4 (single step) to int5 which cau
    ses it to point to iret instruction
```

169

```
150 PRINT"Try shift/PrtSc, press Esc to re-ena
    ble"
160 K$=INKEY$:IF K$<>CHR$(27) GOTO 160
170 '
180 FOR X=0 TO 3:POKE &H14+X,PEEK(&H180+X):NEX
    T 'restore saved int5
190 PRINT"Now shift/Prtsc re-enabled."
```

Double/Single Dots

On the color/graphics adapter board of the PC (*not* the PCjr), to the lower left of the number 6845 (below pins 1 and 2) is a jumper (J3) that can be used in text modes to cause single-dot 5 × 7 characters to be used rather than the double-dot 7 × 7 characters. You will need to solder a wire between the two contact points. These single-dot characters look best on an RGB display. The double-dot characters are meant primarily for composite monitors and television sets. When P3 has been jumpered, the third section of the text character generator ROM is selected. *Caution:* Electronic components are easily damaged. If you're not qualified to perform this modification, get help from a friend who understands electronics.

The first two sections of this ROM contain monochrome characters 0–255 (the first eight rows in the first section of ROM and the remaining rows in the second section). The fourth section holds the default double-dot characters. Figure 4-7 shows the difference in a typical text mode character using double- or single-dot composition. The PCjr has only one character set containing all 256 characters in the 7 × 7 double-dot format. Single-dot characters are not provided. However, a 2716 or 2732 EPROM with any desired character set may be used to replace the MCM68A316E 2K character ROM used in the PCjr.

Figure 4-7. Color/Graphics Single and Double Character

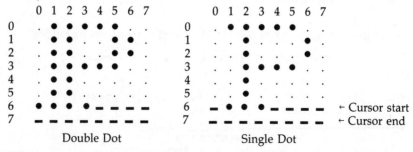

Double Dot   Single Dot

Attributes

Attribute bytes are used in monochrome or color text modes to assign display characteristics to individual characters. For each character displayed on the screen there is an attribute byte that may be used to assign the foreground and background colors, determine whether the character is to blink, and establish one of two brightness levels for the character. Figure 4-8 shows the assignable attributes for the monochrome display adapter.

In the monochrome adapter display buffer, the attribute byte for a character is placed in the byte following the character, with characters occupying even-numbered address positions and attributes located in the odd addresses. The color/graphics adapter also uses this scheme for text modes. Figure 4-9 illustrates the character/attribute arrangement in the text mode display buffer.

Figure 4-8. Monochrome Adapter Display Attributes

	Background				Foreground		
Blink	R	G	B	Intensity	R	G	B

1 = blink   1 = high

Nondisplay ...0   0   0 0   0   0 Dark on dark
Underlined 0   0   0 0   0   1
Normal 0   0   0 1   1   1 Light on dark
Reverse 1   1   1 0   0   0 Dark on light

Figure 4-9. Arrangement of Text Modes Character Attributes

Char1	Attr1	Char2	Attr2	Char3	Attr3	...
B0000h	B0001h	B0002h	B0003h	B0004h	B0005h	...

Characters occupy even-numbered addresses with the associated attribute occupying the next (odd) byte in the display adapter memory.

Even though blink and intensity can be combined with any of the above foreground and background settings (some—such as blinking nondisplay—don't make much sense), the foreground and background attribute settings *cannot* be

171

combined with each other. For example, reverse and under-lined (01110001) would appear as an underlined character, but not reversed. All other unlisted bit combinations cause the associated character to be displayed with the normal attribute, unless the two least significant bits are 01, which will cause the character to be underlined.

The blink and intensity bits function correctly on all un-documented foreground and background combinations. By the way, high intensity and reverse do not combine with an attribute of 78h; the character is displayed in reverse, but not high intensity. High-intensity reverse characters *are* obtainable by playing a trick with the 6845 control register, as we'll see in the next program.

Many authors and the IBM PC *Technical Reference* manual describe the attribute setting of 01110111 (77h) as providing a white box character and say this is the default for unlisted attribute byte settings. This is *not* the case on the PCs and XTs that I have tested; instead, a normal character was displayed when using this attribute. Perhaps only the early monochrome adapters function in the way described in the *Technical Ref-erence* manual.

It's a shame that the unused monochrome attributes could not have been used for additional functions, such as alternate display fonts, field boundaries, nonalterability, auto-skip, and tab stops.

A sample program that displays the possible monochrome and color attributes is presented below. It shows some exciting possibilities for extending the available attributes and also demonstrates a multimonitor access technique used by many popular software packages.

The color/graphics adapter has the same attribute byte format as the monochrome adapter, with the RGB bits determining the foreground and background colors as shown in Figure 4-10.

In the color/graphics display buffer, the attribute byte for a character is placed in the byte following the character, with character numbers occupying even-numbered addresses and attribute bytes located in the odd ones. Figure 4-11 illustrates the character/attribute arrangement in all the text modes.

Figure 4-10. Color/Graphics Adapter Display

	Background				Foreground		
Blink	R	G	B	Intensity	R	G	B

1 = blink   1 = high

Quoted Color	Actual Color	Foreground or Background R G B	Foreground with Intensity Bit Set
Black	Black	0 0 0	Dk Gray
Blue	Blue	0 0 1	Med Blue
Green	Lt Green	0 1 0	Lighter Green
Cyan	Lt Blue	0 1 1	Lighter Blue
Red	Red	1 0 0	Dk Orange
Magenta ...	Purple	1 0 1	Violet
Brown	Orange	1 1 0	Yellow
White	White	1 1 1	Bright White

The intensity bit affects only the foreground color and makes it lighter rather than darker as is meant by intensity when referring to pigments.

Figure 4-11. Arrangement of Text Modes Character Attributes

Contents	Char1	Attr1	Char2	Attr2	Char3	Attr3	... etc.
Location	B8000h	B8001h	B8002h	B8003h	B8004h	B8005h	... etc.

Characters occupy even-numbered addresses with the associated attribute occupying the next (odd) byte in the display buffer.

The demonstration program below (Program 4-15) shows the effect of all 256 possible attribute byte combinations and the hex (or optionally, decimal) value of the attribute byte used to create the effect. The program can be used with either the color/graphics or monochrome adapter, but the user should not attempt to specify a different monitor from what is currently being used unless a monitor-switch routine has been added to the program. The result of specifying an unused monitor is that the captions for the attribute byte will appear on the used monitor, and the actual attribute bytes will be sent to the unused monitor's display buffer.

This capability of displaying on the unused monitor is a feature of many popular programs which first insure that both monitors are available by using a technique similar to the one in Program 4-2 that examines the 3B5h or 3D5h 6845 control port. Obviously, the configuration switches do not give the information needed to determine the actual monitors attached.

Program 4-15 also demonstrates how an additional background intensity attribute can be obtained by turning off the blink capability via bit 5 of a 6845 register located at 3B8h or 3D8h (or via bit 1 of the PCjr VGA register 2). You can see how this affects the screen image by pressing the return key when prompted. This feature gives you an additional dimension in background colors for both monitor types when you don't need blinking characters anywhere on the same screen.

You'll notice that the color monitor displays glitches while the attribute bytes are being POKEd into every other byte of the color display memory (except on the PCjr). We'll soon see how your programs can avoid these glitches.

Program 4-15 uses the first of a series of 6845 or VGA control registers (this one at port 3B8h or 3D8h or 3DAh) to enable or disable the blink attribute for the display adapter. You can also use this port to enable or disable the display of information on the screen. You may want to do this to help preserve the monitor screen phosphorous if the user has obviously left the program unattended for a period of time. Simply check the BASIC TIMER value against the last time an entry was made and issue an INKEY$ to obtain a keypress so that you can reenable the display. In machine language the same can be done using BIOS time-of-day and keyboard services. Program 4-16 shows how to perform these tricks in BASIC for the various screen modes.

Notice how the reverse blinking field becomes high intensity when the blink feature is disabled, giving another type of attribute possibility for the display screen. Also, you'll find that the method used in line 160 to determine the current active screen mode is useful in determining which display adapter is currently active.

You can read about the blink bit and the video enable bit for the PC starting on page 1-141 of the *Technical Reference* manual, and on pages 2-64 and 2-73 for the PCjr.

Even though 16 foreground colors on 16 background colors (using the blink-disable technique) are provided on the PC and PCjr, you may need to create a wider range of shades. Program 4-17 shows how additional colors can be created by

174

mixing foreground and background colors. The program uses CHR$(177), which is a pattern of alternating foreground/ background dots, to demonstrate how the various combinations of colors can be mixed to achieve even more colors. CHR$(178) or CHR$(176) can be substituted for CHR$(177) in line 220 to achieve different shading effects.

You can also use the chart produced to see the effect of mixing graphics PELs of different colors from the palettes available in four-color 320 × 400 graphics mode or the extended modes available on the PCjr.

You'll need to use an RGB color monitor to see the full range of colors available, although a monochrome monitor shows some interesting combinations as well.

The PCjr menu options and routines may be omitted from the program if you do not have access to that machine. The PCjr provides a wonderful capability (besides extended colors in medium and high resolution) in its ability to specify dynamically the color desired for any of the attribute color codes. With this feature, four-color graphics can be much more useful because the colors can be set to the full 0–15 range. You won't find much documentation on this feature in the *Technical Reference* manual, so examine the sample program and observe the effects of menu option 3.

Another feature of the PCjr palettes, the palette mask register of the VGA is even less well-documented. Menu option 4 will show you how this register can be used to turn off the IRGB output lines to the monitor to further customize the palette and create visual effects.

A PCjr palette register is loaded in line 590. The VGA requires that port 3DAh be reset to some value under 10h to reenable video display once any of the palette registers have been changed. You can minimize any video disturbances during the loading of the palette registers by waiting for the vertical retrace period which is indicated by bit 3 after a read of VGA register 3DAh. Or you may use the vector at 34h INT 0D to give control to a vertical retrace routine.

In the PCjr, additional ROM BIOS routines have been added to the video services. These include the tables needed to define the additional modes for the PCjr in service 0, additional color palettes for service Bh, a new service 10h to set the color palette registers, and additional functions in service 5h that can be used to set or read the CRT/processor page register.

175

The color register at port 3D9h is discussed starting on page 1-140 in the PC *Technical Reference* manual. The PCjr manual discusses the palette-related registers on pages 2-50, 2-65, 2-66, and 2-71.

Program 4-15. Demonstration of All Possible Text Mode Attributes

For error-free program entry, be sure to use "The Automatic Proofreader," Appendix H.

```
LB 100 'Videoma; Demonstrate effect of all possib
       le attributes
BK 110 '   on blinking or high intensity backgroun
       ds
HI 120 '
GD 130 DEFINTG=A-Z:DEF SEG=&HFFFF:IF PEEK(&HE)=&H
       FD THEN DEF SEG=&HB800: CTRL.6845=0: BLINK
       .OFF=&H0: BLINK.ON=&H2:SCREEN 0: GOTO 190
       'PCjr
DD 140 CLS: LOCATE 12,19: INPUT "Enter Monitor Ty
       pe: M=monochrome, C=color  ",K$
IH 150 IF K$="C" OR K$="c" THEN DEF SEG=&HB800: C
       TRL.6845=&H3D8: BLINK.OFF=&H9: BLINK.ON=&H
       29: SCREEN 0: GOTO 190 'color adapter
EO 160 IF K$="M" OR K$="m" THEN DEF SEG=&HB000: C
       TRL.6845=&H3B8: BLINK.OFF=&HF: BLINK.ON=&H
       FF: GOTO 190' monochrome adapter
GC 170 GOTO 140 ' incorrect entry
HE 180 '
PN 190 CLS: LOCATE 20,25: COLOR 0,7: PRINT"DISPLA
       Y CHARACTER ATTRIBUTES 0-255": COLOR 7,0
OM 200 LOCATE 1,1: ATTR.LOC=1: FOR ATTR = 0 TO 25
       5 ' set increasing attributes
HI 210 PRINT   "  "+RIGHT$("0"+HEX$(ATTR),2)+" ";
       ' show the attribute in hex
IM 220 'PRINT   "  "+RIGHT$("   "+STR$(ATTR),3)+" ";
       ' show the attribute in dec
LH 230 FOR CAPTION.WIDTH = 1 TO 5: POKE ATTR.LOC,
       ATTR: ATTR.LOC=ATTR.LOC+2: NEXT
DG 240 NEXT ATTR
HP 250 '
MK 260 IF CTRL.6845=0 GOTO 360 'PCjr uses VGA ins
       tead of adapter ports
OG 270 OUT CTRL.6845,BLINK.OFF 'turn off bit 5
HD 280 GOSUB 330
EF 290 OUT CTRL.6845,BLINK.ON 'turn on bit 5
HA 300 GOSUB 340
FH 310 GOTO 270
HK 320 '
DF 330 LOCATE 22,26: INPUT " Press Enter to enabl
       e blink ", K$: RETURN
```

176

```
FF 340 LOCATE 22,26: INPUT "Press Enter to disabl
       e blink", K$: RETURN
HA 350 '
BI 360 X=INP(&H3DA) 'set vga to reg/data sequence
LJ 370 OUT &H3DA,3 'select vga reg three
LJ 380 OUT &H3DA,BLINK.OFF
HG 390 GOSUB 330
KM 400 OUT &H3DA,3 'select vga reg three
AC 410 OUT &H3DA,BLINK.ON
HF 420 GOSUB 340
GL 430 GOTO 360
```

Program 4-16. Disabling/Enabling Blink and the Display

For error-free program entry, be sure to use "The Automatic Proofreader," Appendix H.

```
HP 100 'Videoed; enable/disable blink and display
GG 110 '
DH 120 CLS:LOCATE 5,9:COLOR 0+16,7:PRINT"THIS FIE
       LD HAS BLINK ATTRIBUTES":PRINT
GL 130 COLOR 7,0
DE 140 DEF SEG=&HFFFF: IF PEEK(&HE)=&HFD THEN POR
       T=&H3DA: GOTO 350 'PCjr uses VGA
DE 150 ' Current video is: MONOCHROME        COLO
       R
LA 160 DEF SEG=0: IF PEEK(&H449) = 7 THEN PORT=&H
       3B8 ELSE PORT=&H3D8
IB 170 CURRENT=PEEK(&H465) ' SAVE CONTENTS OF 3B8
       H OR 3D8H PORT
LP 180 GOSUB 290
EK 190 OUT PORT,(CURRENT AND &HDF) ' TURN OFF BLI
       NK, BIT 5
EP 200 GOSUB 300
MN 210 OUT PORT,(CURRENT AND &HD7) 'TURN OFF DISP
       LAY, BIT 3
ID 220 FOR X = 1 TO 2000: NEXT ' WAIT ABOUT 2 SEC
       ONDS
DN 230 OUT PORT,(CURRENT OR &H8) 'TURN ON DISPLAY
       , BIT 3
KN 240 OUT PORT,(CURRENT AND &HDF) 'TURN OFF BLIN
       K, BIT 5
FF 250 GOSUB 310
MC 260 OUT PORT,(CURRENT OR &H20)   'TURN ON BLINK
       , BIT 5
MJ 270 END
HF 280 '
OD 290 PRINT"About to turn off blink, ";: GOTO 32
       0
CJ 300 PRINT"About to turn off display for 2 seco
       nds, ";: GOTO 320
MB 310 PRINT"About to turn on blink, ";: GOTO 320
```

177

```
DE 320 :: PRINT"Press enter to continue": INPUT K
       $: RETURN
HM 330 '
ID 340 ' PCjr uses VGA registers rather than adap
       ter ports
LL 350 GOSUB 290
DC 360 X=INP(PORT)   ' SET VGA TO REG/DATA SEQUENC
       E
IP 370 OUT PORT,3: OUT PORT,0   ' TURN OFF BLINK,
       BIT 1
FA 380 GOSUB 300
CB 390 OUT PORT,0: OUT PORT,0   ' TURN OFF DISPLAY
       , BIT 3
IB 400 FOR X = 1 TO 2000: NEXT ' WAIT ABOUT 2 SEC
       ONDS
BM 410 OUT PORT,0: OUT PORT,9   ' TURN ON DISPLAY,
       BIT 3
FB 420 GOSUB 310
GE 430 OUT PORT,3: OUT PORT,2   ' TURN ON BLINK, B
       IT 1
LF 440 END
```

Program 4-17. Color Swatches and PCjr Palette Registers

For error-free program entry, be sure to use "The Automatic Proofreader," Appendix H.

```
ED 100 'VIDEOCO; demonstrate color swatches and j
       r palette capabilities
GG 110 '
EC 120 DEFINTG=A-Z: SCREEN 0,1,0: WIDTH 80: COLOR
       15,0: CLS
HK 130 '
HM 140 LOCATE 13,2: PRINT "bkgd";: LOCATE 14,2: P
       RINT "colors"
DJ 150 LOCATE 2,9: PRINT "foreground colors"
HA 160 '
NL 170 FOR FRGD.SECT=0 TO 7
PO 180 FOR FRGD=FRGD.SECT TO FRGD.SECT+24 STEP 8
KE 190 COLOR FRGD,0: LOCATE 4,8+(2*FRGD): PRINT M
       ID$(STR$(FRGD),2,2);
AC 200 FOR BKGD=0 TO 7
NB 210 IF FRGD=0 THEN COLOR BKGD,0: LOCATE BKGD+5
       ,1: PRINT "  ";BKGD;
DO 220 COLOR FRGD,BKGD: LOCATE BKGD+5,8+(2*FRGD):
       PRINT CHR$(177);CHR$(177)
FK 230 NEXT: NEXT: NEXT
HN 240 '
OE 250 DEF SEG=&HFFFF: IF PEEK(&HE)=&HFD THEN CTR
       L.6845=0: BLINK.OFF=&H0: BLINK.ON=&H2: GOT
       O 440 'PCjr
```

178

```
MC 260 DEF SEG=0: CTRL.6845=&H3D8:BLINK.OFF=&H9:B
       LINK.ON=&H29
QL 270 IF PEEK(&H449)=7 THEN CTRL.6845=&H3B8:BLIN
       K.OFF=&HF:BLINK.ON=&HFF
FH 280 GOTO 440
HH 290 '
CB 300 IF CTRL.6845=0 GOTO 350 'jr
AE 310 OUT CTRL.6845,BLINK.OFF :GOTO 520 ' turn o
       ff bit 5
JN 320 IF CTRL.6845=0 GOTO 390 'jr
HJ 330 OUT CTRL.6845,BLINK.ON :GOTO 520 '   turn o
       n bit 5
HO 340 '
AG 350 X=INP(&H3DA) 'set vga to reg/data sequence
KH 360 OUT &H3DA,3 'select vga reg three
KH 370 OUT &H3DA,BLINK.OFF
FM 380 GOTO 520
BO 390 X=INP(&H3DA) 'set vga to reg/data sequence
KM 400 OUT &H3DA,3 'select vga reg three
AC 410 OUT &H3DA,BLINK.ON
EB 420 GOTO 520
HN 430 '
DG 440 COLOR 7,0:LOCATE 14,18: PRINT"-------------
       ------- MENU --------------------"
QI 450 COLOR 15,0
NA 460 LOCATE ,22:PRINT"1 = ENABLE BLINK"
CB 470 LOCATE ,22:PRINT"2 = DISABLE BLINK"
IC 480 LOCATE ,22:PRINT"3 = JR, CHANGE PALETTE CO
       LORS"
MI 490 LOCATE ,22:PRINT"4 = JR, CHANGE PALETTE CO
       LOR MASK"
NN 500 LOCATE ,22:PRINT"5 = JR, RESET PALETTES &
       MASK"
BO 510 LOCATE ,22:PRINT"6 = EXIT program"
CA 520 K$=INPUT$(1):K=VAL(K$):IF K<1 OR K>6 THEN
       BEEP: GOTO 520
FL 530 ON K GOTO 320,300,550,620,670: END
HA 540 '
OO 550 LOCATE 22,5: INPUT "Enter FROM color numbe
       r (0-15) ... ",FC$
FK 560 FC=VAL(FC$): IF FC>15 GOTO 550
PC 570 LOCATE 22,5: INPUT "Enter  TO  color numbe
       r (0-15) ... ",TC$
KE 580 TC=VAL(TC$): IF TC>15 GOTO 570
OP 590 X=INP(&H3DA):OUT &H3DA,FC+&H10: OUT &H3DA,
       TC: OUT &H3DA,0
DC 600 LOCATE 22,1: PRINT SPACE$(79);: GOTO 520
HL 610 '
JA 620 LOCATE 22,5: INPUT "Enter IRGB hex value (
       0-F) see TRM 2-53 ... ",TC$
```

179

```
OF 630 TC=VAL("&h"+TC$): IF TC>15 OR TC<0 GOTO 62
       0
JF 640 X=INP(&H3DA):OUT &H3DA,1: OUT &H3DA,TC
EM 650 LOCATE 22,1: PRINT SPACE$(79);: GOTO 520
HF 660 '
HD 670 X=INP(&H3DA): FOR X=0 TO 15: OUT &H3DA,X+&
       H10: OUT &H3DA,X: NEXT
GN 680 OUT &H3DA,1: OUT &H3DA,&HF
FB 690 GOTO 520
```

Screen Paging

When using the color adapter in text mode, several screen
pages of information can be prepared ahead and stored in the
display buffer in anticipation of display. Recall the possible
text modes for the color adapter as shown in Table 4-5.

These modes use either 2K or 4K of the video memory,
depending on the number of columns displayed, leaving room
(on the PC) for three or seven more screen pages waiting to be
instantaneously displayed. BIOS INT 10, service 5 is provided
to allow the selection of one of these pages for display. The
cursor location can be tracked and set in all the pages for fast
switching between the pages without any confusion regarding
the cursor location. Services 2 and 3 of INT 10 are available
for cursor functions.

Although the PCjr can hold many more pages of screen
information than the PC, only eight cursors can be tracked at
any time. And these cursor locations all refer to the current 16K
display buffer. The eight cursor locations are stored in locations 450h through 45Fh, as in the PC. The cursor-tracking
locations in the PCjr correspond to the pages within an individual 16K display buffer.

Table 4-5. Summary of Available Color Text Modes

449h ROM BIOS CRT Mode	Display Screen Characteristics	BASIC Screen/ Width/Burst	465h 6845 Mode PC	PCjr	44Ch Page Length	462h Buffer Pages
00h	40×25 b/w text	0/40/off	2Ch	Ch	800h*	8
01h	40×25 16-color text	0/40/on	28h	8h	800h*	8
02h	80×25 b/w text	0/80/off	2Dh	Dh	1000h*	4
03h	80×25 16-color text	0/80/on	29h	9h	1000h*	4

*The PCjr may have up to eight display buffers of 16K, each segmented into screen
pages of the appropriate length.

180

For both the PC and PCjr, BIOS supplies INT 10 services to allow characters to be written into or obtained from any screen page. Other services, such as scrolling up or down, are performed only on the page currently being displayed. INT 10, service Fh returns the active page number if your program needs to know. The BASIC SCREEN statement allows the programmer to specify which page is being displayed and which page in the current display buffer that output is to be directed to.

The number of the active page of the display buffer is kept in location 462h by ROM BIOS; the length of the page is maintained in location 44Ch (with an incorrect length of 4000h for monochrome—it should be 1000h). The offset of the page is saved in location 44E–44Fh and in the 6845 registers 12–13h. The location of the cursor for each page is stored in the series of bytes between 450–45Fh. Each page has a two-byte area in this range where the column and row of the cursor are saved. Registers 14–15h of the 6845 track the location of the cursor for the active page.

Program 4-18 displays the page-related information from the BIOS CRT information block in memory.

Program 4-19 shows how to use the capabilities of the multipage display buffer on both the PC and the PCjr. First, all four 80 × 25 pages within the 16K display buffer are filled with a character (two 16K buffers on the PCjr). Then the program allows the user to select the page to be displayed. The PCjr user can also select which buffer the page to be displayed is located in, and the program adjusts the CRT/processor page register to the correct buffer. You can see how quickly the 6845 registers that control the starting position in the display buffer can cause the new information to be displayed on the screen. Since Program 4-19 doesn't set the attribute byte associated with each text byte, you may see some rather strange colors on the screen when switching to some pages. This will not hurt and as a side benefit will help identify the page being viewed.

When the PCjr version of the program ends, the default display buffer at the high end of memory (called "buffer1" in the program) will be automatically switched to by BASIC, causing the screen to display the "e" screen rather than the "a" screen. This is consistent with the rules stated for the SCREEN statement in the BASIC manual.

You'll see the PCjr switch to the "e" screen as it begins to fill the pages in the second buffer. This need not happen if the CRT/processor register is changed so that only the processor portion of the register is affected. Currently, the program changes both the CRT and processor portions of the register.

When the program ends and you are left with a screen with lots of letters on it, use Ctrl-End to clear the line the cursor is on or Ctrl-Home to clear the whole screen. (On the PCjr, while holding down Ctrl, press Fn followed by either End or Home.) Incidentally, you'll notice that the KEY line becomes filled with the fill character. That tells you that the only thing preventing the use of the twenty-fifth line is BASIC's screen management and not any special restrictions in BIOS or the display circuitry. But we already have seen this to be true from other demonstration programs.

PRINT statements could be used instead of POKE to fill the pages, but then SCREEN statements would be needed to switch the current APAGE to correspond to the desired display page. This would seem only to slow us down more. The speed of either POKE or PRINT is probably not satisfactory for real applications. Machine language routines can build display pages at sufficient speed to be effective.

Program 4-18. Program to Display Page Information

For error-free program entry, be sure to use "The Automatic Proofreader," Appendix H.

```
EI 100 'Videost; Display Video status data
GG 110 '
QO 120 DEF SEG=0:CLS:PRINT " --- Current Video St
       atus ---":LOCATE 3,1
AF 130 PRINT "MODE            449h =" PEEK(&H449)
GB 140 PRINT "COLUMNS      44A-44Bh =" PEEK(&H44A)+
       256*PEEK(&H44B)
FJ 150 PRINT "PAGE SIZE    44C-44Dh =" PEEK(&H44C)+
       256*PEEK(&H44D) 'MONOCHROME wrong !!
MD 160 PRINT "PAGE START   44E-44Fh =" PEEK(&H44E)+
       256*PEEK(&H44F)
FA 170 PRINT "PAGE NUMBER      462h =" PEEK(&H462)
CJ 180 PRINT "CRSR LOC     450-45Fh = PAGE, ROW, CO
       L"
AA 190 FOR X=&H450 TO &H45F STEP 2
JJ 200 PRINT TAB(23);(X-&H450)/2;TAB(29);PEEK(X+1
       );TAB(34);PEEK(X):NEXT
JA 205 PRINT
LB 210 PRINT "PCjr CRT/PROCESSOR PAGE REGISTER:"
EI 220 PRINT "CONTENTS of    48Ah =" HEX$(PEEK(&H
       48A));"h"
```

HI 230 PRINT "   CRT 16K page =" PEEK(&H48A)
         AND &H7
DB 240 PRINT "   PROC 16K page =" (PEEK(&H48A)
         AND &H38)/8

Program 4-19. Demonstration of Display Buffer/Page Switching

For error-free program entry, be sure to use "The Automatic Proofreader," Appendix H.

```
.L 100 'VIDEOBP; demonstrate video buffer/pages u
       sage
GG 110 '
HG 120 ' After pages filled, 0-3 =page number to
       display, 8=jr buffer0, 9=jr buffer1
KM 130 ' --- Reserve 2 16K buffers if PCjr ---
BP 140 DEF SEG=&HFFFF: IF PEEK(&HE)=&HFD THEN CLE
       AR ,,32768!: PCJR=-1
DF 150 ' --- Initialization ---
GL 160 DEFINTG=A-Z: SCREEN 0: WIDTH 80: CHAR=ASC(
       "a")-1
OI 170 ' --- If PCJR, fill two 16K buffers ---
AC 180 IF NOT PCJR GOTO 210
GH 190 FOR BUFFER=6 TO 7: OUT &H3DF,BUFFER+(BUFFE
       R*8): CLS: DEF SEG=&HB800: GOSUB 230: NEXT
       : GOTO 280
JL 200 ' --- If not PCjr, fill one 16K buffer ---
OI 210 FOR BUFFER=0 TO 0: DEF SEG=&HB800: GOSUB 2
       30: NEXT: GOTO 280
GB 220 ' --- Subroutine to fill four pages with i
       ncrementing characters ---
PM 230 FOR PAGE=0 TO 3: CHAR=CHAR+1: LOCATE 1,1
AE 240   PRINT" Filling buffer"BUFFER"/ page "PA
       GE"with "CHR$(CHAR)" "
IH 250   FOR OFFSET=0 TO 4095 STEP 2
GI 260   POKE PAGE*4096+OFFSET,CHAR: NEXT: NEXT:
       RETURN
KK 270 ' --- Let the user select which page to di
       splay ---
CB 280 LOCATE 1,1
IC 290 IF PCJR THEN PRINT" select page (0-3) to d
       isplay, esc to exit, 8=buffer0, 9=buffer1
       ";
CL 300 IF NOT PCJR THEN PRINT" select page (0-3)
       to display, esc to exit ";
EF 310 K$=INKEY$: IF K$=CHR$(27) GOTO 420 ELSE IF
       K$="" GOTO 310
DI 320 K=VAL(K$)
NE 330 ' --- Set the buffer or page selected ---
PO 340 IF (K=8 OR K=9) AND PCJR GOTO 360
LD 350 IF K>3 THEN BEEP: GOTO 310
```

183

```
BF 360 IF K=8 THEN OUT &H3DF,6+8*6: GOTO 310 '8=j
       r buffer0
MO 370 IF K=9 THEN OUT &H3DF,7+8*7: GOTO 310 '9=j
       r buffer1
IA 380 OUT &H3D4,&HC: OUT &H3D5,((4096*K)/2)/256
       'set 6845 reg to page offset
GG 390 OUT &H3D4,&HD: OUT &H3D5,0
LE 400 DEF SEG=0: POKE &H44E,(4096*K)/256: POKE &
       H44F,0 ' maintain video tracking
CA 410 GOTO 310
HN 420 ' --- Reset 6845 page offset registers ---
FK 430 OUT &H3D4,&HC: OUT &H3D5,0
GN 440 OUT &H3D4,&HD: OUT &H3D5,0
AF 450 DEF SEG=0: POKE &H44E,0: POKE &H44F,0
MJ 460 END
```

Graphics

The graphics screen modes use a different technique from the text screen modes to specify the images that are to appear on the screen and the colors associated with them. Rather than the display buffer being filled with ASCII character codes and attribute bytes (as in text mode), the graphics modes incorporate color information directly in the bit settings that are used to define which PELs are on or off on the display screen.

A graphics screen measures 320 × 200 or 640 × 200 PELs (also 160 × 200 on the PCjr) rather than being measured in character lines and columns. Text characters can be placed on the graphics screen (in 40- or 80-column sizes), but they are actually drawn PEL-by-PEL by the BIOS from BIOS- or RAM-resident PEL maps rather than being constructed by the shift register and character set ROM in the display adapter.

Table 4-6 summarizes the available graphics modes. The 320 × 200 four-color graphics mode assigns two bits to each PEL position on the screen. Since two bits can represent binary digits with four possible values (0–3), any one of four different colors can be selected. A binary value of 00 selects the current background color, causing no PEL to be visible at that position. The meaning of values 1–3 depends on which color palette is being used.

The PCjr allows any 4 of 16 colors to be used by setting the PCjr VGA palette registers. Because of this capability, the number of palettes available in PCjr graphics modes is not relevant.

184

Table 4-6. Summary of Available Graphics Modes Characteristics

449h ROM BIOS CRT Mode	Display Screen Characteristics	BASIC Screen/ Width/Burst	465h 6845 Mode PC	PCjr	44Ch Page Length	462h Buffer Pages
04h	320×200 4-col graphics	1,2,3,4/40/on	2Ah	Ah	4000h*	1
05h	320×200 b/w graphics	1,2,3,4/40/off	2Eh	Eh	4000h*	1
06h	640×200 b/w graphics	1,2,3,4/80/off	1Eh	Eh	4000h*	1
08h	PCjr 160×200 16-col graphics	3/20/on	n/a	1Ah	4000h*	1
09h	PCjr 320×200 16-col graphics	5,6/40/on	n/a	1Bh	8000h*†	
0Ah	PCjr 640×200 4-col graphics Key	5,6/80/on	n/a	Bh	8000h*†	

* The PCjr may have up to eight display buffers of 16K, each segmented into screen pages of the appropriate length.

† Requires PCjr 64K display/memory enhancement.

n/a Not applicable.

Non-PCjr palette 1 (cyan, magenta, white) or palette 0 (green, red, brown) is chosen by using bit 5 of port 3D9h, and it may be examined in bit 5 of memory location 466h. The background/border color is selected by setting bits 0–3 (IRGB) of the same port, and the current setting can be seen in bits 0–3 of location 466h. The 320 × 200 b/w graphics mode presents the four color possibilities for each PEL as shades of gray.

Palette	00	01	10	11
0	Bkgd	Green	Red	Yellow
1	Bkgd	Cyan	Purple	White
2	Bkgd	Cyan	Red	White

In the 320 × 200 four-color mode, you can create a third palette on RGB monitors by turning on bit 2 of port 3D8h. Turning on this bit gives a third palette composed of the colors cyan, red, and white. The current palette selection has no effect on the colors in the palette when this bit is turned on. Turning off the bit returns the original palette selection. While the third palette is not a big change from palette 1, it may be handy to be able to use red with cyan and white. Program 4-20 demonstrates the effect of using this bit to obtain another palette.

Program 4-20. Third Palette, 320 × 200

For error-free program entry, be sure to use "The Automatic Proofreader," Appendix H.

```
JP 100 'VIDEOP3; demonstrate third palette - cyan
       , red, white
GG 110 '
FM 120 SCREEN 1:CLS:DEF SEG=0
JC 130 FOR X=0 TO 1 ' palettes
HA 140 COLOR 8,X
PB 150 LOCATE 1,1:PRINT " palette "X;:Z=0
QI 160 FOR Y=100 TO 300 STEP 100:Z=Z+1 ' z is col
       ors in palette, y is circle location
LJ 170 CIRCLE (Y,50),10,Z:PAINT (Y+5,51),Z:NEXT
FD 180 K$=INKEY$:IF K$="" GOTO 180 'wait for keyp
       ress
KD 190 IF K$=CHR$(27) THEN END
AH 200 OUT &H3D8,(PEEK(&H465) OR 4) 'enable palet
       te 2
JK 210 LOCATE 1,1:PRINT "bit 2 on "
LB 220 K$=INKEY$:IF K$="" GOTO 220 'wait for keyp
       ress
EL 230 OUT &H3D8,(PEEK(&H465) AND (255-4)) ' disa
       ble palette 2
NG 240 NEXT
AH 250 GOTO 130 ' loop
```

Every byte of the color display adapter memory starting at B8000h contains the color information for four PELs: 320 across times 200 down is 64,000 PELs, divided by 4 PELs per byte equals 16,000 bytes needed to define a full screen; this leaves 384 bytes of the display adapter memory unused (6*1024=16384=4000h). But these 384 spare bytes are *not* all at the end of the display adapter's memory as you might assume. We'll see in a moment where these free bytes are actually located.

Since each scan line has 320 PELs on it and each byte can hold PEL information for 4 PELs, we'll need 320 divided by 4, or 80 (50h) bytes for each scan line. Again, 200 scan lines times 80 bytes per line is 16,000 bytes—384 bytes short of the display buffer size.

The layout of memory usage for 640 × 200 b/w mode is the same as for the 320 × 200 mode, but each byte holds the on/off information for eight PELs. Since twice as many PELs can be defined in a byte, we can double the number of PELs described in the same amount of memory as the 320 × 200 mode. But we have room only in the one bit per PEL to choose one of two colors, the background or the foreground color.

The PCjr 160 × 200 graphics mode uses four bits to describe each PEL, allowing the choice of 16 colors per PEL, with half the number of PELs able to be described in the 16K display buffer.

The 320 × 200, 160 × 200, and 640 × 200 graphics modes each use the display adapter memory in halves. The first 8000-byte half (0–1F3Fh) is used for the even-numbered scan lines on the screen, and the second 8000-byte half (2000–3F3Fh) is used for the screen's odd-numbered scan lines. This arrangement complicates the rapid mapping of a picture into the video adapter memory.

Figure 4-12 illustrates the layout of color adapter memory for 320 × 200, 160 × 200, and 640 × 200 graphics modes.

Figure 4-12. Color Adapter Memory Usage

B800:		
	0000–004Fh	Scan line 0
	0050–009Fh	Scan line 2
	00A0–00EFh	Scan line 4
	. .	.
	. .	.
	. .	.
	1EF0–1F3Fh	Scan line 198
	1F40–1FFFh	192 (C0h) unused
	2000–204Fh	Scan line 1
	2050–209Fh	Scan line 3
	20A0–20EFh	Scan line 5
	. .	.
	. .	.
	. .	.
	3EF0–3F3Fh	Scan line 199
	3F40–3FFFh	192 (C0h) unused

The PCjr extended graphics modes of 320 × 200 16-color graphics and 640 × 200 4-color graphics require 128K of RAM and use two contiguous 16K graphics display buffers to map the PELs into. The 320 × 200 16-color mode permits one byte to hold the color information for two PELs, while 640 × 200 4-color mode packs four PELs into each byte. Once again

187

Figure 4-13. PCjr 128K Color/Graphics Memory Usage

B800:

0000–004Fh	Scan line 0
0050–009Fh	Scan line 4
00A0–00EFh	Scan line 8
. .	.
. .	
. .	.
1EF0–1F3Fh	Scan line 196
1F40–1FFFh	192 (C0h) unused
2000–204Fh	Scan line 1
2050–209Fh	Scan line 5
20A0–20EFh	Scan line 9
. .	.
. .	
. .	.
3EF0–3F3Fh	Scan line 197
3F40–3FFFh	192 (C0h) unused
4000–404Fh	Scan line 2
4050–409Fh	Scan line 6
40A0–40EFh	Scan line 10
. .	.
. .	
. .	.
5EF0–5F3Fh	Scan line 198
5F40–5FFFh	192 (C0h) unused
6000–604Fh	Scan line 3
6050–609Fh	Scan line 7
60A0–60EFh	Scan line 11
. .	.
. .	
. .	.
7EF0–7F3Fh	Scan line 199
7F40–7FFFh	192 (C0h) unused

we see that twice the resolution of PELs reduces the number of available colors to 4. Of course, the PCjr, unlike the PC, allows (via the VGA color registers) great latitude in choosing which 4 colors are to be used.

Figure 4-13 illustrates the layout of color memory for PCjr 320 × 200 16-color and 640 × 200 4-color graphics modes.

Program 4-21 demonstrates several aspects of the graphics mode memory that are common between the PC and the PCjr. First, 320 × 200 mode is entered, and all four colors are shown from your choice of the two supported palettes. Each byte in a four-byte segment is filled with the binary code to cause that byte to be displayed in one of the four colors. Notice how every other line is filled in from top to bottom; then the blank lines are filled in the same method because of the separation of the even and odd scan lines in the graphics memory. The background color could also be specified by the user when the palette is chosen; black is used to maintain a constant for contrast purposes.

Removing the STEP 4 from line 160 and replacing line 170 with POKE L,TIMER MOD 256:NEXT produces a pleasing color pattern.

Next, the 640 × 200 mode shows the range of shading that can be obtained by using bytes with various combinations of the bits from 0 to 255. Again, every other line is filled and then the blank lines are filled in.

By making minor changes, you can have hours of fun creating different visual patterns from this program.

Program 4-21. Graphics Memory Filler Program

For error-free program entry, be sure to use "The Automatic Proofreader," Appendix H.

```
PC 100 'Videogm; demonstrate graphics memory arra
       ngement
GG 110 '
PB 120 SCREEN 1:DEF SEG=&HB800:KEY OFF:CLS
HK 130 '
QP 140 INPUT "Palette (0-1)";PAL
FI 150 COLOR 0,PAL:CLS
OD 160 FOR L=0 TO &H3F3F STEP 4
EM 170 POKE L,&H55:POKE L+1,&H0:POKE L+2,&HAA:POK
       E L+3,&HFF:NEXT
JP 180 'above statement fills 4 bytes with 010101
       01,00000000,10101010,11111111
AG 190 LOCATE 25,1:INPUT"Press enter for screen 2
       ",X$
```

```
6F 200 '
HM 210 SCREEN 2
OK 220 FOR L=0 TO &H3F3F
HC 230 POKE L,L MOD 256:NEXT
AB 240 'above statement fills every 256 bytes wit
       h 0-255 bit pattern
KH 250 LOCATE 25,1:INPUT"Press enter to end",X$
HB 260 '
IA 270 SCREEN 0:KEY ON:END
```

There is a set of video service routines in ROM BIOS that make it easy to perform text and graphics functions in the IBM-supported manner. To illustrate their use, let's use a few of the services in a simple program that generates bar charts. Program 4-22 can be entered with DEBUG and saved as VIDEOBIO.COM, using the the N (Name) command provided by DEBUG. Set register BX to 0 and CX to 100h, using the R (Register) command before giving the W (Write) command to insure that the whole program is saved to disk.

This sample program is *not* intended to be a lesson in the finer points of programming, but rather a collection of demonstration routines that can be easily understood. I'm confident that you will write more efficient, generalized, and clever code in your own programs. But this grab bag of routines gives you a quick and easily understood demonstration of some basic BIOS call routines for graphics programming. Included are routines that set the screen mode, palette and background colors; place a graphics dot; position the cursor; write TTY-style text; and wait for keypress to continue.

You may want to experiment with extending the program by adding scaling lines; using color-mixing techniques in the bars to achieve more apparent colors; generalizing the draw routine further to include any rectangular shape anywhere on the screen; and adding keyboard-entered values for the bars, bar labeling, and so forth. The more you try, the more you will learn about the ROM BIOS service routines for video.

The DOS interrupts and function calls do not provide any services that are strictly graphics, but rather make available text character services that may be used in graphics or text modes. Obviously, these eventually reduce to the BIOS service routines. All BIOS and DOS interrupts and functions for video support are listed at the end of this chapter.

Program 4-22. Bar Chart Graphics Program Using BIOS Calls

```
0100  E81500      CALL    0118        ; Set video mode and colors
0103  E82C00      CALL    0132        ; Draw bar 1
0106  E84200      CALL    014B        ; Draw bar 2
0109  E85800      CALL    0164        ; Draw bar 3
010C  E86E00      CALL    017D        ; Draw bar 4
010F  E89E00      CALL    01B0        ; Show caption
0112  E8CB00      CALL    01E0        ; Wait for keypress
0115  E9DE00      JMP     01F6        ; Reset video mode and end
0118  B400        MOV     AH,00       ; Called to set 320 X 200,
011A  B005        MOV     AL,04       ; 4-color mode
011C  CD10        INT     10          ; via BIOS,
011E  90          NOP                 ; then
011F  B40B        MOV     AH,0B       ; Set color palette
0121  B700        MOV     BH,00       ; background
0123  B301        MOV     BL,01       ; to blue,
0125  CD10        INT     10          ; via BIOS,
0127  90          NOP                 ; then
0128  B40B        MOV     AH,0B       ; Set color palette
012A  B701        MOV     BH,01       ; foreground
012C  B301        MOV     BL,01       ; to cyan, magenta, white
012E  CD10        INT     10          ; via BIOS
0130  C3          RET                 ; And return.
0131  90          NOP                 ; Called to draw bar 1,
0132  BA8000      MOV     DX,0080     ; from row 80h
0135  8916F001    MOV     [01F0],DX   ;
0139  BB0100      MOV     BX,0001     ; in color 1 (cyan)
013C  881EF401    MOV     [01F4],BL   ;
0140  B94000      MOV     CX,0040     ; from column 40h
0143  BB2000      MOV     BX,0020     ; 20h PELs wide
0146  E84D00      CALL    0196        ; call drawing routine
0149  C3          RET                 ; And return.
014A  90          NOP                 ; Called to draw bar 2,
014B  BA6000      MOV     DX.0060     ; from row 60h
014E  8916F001    MOV     [01F0],DX   ;
0152  BB0200      MOV     BX,0002     ; in color 2 (magenta)
0155  881EF401    MOV     [01F4],BL   ;
0159  B97000      MOV     CX.0070     ; from column 70h
015C  BB2000      MOV     BX,0020     ; 20h PELs wide
015F  E83400      CALL    0196        ; call drawing routine
0162  C3          RET                 ; And return.
0163  90          NOP                 ; Called to draw bar 3,
0164  BA4000      MOV     DX,0040     ; from row 40h
0167  8916F001    MOV     [01F0],DX   ;
016B  BB0300      MOV     BX,0003     ; in color 3 (white)
016E  881EF401    MOV     [01F4],BL   ;
0172  B9A000      MOV     CX,00A0     ; from column A0h
0175  BB2000      MOV     BX,0020     ; 20h PELs wide
0178  E81B00      CALL    0196        ; call drawing routine
```

```
017B  C3              RET                      ; And return.
017C  90              NOP                      ; Called to draw bar 4,
017D  BA2000          MOV     DX,0020          ; from row 20h
0180  8916F001        MOV     [01F0],DX        ;
0184  BB8100          MOV     BX,0081          ; in color 1 (cyan) XORed
0187  881EF401        MOV     [01F4],BL        ;
018B  B9D000          MOV     CX,00D0          ; from column D0h
018E  BB2000          MOV     BX,0020          ; 20h PELs wide
0191  E80200          CALL    0196             ; call drawing routine
0194  C3              RET                      ; And return.
0195  90              NOP                      ; Called to draw bars on screen
0196  53              PUSH    BX               ; Save width of bar
0197  B40C            MOV     AH,0C            ; Request put-dot service
0199  A0F401          MOV     AL,[01F4]        ; in caller's selected color
019C  CD10            INT     10               ; via BIOS with DX=row,
                                               ; CX=col
019E  42              INC     DX               ; do next row till
019F  81FAC700        CMP     DX,00C7          ; bottom of screen
01A3  75F2            JNZ     0197             ;
01A5  8B16F001        MOV     DX,[01F0]        ; then back to starting row
01A9  41              INC     CX               ; and next column
01AA  5B              POP     BX               ; subtracting 1 from width
01AB  4B              DEC     BX               ; for the column just done
01AC  75E8            JNZ     0196             ; till all columns are done
01AE  C3              RET                      ; then return.
01AF  90              NOP                      ; Called to caption the screen
01B0  B402            MOV     AH,02            ; position the cursor
01B2  BA0804          MOV     DX,0408          ; at row 4, column 8
01B5  CD10            INT     10               ; via BIOS
01B7  BED001          MOV     SI,01D0          ; Point to caption start
01BA  B90E00          MOV     CX,000E          ; load loop counter with length
01BD  8A04            MOV     AL,[SI]          ; load a byte of the caption
01BF  46              INC     SI               ; point to the next caption byte
01C0  B40E            MOV     AH,0E            ; request TTY output
01C2  B303            MOV     BL,03            ; in color white
01C4  CD10            INT     10               ; via BIOS
01C6  E2F5            LOOP    01BD             ; until all of caption done
01C8  C3              RET                      ; then return.
01C9  909090909090    NOPs                     ; Unused filler
01CF  90              NOP                      ; Unused filler
01D0  53616C657320    "Sales "                 ; Caption
01D6  466F72656361    "Foreca"                 ; for
01DC  7374            "st"                     ; screen
01DE  9090            NOPs                     ; Called to wait for keypress
01E0  B401            MOV     AH,01            ; using service 1
01E2  CD16            INT     16               ; of BIOS
01E4  74FA            JZ      01E0             ; spin till key pressed
01E6  C3              RET                      ; then return.
01E7  909090909090    NOPs                     ; Unused filler
01ED  909090          NOPs                     ; Unused filler
```

01F0	0000			; Row save area
01F2	9090	NOPs		; Unused filler
01F4	00			; Color save area
01F5	90	NOP		; Jump here to
01F6	B400	MOV	AH,00	; reset screen mode to
01F8	B003	MOV	AL,03	; 80 X 25 color
01FA	CD10	INT	10	; via BIOS
01FC	CD20	INT	20	; and exit program.
01FE	9090	NOPs		; Unused filler

Writing Glitch-free Screens on Color

When the color/graphics adapter is used in text mode, *glitches* (random small lines of various colors) will appear on the screen when the color/graphics buffer is being written to. These do not occur on the PCjr, thanks to its VGA memory access circuitry.

The PC glitches occur because the character generator's process of building each character on the screen is being disrupted by writing to the color adapter memory. Sometimes these glitches can be annoying and if excessive may cause doubt in the user about the quality level of the software or hardware.

You'll notice that the glitches do not necessarily appear at the position on the screen corresponding to the data being placed in screen memory. Rather, they can appear anywhere, based on the circumstances in which characters were being constructed on the screen by the character generator at the instant of the program's memory write.

The BIOS text character service routines prevent these glitches from appearing when they are placing data in the screen memory, so we can use these service routines to prevent glitches from appearing. BASIC uses the screen services of BIOS since DOS may be absent. You won't have any problems with glitches in BASIC unless you POKE directly to the color adapter memory.

When it isn't possible to use the BIOS routines to place text on the screen (because of performance or special control requirements), we can use the same techniques that the BIOS routines use to eliminate screen glitches.

Program 4-23 experiments with the various methods of suppressing screen glitches. It can be entered with DEBUG, or you can follow the discussion of the methods and then use the appropriate routines in your own machine language programs

193

or call them from your BASIC programs when doing screen memory POKEs.

First, issue a MODE CO80 command from DOS to insure that the color adapter is properly initialized, enter and save the program using DEBUG, and then run the program from within DEBUG. The program pauses after each write to screen memory so that you can see the effect of the process in pulses. The screen does not appear to change, but it is actually being rewritten at every pulse. You'll have no problem seeing the pulses. Press any key to end the program.

You'll notice that the program produces randomly located glitches on the screen since the antiglitch routine called by the instruction at 132h is a dummy routine. Also, the screen-enable call at 13Fh does nothing now since the screen is not being disabled in this version of the program. By altering the number of bytes to be placed in the screen memory (by changing the value loaded into CX by the instruction at location 129h) up to the maximum of 7D0h, the glitches can become quite prevalent. If the screen mode in the instruction at address 102h is changed to any of the graphics or 40-column text modes, the problem disappears. The problem occurs only in screen modes 2 and 3 (b/w or color 80 $\times$ 25 text). This tells us that any of the other modes can be used to escape the glitch problem.

We can use the BIOS method of waiting for a horizontal retrace before putting a byte in screen memory by changing the instruction at 132h to CALL 146 and the LOOP instruction at 13Dh to LOOP 132 with the DEBUG Assemble command.

Now a character is placed on the screen only during the quiet period while the monitor scan line is being repositioned to the left of the screen from the right-hand edge.

This sample program may still show glitches in the left-hand 10 or 12 columns, but these will not be present in normal usage of this technique of waiting for the horizontal retrace before placing characters. Waiting for the retrace period does not slow the display of characters much, since the 12-microsecond retrace occurs 12,000 times per second.

The monitor also has a vertical retrace period 60 times per second. This is the period during which the scan line is repositioned to the top left of the screen from the bottom-right corner. This process takes 1.02 milliseconds, but occurs infrequently enough that waiting for this period can drastically slow down the screen display. You can try waiting for this re-trace period by changing the instruction at 132h to CALL 159.

You may also want to change the instruction at 13Dh to LOOP 135 to see how much glitch prevention is accomplished by trying to write all the characters going to the screen during a single vertical retrace period. Try different character lengths by varying the value placed in the CX register at location 129h.

Replacing the instruction at 132h with CALL 191 and the one at 13Dh with LOOP 135 activates the third antiglitch technique—disabling the screen display while the screen is written to, then reenabling it. This method causes the familiar blinking that many color-text programs are known for, depending on the amount of time that the screen is disabled. The BIOS INT 10 services for scrolling the screen up and down use this technique.

Program 4-23. Glitch Elimination Experiments

```
0100  B400    MOV    AH,00           ; Set mode
0102  B003    MOV    AL,03           ; to screen 3 (80 X 25 color text)
0104  CD10    INT    10              ; via BIOS
0106  90      NOP                    ;
0107  E81600  CALL   0120            ; Write to screen memory
010A  E2FE    LOOP   010A            ; Wait till CX is exhausted
010C  E2FE    LOOP   010C            ; then again, to create pause
010E  90      NOP                    ;
010F  B401    MOV    AH,01           ; Get key status
0111  CD16    INT    16              ; via BIOS
0113  74F2    JZ     0107            ; none yet, so fill memory again
0115  90      NOP                    ;
0116  B400    MOV    AH,00           ; Reset mode
0118  B003    MOV    AL,03           ; to 80 X 25 color
011A  CD10    INT    10              ; via BIOS
011C  90      NOP                    ;
011D  CD20    INT    20              ; and EXIT program
011F  90      NOP                    ;
0120  90      NOP                    ; - FILL SCREEN MEMORY -
0121  B800B8  MOV    AX,B800         ; Location of screen memory
0124  50      PUSH   AX              ; to register
0125  07      POP    ES              ; ES
0126  BF0000  MOV    DI,0000         ; Offset within ES starts at 0
0129  B90002  MOV    CX,0200         ; Number of bytes times 2
012C  B80000  MOV    AX,0000         ; Initialize character number to 0
012F  B401    MOV    AH,01           ; Blue on black attribute for all
0131  FA      CLI                    ; Disable interrupts
0132  E86200  CALL   0197            ; Call antiglitch routine
0135  26      ES:                    ; Target segment is screen memory
0136  8905    MOV    [DI],AX         ; Place the character and attribute
```

195

```
0138  FEC0    INC    AL        ; Next character number
013A  90      NOP              ;
013B  47      INC    DI        ; Next char/attr offset in screen
                               ; memory
013C  47      INC    DI        ;
013D  E2F6    LOOP   0135      ; Keep filling till CX=0
013F  E83D00  CALL   017F      ; Reenable the screen display
0142  FB      STI              ; Reenable interrupts
0143  C3      RET              ; Return to caller
0144  90      NOP              ;
0145  90      NOP              ;
0146  50      PUSH   AX        ; - WAIT FOR HORIZONTAL
                               ; RETRACE -
0147  BADA03  MOV    DX,03DA   ; Color adapter status byte
014A  EC      IN     AL,DX     ; Read into AL
014B  A801    TEST   AL,01     ; bit 0 = horizontal retrace
014D  75FB    JNZ    014A      ; Loop till off to get full cycle
014F  90      NOP              ;
0150  EC      IN     AL,DX     ; Now wait for the retrace bit
0151  A801    TEST   AL,01     ; to be set so that we get
0153  74FB    JZ     0150      ; a full retrace cycle
0155  90      NOP              ;
0156  58      POP    AX        ; In horizontal retrace
0157  C3      RET              ; Return to caller
0158  90      NOP              ; - WAIT FOR VERTICAL RETRACE -
0159  50      PUSH   AX        ;
015A  BADA03  MOV    DX,03DA   ; Color adapter status byte
015D  EC      IN     AL,DX     ; Read into AL
015E  A808    TEST   AL,08     ; bit 3 = vertical retrace
0160  75FB    JNZ    015D      ; Loop till off to get full cycle
0162  90      NOP              ;
0163  EC      IN     AL,DX     ; Now wait for the retrace bit
0164  A808    TEST   AL,08     ; to be set so that we get
0166  74FB    JZ     0163      ; a full retrace cycle
0168  90      NOP              ;
0169  58      POP    AX        ; In vertical retrace
016A  C3      RET              ; Return to caller
016B  90      NOP              ;
016C  90      NOP              ; - DISABLE SCREEN DISPLAY -
016D  50      PUSH   AX        ;
016E  31C0    XOR    AX,AX     ;
0170  50      PUSH   AX        ;
0171  1F      POP    DS        ; Data segment 0
0172  A06504  MOV    AL,[0465] ; Get current adapter mode byte
0175  24F7    AND    AL,F7     ; Turn off bit 3
0177  BAD803  MOV    DX,03D8   ; Send to adapter
017A  EE      OUT    DX,AL     ; mode register
017B  0E      PUSH   CS        ; Restore DS
017C  1F      POP    DS        ;
017D  58      POP    AX        ;
```

196

```
017E  C3       RET                    ; Return to caller
017F  50       PUSH  AX               ; - ENABLE SCREEN DISPLAY -
0180  31C0     XOR   AX,AX            ;
0182  50       PUSH  AX               ;
0183  1F       POP   DS               ; Data segment 0
0184  A06504   MOV   AL,[0465]        ; Get current adapter mode byte
0187  0C08     OR    AL,08            ; Turn on bit 3
0189  BAD803   MOV   DX,03D8          ; Send to adapter
018C  EE       OUT   DX,AL            ; mode register
018D  0E       PUSH  CS               ; Restore DS
018E  1F       POP   DS               ;
018F  58       POP   AX               ;
0190  C3       RET                    ; Return to caller
0191  E8B2FF   CALL  0146             ; Call for horizontal retrace
0194  E8D6FF   CALL  016D             ; Call for disable screen
0197  C3       RET                    ; Return to caller
0198  90       NOP                    ; Unused
0199  00       DB    00               ; filler
```

rcx (Set register CX to the program length)
:99
w (Write the program to disk)

Incidentally, the PCjr vertical retrace can be detected by testing bit 3 after reading port 3DAh, or you may use the vector at 34h INT 0D to drive a vertical retrace routine. See pages 2-72 and 2-73 of the PCjr *Technical Reference* manual. Horizontal retrace is not signaled in the PCjr.

There's still one more method for the elimination of glitches and it's extremely powerful. Glitch suppression is only a side benefit from a much more versatile capability. Remember that in 80 × 25 text mode there is room in the color adapter memory for four screen images?

By writing to a screen image currently not being displayed, the character generator is never bothered by the program's screen memory accesses. Also, you can build screens before needing them and then instantly (without blinking or glitches) switch to the one that you want displayed. The BASIC SCREEN statement supports this function with the APAGE (active page being written to) and VPAGE (page currently being viewed) parameters. Many of the BIOS character services also allow a screen page number to be specified, including the routine for positioning the cursor.

Since we've previously explored the use of display buffer pages, we won't reexamine the whole subject here, but we will demonstrate its use in glitch elimination.

Program 4-24 is much like the preceding program, but it uses no antiglitch routines. It switches between screen page 0 and page 1 to demonstrate that smooth and instantaneous switching between screens can be done. Press any key to end the demonstration. The length of characters loaded into the CX register by the instruction at location 121h is set so that page 0 is filled and page 1 is only partially filled—this let's you distinguish between them.

Program 4-24. Screen Paging in Text Modes

DEBUG VIDEOSP.COM a (Enter the assembler language operation code and parameters)

```
                                    - MAINLINE -
0100  B400    MOV    AH,00    ;Set mode
0102  B003    MOV    AL,03    ;to screen 3 (80 × 25 color text)
0104  CD10    INT    10       ; via BIOS
0106  E80F00  CALL   0118     ; Write to screen pages 0 and 1
0109  90      NOP             ;
010A  E82900  CALL   0136     ; Switch between the two pages
010D  90      NOP             ; till a key is pressed
010E  B400    MOV    AH,00    ; Reset mode
0110  B003    MOV    AL,03    ; to 80 × 25 color
0112  CD10    INT    10       ; via BIOS
0114  90      NOP             ;
0115  CD20    INT    20       ; and EXIT program
0117  90      NOP             ;
0118  90      NOP             ; - WRITE TO SCREEN PAGES -
0119  B800B8  MOV    AX,B800  ; Location of screen memory
011C  50      PUSH   AX       ; to register
011D  07      POP    ES       ; ES
011E  BF0000  MOV    DI,0000  ; Offset within ES starts at 0
0121  B9000C  MOV    CX,0C00  ; Number of bytes times 2
0124  B80000  MOV    AX,0000  ; Initialize character number to 0
0127  B401    MOV    AH,01    ; Blue on black attribute for all
0129  90      NOP             ;
012A  26      ES:             ; Target segment is screen memory
012B  8905    MOV    [DI],AX  ; Place the character and attribute
012D  FEC0    INC    AL       ; Next character number
012F  90      NOP             ;
0130  47      INC    DI       ; Next char/attr offset in screen
                              ; memory
0131  47      INC    DI       ;
0132  E2F6    LOOP   012A     ; Keep filling till CX=0
0134  C3      RET             ; Return to caller
0135  90      NOP             ;
0136  B80000  MOV    AX,0000  ;
0139  31C9    XOR    CX,CX    ; Pause while a screen page
013B  E2FE    LOOP   013B     ; is being displayed
```

```
013D  E2FE   LOOP  013D    ;
013F  3401   XOR   AL,01   ; Select the other page
0141  50     PUSH  AX      ;
0142  B405   MOV   AH,05   ; with active page service
0144  CD10   INT   10      ; via BIOS
0146  B401   MOV   AH,01   ; Test for a keypress
0148  CD16   INT   16      ; via BIOS
014A  7403   JZ    014F    ; If not, repeat the loop
014C  58     POP   AX      ; Else
014D  C3     RET           ; return to caller
014E  90     NOP           ;
014F  58     POP   AX      ;
0150  EBE7   JMP   0139    ;
0152  00     DB    00      ;
0155  90     NOP           ;
```

rcx (Set the length of the program in the cx register)
:55
w (Save the program on disk)

You can use the multiple screen capabilities of the color adapter and PCjr while doing BASIC programming by simply listing a reference section of code in one or more screens and using the SCREEN statement to switch to an unused screen to enter additional statements. Switch to the other screens whenever you need to reference the listed information.

The BIOS routine to select the active page for display simply adjusts some of the display adapter 6845 registers and records the current screen status information in the video-related memory locations from 449h through 466h. Changing these 6845 registers will cause the information on the display screen to scroll instantly, not only to a different screen page, but also to any position you desire within the active or inactive pages. The video display page starting address is stored in 44Eh, and the active page number in 462h. Be sure to keep these accurate.

Program 4-24 can be modified to demonstrate the results of using the 6845 scrolling registers (C–Dh) to reposition the active page at any character position desired. Program 4-25 contains the replacement routine to do this. The routine does not update locations 44Eh and 462h since it is experimental only, but in your programs be sure to keep these locations updated with the current video environment. You can change the number of bytes to scroll by using different values in the instruction at 13Fh. Be sure that the instruction at 121h causes enough bytes to be written to the display buffer for your scrolling trial. The samples, as written, provide enough characters to demonstrate the scrolling effect.

If the end of the display buffer is encountered during screen character generation (because of scrolling within the last video page), the adapter wraps around to the beginning of the adapter memory to obtain the remainder of the information needed to fill a screen. Thus, you can use scrolling as a window into a much larger stream of text located in the display adapter's memory. The scrolling techniques work in either text or graphics modes. Try changing the mode selected by the instruction at 102H to 5 to see the effect in 320 × 200 color/graphics. The monochrome display adapter can also be programmed to perform scrolling, but since there is only one video page, it's hard to imagine a reason for doing this. You can try this by setting video mode 7, changing B800h to B000h, and 3D4h to 3B4h in the example routine.

Program 4-25. Text Scrolling

DEBUG VIDEOSP.COM
-n VIDEOSS.COM (Assign a new name to the program)
-a (Enter the assembler language operation code and parameters)

```
0136 B80000   MOV    AX,0000  ;
0139 31C9     XOR    CX,CX    ; Pause while a screen page
013B E2FE     LOOP   013B     ; is being displayed
013D E2FE     LOOP   013D     ;
013F B92000   MOV    CX,0020  ; Scroll 32 characters into page 0
0142 BAD403   MOV    DX,03D4  ; 6845 register port
0145 B00C     MOV    AL,0C    ; Select register 12
0147 EE       OUT    DX,AL    ; Tell 6845 to address reg Ch
0148 42       INC    DX       ; Register contents to port 3D5h
0149 88E8     MOV    AL,CH    ; MSB of scroll amount
014B EE       OUT    DX,AL    ; to register 12
014C 4A       DEC    DX       ; Back to 6845 register port
014D B00D     MOV    AL,0D    ; Select register 13
014F EE       OUT    DX,AL    ; Tell 6845 to address reg Dh
0150 42       INC    DX       ; Register contents to port 3D5h
0151 88C8     MOV    AL,CL    ; LSB of scroll amount
0153 EE       OUT    DX,AL    ; to register 13
0154 B401     MOV    AH,01    ; Spin here till key is pressed
0156 CD16     INT    16       ; Via BIOS
0158 74FA     JZ     0154     ;
015A C3       RET             ; Return to caller
```

rcx (Set the length of the program in the cx register)
:5A
w (Save the program on disk)

Ports and Registers

The display adapter ports and 6845 registers are fairly well described in the *Technical Reference* manual, and the Port Map Appendix in this book restates and expands on the manual information. *Be extremely careful when experimenting with the first ten 6845 registers; incorrect values in these registers can damage the display adapter or monitor.* You may want to wait for others to play with these registers and report their findings. Some fairly innocuous registers are those for the cursor start/end, the scrolling registers we've explored, and the cursor address registers. Look at the BIOS video routines for examples of how these registers are used.

Some clarification of the information in the *Technical Reference* manual about the ports and registers is necessary. Ports 3B4/3D4h can actually be accessed through ports 3X0, 3X2, 3X4, and 3X6h (replace X with B for monochrome or D for color). Likewise, port 3X5h may be reached via port 3X1, 3X3, 3X5, or 3X7h. This is why you'll see these other ports not used. Of all the video ports in the adapter, only 3X5h and 3XAh can be read; all others are write-only.

Of the 6845 registers, only C–11h may be read (through 3X5h). Registers C–Fh should contain half the offset from the beginning of the display buffer rather than the full amount. The cursor location registers (E–Fh) should be the same as the page start registers (C–Dh) plus the number of positions into the page.

For the PCjr, the 6845 registers and their contents are described starting on page 2-75 of the *Technical Reference* manual. The ports are mentioned briefly on page 2-80. The VGA registers are described starting on page 2-63, and the contents of the VGA registers for various modes are listed in a table on page 2-81. The ROM BIOS video routines (INT 10) are listed starting on page A-29, with page A-31 containing the addresses of all the service routines.

The *Technical Reference* manual for the PC describes the monochrome 6845 registers on page 1-115, the monochrome port addresses on page 1-117, the color 6845 registers on page 1-138, and the color ports starting on page 1-139. The ROM

BIOS video service (INT 10) routines are listed starting on page A-46, with A-48 containing a list of the addresses for all the subordinate services.

The video-tracking information maintained by BIOS in locations 449–466h is at least as important as the display adapter ports, VGA registers, and 6845 registers, but these locations are largely undocumented. Since most of the display adapter ports, VGA registers, and 6845 registers are write-only (you can't read their contents), the video-tracking locations provide the only means of determining the current settings of ports and registers. Also, this section of memory is independent of the display adapter in that the information stored there reflects the state of the current video adapter, whichever type is currently in use.

We've been using many of these locations in the sample programs and diagrams in this chapter, and they are mapped in detail in the Memory Map Appendix of this book. A summary of the information contained in them will clarify their relationship to the display adapter ports and registers. Table 4-7 summarizes these video-tracking locations and the more usable video ports, 6845 registers, and VGA registers.

Table 4-7. Summary of Video Tracking, Ports, 6845 Registers, VGA Registers

Purpose	Tracking	PC	PCjr
BIOS video mode	449h		
Mode selection	465h	*Port: 3X8h	*VGA: 0, 4
PCjr CRT/processor page	48Ah		*Port: 3DFh
Columns	44A–44Bh		
Page length	44C–44Dh		
Page beginning	44E–44Fh	6845: C–Dh	6845: C–Dh
Page number	462h		
Current adapter port base	463–464h		
Status		Port: 3XAh	Port: 3DAh
Palette	466h	*Port: 3X9h	*VGA: 1, 2, 10–1Fh
Cursor start/end	460–461h	*6845: A–Bh	*6845: A–Bh
Cursor position	450–45Fh	*6845: E–Fh	6845: E–Fh
Other pages' cursor position	450–45Fh		
Light pen position		6845: 10–11h	6845: 10–11h
Light pen latches		*Port: 3DB–3DCh	*Port: 3DB–3DCh
PCjr horizontal adjust	489h		6845: C–Dh

* = Not readable
X = B (monochrome) or D (color)

As you can see, about the only unique display adapter port and register information not reflected in the video-tracking locations is the status register at port 3BAh or 3DAh (apart

from the esoteric vertical/horizontal–synch/adjust and light
pen location values).

PCjr Cartridge BASIC Video Enhancements

The PCjr BASIC cartridge includes video support that is not
available from ROM BASIC, Disk BASIC, or BASICA. Because
of this, the BASIC cartridge is needed to exploit the full
capabilities of the PCjr graphics enhancements. Here are some
of the major areas of added video support in the PCjr
cartridge.

> SCREEN modes include 3, 4, 5, and 6
> SCREEN parameter ERASE is added
> SCREEN parameters VPAGE and APAGE are valid for
> graphics modes
> SCREEN parameter BURST is always set on for modes 2,
> 3, 5, and 6
> CLEAR parameter V allocates video memory space
> PALETTE and PALETTE USING for adjusting the VGA
> color registers
> COLOR parameter FOREGROUND available for modes 3,
> 4, 5, and 6
> Colors 0–15 supported in CIRCLE, DRAW, LINE, PAINT
> PCOPY may be used to copy screens in all modes, not
> just graphics

Video-Related Locations and References

Locations show PC values, then PCjr if they differ. The TRM
page indicated is the beginning or most significant page as
found in the XT *Technical Reference* manual (see the Introduction concerning the edition of manuals referenced in this
book). You should also examine the context of the surrounding pages.

Memory Video Support References

Location: **14h**
Label   : (INT 5)
Usage   : Vector to PRINT_SCREEN if GRAPHICS not loaded
           FFF54h; PCjr: FFF54h
TRM pg : A-81; PCjr: A-108

Location: PCjr: **34h**
Label   : (INT D, IRQ-5)
Usage   : Vector to PCjr vertical retrace dummy routine; PCjr:
           FF815h
TRM pg : PCjr: A-96

Location: **40h**
Label   : (INT 10) VIDEO_INT
Usage   : Vector to VIDEO-IO video service routines FF0A4H; PCjr:
           FF0A4h
TRM pg : A-46; PCjr: A-29

Location: **74h**
Label   : (INT 1D) PARM_PTR
Usage   : Vector to VIDEO-PARMS 6845 register tables FF0A4H;
           PCjr: FF0A4h
           Parms may be changed by copying tables to RAM, then
           changing this vector
TRM pg : 2-5, A-48; PCjr: 5-9, A-8

Location: **7Ch**
Label   : (INT 1F) EXT_PTR
Usage   : Vector to CRT_CHARH, graphics characters 128–255 PEL
           maps
           PC: 00000 (user sets); PCjr: FE05Eh
           PCjr: vector to first set 0–127 (0–7Fh) at 110h INT 44
TRM pg : 2-6; PCjr: 5-9, A-54

Location: PCjr: **110h**
Label   : (INT 44) CSET_PTR
Usage   : Vector to CRT_CHAR_GEN, graphics characters 0–127
           PEL maps
           PCjr: FFA6Eh
           Vector to second set 128–255 (80–FFh) at 7Ch INT 1F
TRM pg : PCjr: 5-9, A-103

Location: **410h**
Label   : EQUIP-FLAG
Usage   : Installed hardware found or switches set at boot
           bits 4–5; initial video mode
           00=unused, 01=40×25 color, 10=80×25 color,
           11=80×25 mono
           PCjr default is 40×25, bits changed with video mode
TRM pg : 1-10, A-71; PCjr: A-97

Location: **449h**
Label   : CRT_MODE
Usage   : Current BIOS video mode number
TRM pg : A-4; PCjr: A-5

Location: **44A–44Bh**
Label   : CRT_COLS
Usage   : Current number of columns on screen
TRM pg : A-4; PCjr: A-5

Location: **44C–44Dh**
Label   : CRT_LEN
Usage   : Current length of page
TRM pg : A-4; PCjr: A-5

Location: **44E–44Fh**
Label   : CRT_START
Usage   : Current offset of page in display buffer
              See 6845, reg C–Dh
TRM pg : A-4; PCjr: A-5

Location: **450–45Fh**
Label   : CURSOR_POSN
Usage   : Cursor location for each of up to eight pages
              See 6845, reg E-Fh
TRM pg : A-4; PCjr: A-5

Location: **460–461h**
Label   : CURSOR_MODE
Usage   : Cursor start and end lines
              See 6845, reg A–Bh
TRM pg : A-4; PCjr: A-5

Location: **462h**
Label   : ACTIVE_PAGE
Usage   : Current page number being displayed
TRM pg : A-4; PCjr: A-5

Location: **463–464h**
Label   : ADDR_6845
Usage   : Current base vector for the active display card
              3B4 mono, 3D4 color
TRM pg : A-4; PCjr: A-5

Location: **465h**
Label   : CRT_MODE_SET
Usage   : Current video mode 6845 mode register setting
              See port 3B8/3D8h, VGA reg 0,4
TRM pg : 1-118, 1-141, A-4; PCjr: 2-64, 2-66, 2-81, A-5

Location: **466h**
Label   : CRT_PALETTE
Usage   : Current color register setting
              See port 3B9/3D9h, VGA reg 1, 2, 10–1fh
TRM pg : 1-140, A-4; PCjr: 2-66, 2-81, A-5

Location: PCjr: **489h**
Label   : HORZ-POS
Usage   : Current PCjr screen horizontal adjustment
TRM pg : PCjr: A-5

Location: PCjr: **48Ah**
Label   : PAGDAT
Usage   : Current CRT/processor page register contents
          See port 3DFh
TRM pg : PCjr: 2-47, 2-79

Location: **B0000h–B0FFFh**
Label   : VIDEO_MONO
Usage   : 4K monochrome display buffer
TRM pg : 1-117

Location: **B8000h–BBFFFh**
Label   : VIDEO_COLOR
Usage   : 16K color display buffer
TRM pg : 1-133, 1-136, 1-145; PCjr: 2-61

Port Video Support References

Location: PCjr: **Port 21h**
Label   : INT A01
Usage   : IRQ5 bit 5 on if vertical retrace in progress
TRM pg : PCjr: 2-82

Location: PCjr: **Port 61h**
Label   : PORT_B
Usage   : bit 2 alpha/graphics steerer
TRM pg : PCjr: 2-31

Location: **Port 62h**
Label   : PORT_C
Usage   : Configuration switch 5–6 input, default monitor type
          PCjr: 64K display expansion installed
TRM pg : 1-10; PCjr: 2-30

Location: **Port 3B4h**
Usage   : Monochrome 6845 index register
TRM pg : 1-115

Location: **Port 3B5h**
Usage   : Monochrome 6845 data register
TRM pg : 1-115

Location: **Port 3B8h**
Usage   : Monochrome mode register
          See memory 465h
TRM pg : 1-118

Location: **Port 3BAh**
Usage   : Monochrome status
TRM pg : 1-118

Location: **Port 3D4h**
Usage   : Color 6845 index register
TRM pg : 1-138; PCjr: 2-76, 2-80

Location: **Port 3D5h**
Usage   : Color 6845 data register
TRM pg : 1-138; PCjr: 2-76, 2-80

Location: **Port 3D8h**
Usage   : Color mode register
         See memory 465h; PCjr: VGA 0,4
TRM pg : 1-141

Location: **Port 3D9h**
Usage   : Color-select register
         See memory 466h; PCjr: VGA 1, 2, 10–1Fh
TRM pg : 1-140

Location: **Port 3DAh**
Usage   : Color status register
TRM pg : 1-143; PCjr: 2-73, 2-80

Location: PCjr: **Port 3DAh**
Usage   : Video gate array access port
TRM pg : PCjr: 2-63, 2-80, 2-81

Location: **Port 3DBh**
Usage   : Clear light pen latch
TRM pg : 1-139; PCjr: 2-74, 2-80

Location: **Port 3DCh**
Usage   : Preset light pen latch
TRM pg : 1-139; PCjr: 2-74, 2-80

Location: PCjr: **Port 3DFh**
Usage   : CRT/processor page register
         See memory 48Ah
TRM pg : PCjr: 2-47, 2-79, 2-80

ROM BIOS Video Support References

PC2 ROM BIOS

INT	Serv	Address	PC2 ROM BIOS
		FE1EFh	fill INT 10–1F vectors from FFF03h
		FE202h	save configuration switches in equipment flag
		FE3DEh	set up INT 0–15 vectors
10		FF045h	INT 10, video I/O
1D		FF0A4h	mode parameter tables
10	00	FF0FCh	set mode
10	01	FF1CDh	set cursor type
10	02	FF1EEh	set cursor position
10	05	FF217h	set video page
10	03	FF239h	read cursor position
10	0B	FF24Eh	set colors
10	0F	FF274h	read video state
		FF285h	calculate display buffer address of character
10	06	FF296h	scroll up
10	07	FF338h	scroll down
10	08	FF374h	read attribute and character at cursor
10	09	FF3B9h	write attribute and character at cursor
10	0A	FF3ECh	write character at cursor
10	0D	FF41Eh	read dot
10	0C	FF42Fh	write dot
		FF452h	calculate buffer location for dot
10	06	FF495h	graphics scroll up
10	07	FF4EEh	graphics scroll down
		FF578h	graphics write character
		FF629h	graphics read character
		FF6AEh	expand medium color
		FF6C3h	expand byte
		FF6E5h	read medium byte
		FF702h	calculate medium cursor position in display buffer
10	0E	FF718h	write TTY
10	04	FF794h	read light pen
		FFA6Eh	PEL maps for graphics characters 0–127
05		FFF54h	INT 5 screen print

PCjr ROM BIOS

INT	Serv	Address	PCjr ROM BIOS
		F0103h	VGA and 6845 set up
		F0C21h	put logo on screen
10		F0CE9h	INT 10, video I/O
10	00	F0DA5h	set mode
10	0E	F1992h	write TTY
1F		FE05Eh	PEL maps for graphics characters 128–255
10	01	FE45Eh	set cursor type
10	02	FE488h	set cursor position
10	05	FE4B3h	set video page
10	05	FE4DBh	read/set CRT/CPU registers
10	03	FE52Dh	read cursor position
10	0B	FE543h	set colors
10	0F	FE5B1h	read video status
		FE5C2h	calculate display buffer address of character
10	06	FE5D3h	scroll up
10	07	FE63Fh	scroll down
		FE675h	read 256 bytes in 512 bytes
10	10	FE685h	set VGA palette registers
1D		FF0A4h	mode parameter tables
10	08	FF0E4h	read attribute and character at cursor
10	09	FF113h	write attribute and character at cursor
10	0A	FF12Ch	write character at cursor
10	0D	FF146h	read dot at cursor
10	0C	FF1D9h	write dot at cursor
10	06	FF259h	graphics scroll up
10	07	FF305h	graphics scroll down
		FF3F1h	write graphics character
		FF531h	read graphics character
		FF659h	expand medium color
		FF67Eh	expand byte
		FF6A0h	expand nybble
		FF6C3h	read medium byte
		FF6FCh	read medium byte
		FF729h	calculate medium cursor position in display buffer
10	04	FF746h	read light pen
44		FFA6Eh	PEL maps for graphics characters 0–127
05		FFF54h	INT 5 screen print

Additional Video Information

Subject	TRM
Attribute meaning for 0–255 ASCII codes	C-1; PCjr: C-1
Color display description	1-149, E-2; PCjr: 3-81, D-5
Monochrome display description	1-121
Monitor type switch settings	G-4
Video parameters table	2-5; PCjr: 5-9
PCjr: Memory interleave and video refresh	PCjr: 2-17
PCjr: 64K memory and display expansion	PCjr: 3-5
PCjr: Adapter cable for color display	PCjr: 3-93
PCjr: Connector for television	PCjr: 3-85
PCjr: Video/display buffer compatibility with PC	PCjr: 4-12
PCjr: Screen horizontal adjustment keys	PCjr: 5-37

BASIC Video Support

BASIC provides many statements that can be used for video functions. Check your BASIC manual for the following statements: CIRCLE, CLEAR, CLS, CSRLINE, COLOR, DRAW, GET, KEY, LINE, LOCATE, ON PEN, PAINT, PALETTE, PCOPY, PEN, PMAP, POINT, POS, PRINT, PRESET, PSET, PUT, SCREEN, SPC, TAB, VIEW, WIDTH, WINDOW, WRITE.

DOS Video Support References

Subject	DOS Page
ANSI.SYS screen device driver	Chapter 13 of DOS 2.0, Chapter 2 of DOS 2.10 TRM
DOS CLS internal command	6-58 of DOS 2.0, 2-42 of DOS 2.1
DOS GRAPHICS external command	6-106 of DOS 2.0, 2-96 of DOS 2.1
DOS display/standard output callable functions	D-18 of DOS 2.0, 5-18 of DOS 2.1 TRM

DOS Video Interrupts and Services

21 DOS Function Request
  02 display character (with break)
  06 direct console I/O (no wait, break, or echo)
  DL<>ff output character
  09 display string till $ (with break)

Appendix A
Memory Map

Appendix A
Memory Map

A number of the memory locations explored in this memory map are shown in the *Technical Reference* manual, but they suffer from little information, cryptic explanations, or none at all. Their interdependences with other locations and usage by the system are left to the programmer to discover by paging through the entire machine language listing. This memory map will give you a more lucid picture of the use of memory locations, as well as point you to *Technical Reference* manual references (XT and PCjr manual), example programs, and detailed explanations in the various chapters in this book. Additionally, a combined index of ROM BIOS routine starting addresses is included so that you can quickly identify and locate the appropriate ROM BIOS routine in any of the PC models.

This Appendix details the contents of the PC memory address space as though it were laid out top to bottom in low-memory to high-memory order, as Figure A-2 shows.

Each byte of memory is composed of eight bits, each containing either a one or a zero. Figure A-1 shows the bit format of a byte, the bit numbering scheme, and the values represented by each bit.

Figure A-1. Bit Contents of a Byte

7	6	5	4	3	2	1	0	Bit number, 2^n = value

| 80 | 40 | 20 | 10 | 8 | 4 | 2 | 1 | Hexadecimal values |
| 128 | 64 | 32 | 16 | 8 | 4 | 2 | 1 | Decimal values |

Example: Bit 5 = 2^5 = 20h = 32
0101 0101 = 55h = 85

Figure A-2. Map of Typical PC Memory Usage

Using DOS 2.10, No CONFIG.SYS or AUTOEXEC.BAT, 384K Memory

0K		8088 Vectors INT 0–7 8259 Vectors INT 8–F BIOS Vectors INT 10–1F DOS Vectors INT 20–2F Assignable INT 40–FF	
1K	400h	ROM BIOS Communications Area	
	500h		
1.5K	700h	DOS Data Areas	
3.5K		IBMBIO 72Fh of 1280h	DEBUG Search Pattern "VER 2.15"
	E30h		DEBUG Search Pattern E9 87 3F 03 44 45 56
19K		IBMDOS 3F89h of 4280h Storage Chain Anchor → 5100h	← INT 20,25,26,27
	4DB9h	Device Drivers User extensions of IBMBIO such as ANSI.SYS CONFIG.SYS: buffers, files	
21K	53F0h	*P Resident COMMAND	← INT 21,22,23,24
24K	5FD0h	* Master ENVIRONMENT for COMMAND A0h bytes, expandable to 32K if no programs have been made resident	
24.1K	6080h	* ENVIRONMENT for Next Program	
	60B0h	*P BASIC Extensions Disk=12K, Advanced=22K	
		Start of BASIC 64K Workspace: (/M or CLEAR may be used to size) DS:0 4K interpreter work area	← Redirected INT 0,4,9,B, 1B,1C, 23,24
		Communications (/C) Buffers 180h Default Size	
		RS-232 Routines 5E0h Default Size	
		File (/F) Control Blocks 234h Default Size	
		File (/S) Random Buffers 80h Default Size	
		DS:30–31h BASIC Program Text	
		DS:358–9h Scalars, toward FFFFh	
		DS:35A–Bh Arrays, toward FFFFh	↓
		DS:35C–Dh Free Space	

```
                      ┌──────────────────────────────────────┐
                      │ DS:32F–0h Strings, toward 0000h     ↑ │
                      │ DS:30A–Bh                             │
                      ├┄┄┄┄┄┄┄┄┄┄┄┄┄┄┄┄┄┄┄┄┄┄┄┄┄┄┄┄┄┄┄┄┄┄┄┄┄┄┄┤
                      │        DS:2C–Dh Stack 200h Bytes      │
                      │     (/M or CLEAR may be used to size)  │
 64K                  ├──────────────────────────────────────┤
 BASIC ext.+          │         Unused and Available          │
         1C000h       ├──────────────────────────────────────┤
 Jr:128K–16K          │          Video Buffer in Jr           │
   end–3410h          ├──────────────────────────────────────┤
 Jr:end=112K          │          Transient COMMAND            │     DEBUG Search Pattern:
                      │ end–FA8h  Error messages              │     B4 0E CD 21 2E 8E 1E
                      │ end–B10h  Internal command table      │
                      │ end–9F5h  Last command text           │
                      │ end–9F6h  Length of last command      │
                      │ end–8AEh  Formatted filespec          │
                      ├──────────────────────────────────────┤
                      │ ::::::END OF RAM MEMORY EXPANSION::::::│
 640K    A0000h       ├──────────────────────────────────────┤
                      │   Reserved for Future Video Buffers   │
 704K    B0000h       ├──────────────────────────────────────┤
                      │       Monochrome Video Buffer         │
 708K    B1000h       ├──────────────────────────────────────┤
                      │   Reserved for Future Video Buffers   │
 736K    B8000h       ├──────────────────────────────────────┤
                      │         Color Video Buffer(s)         │
 752K    BC000h       ├──────────────────────────────────────┤
                      │   Reserved for Future Video Buffers   │
 768K    C0000h       ├──────────────────────────────────────┤
                      │             Jr: Cartridge             │
                      │          PC: ROM Expansion            │
 800K    C8000h       ├──────────────────────────────────────┤
                      │             Jr: Cartridge             │
                      │       C8000h XT: Hard Disk ROM        │
 832K    D0000h       ├──────────────────────────────────────┤
                      │             Jr: Cartridge             │
                      │          PC: ROM Expansion            │
 864K    D8000h       ├──────────────────────────────────────┤
                      │             Jr: Cartridge             │
                      │          PC: ROM Expansion            │
 896K    E0000h       ├──────────────────────────────────────┤
                      │             Jr: Cartridge             │
                      │          PC: ROM Expansion            │
 928K    E8000h       ├──────────────────────────────────────┤
                      │          Jr: BASIC Cartridge          │
                      │          PC: ROM Expansion            │
 960K    F0000h       ├──────────────────────────────────────┤
                      │     Jr: POST/Keyboard Adventure       │
                      │          PC: ROM Expansion            │
                      │             Jr: Cartridges            │
 984K    F6000h       ├──────────────────────────────────────┤
                      │            Cassette BASIC             │
                      │             Jr: Cartridges            │
1016K    FE000h       ├──────────────────────────────────────┤
                      │              ROM BIOS                 │
                      │             Jr: Cartridges            │
1024K    100000h      └──────────────────────────────────────┘
```

* = Storage chain block, 10h bytes
P = Program segment prefix, 100h bytes

How the Map Entries Are Formated

Here is the explanation of a typical memory map interrupt vector:

14 Print Screen Image
INT 5, All PCs, Points: BIOS, Set: BIOS, Contents: FFF54
BIOS calls this interrupt when Shift-PrtSc or Fn-P is pressed. GRAPHICS.COM changes this vector to point to itself. See also location 500h.

Location 14 hexadecimal contains a vector that is used to point to Print Screen Image (which corresponds to interrupt 05h) and is used for the same purpose in the PC1, PC2, XT, and PCjr.

The vector points to memory occupied by ROM BIOS. This vector is set by ROM BIOS and its typical absolute memory location contents are as shown. Any differences in typical contents between models of the PC would also be shown, so they must all use the same address in this vector. The vector's actual (nonabsolute) four-byte memory contents are composed of a two-byte IP offset (LSB, MSB), then a two-byte CS segment (LSB, MSB). See Chapter 1 if you're unfamiliar with the use of this address format.

Memory location 500h contains some information related to this subject, and further information may be present immediately following 500h. An asterisk (*) would be placed before the "INT 5" if the interrupt or function was new in DOS 2.x, or a dagger (†) if it was new in DOS 3.x. Since memory contents are somewhat configuration-dependent, use Program 1-9, VECTORSD, or 1-8, VECTORSB, in Chapter 1 to determine and document the vector contents for the configuration of your computer. The typical contents listed here were obtained on the following systems:

PC1: DOS 2.1, 384K, color and monochrome monitors, parallel printer, using BASICA, two floppy disks.
XT: DOS 2.1, 384K, color and monochrome monitors, parallel printer, using BASICA, one floppy disk, one hard disk.
PCjr: DOS 2.1, 384K (128K base and 256K expansion), color monitor, parallel printer, using BASIC cartridge, one floppy disk.

In order to increase the possiblity of compatibility with future PCs, some locations should not be accessed directly. For

216

these locations, we have included the expression *upward-compatible* manner or method. You should use the method indicated to obtain the value of the memory location being discussed.

Locations: 0–3FFh
1024 Bytes for 256 Interrupt Vectors
Interrupts may be caused by a signal on the INTR pin of the 8088. The 8088 detects the interrupt at the end of execution of the current instruction. The flag register, CS (code segment), and IP (instruction pointer) are pushed on the stack to save the current state of the system. The trap and interrupt bits of the flag register are cleared to prevent any further interrupts while the interrupt is being handled. The interrupt vector selected is based on the interrupt number, and the vector is used to proceed to the interrupt routine. The routine issues an IRET instruction when it has finished processing the interrupt condition. This causes the saved system state to be restored, and the interrupted process continues.

Interrupts can be ignored by using the CLI operation code which clears the interrupt bit in the flag register. The NMI interrupt cannot be ignored. It is triggered by a signal on the 8088 NMI pin.

8088 Interrupts
00 8088 Divide by Zero Error
INT 0, All PCs, Points: IRET, Set: DOS/BASIC, Contents: 067B6, Jr=E8DEE
Produces *divide overflow* or BASIC's *Division by zero* message, then continues.

04 8088 Single Step
INT 1, All PCs, Points: IRET, Set: DOS, Contents: 847
Performs routine after each instruction; trap flag automatically set off during the routine. Activated by trap bit in flag register, used by DEBUG *trace*.

08 Parity Error Non-Maskable-Interrupt (NMI)
INT 2, not Jr, Points: BIOS, Set: BIOS, Contents: FF85F, PC1=FE2C3
Produces *parity check 1* or *parity check 2* message, then halts.

08   Keyboard Non-Maskable-Interrupt (NMI)
INT 2, Jr, Points: BIOS, Set: BIOS, Contents: F0F78
Keyboard read and assemble bits routine.

0C   8088 Breakpoint
INT 3, All PCs, Points: BIOS, Set: BIOS, Contents: 847
Routine to be executed when instruction CCh (or INT 3) is
reached. Used by DEBUG *go* with breakpoints.

10   8088 Overflow
INT 4, All PCs, Points: IRET, Set: DOS/BASIC, Contents:
067B2, Jr=E8DEA
Used with INTO operation code to activate user overflow
handler routine.

14   Print Screen Image
INT 5, All PCs, Points: BIOS, Set: BIOS, Contents: FFF54
BIOS calls this interrupt when Shift-PrtSc or Fn-P is pressed.
GRAPHICS.COM changes this vector to point to itself. See
also location 500h.

18   Reserved for Future Use
INT 6, All PCs, Points: IRET, PC1=0, Set: BIOS, Contents:
FFF23, PC1=0, Jr=FF815

1C   Reserved for Future Use
INT 7, All PCs, Points: IRET, PC1=0, Set: BIOS, Contents:
FFF23, PC1=0, Jr=FF815

8259 Interrupt Requests (IRQ)
The 8259 Interrupt Controller chip receives interrupts from
various other devices and presents these prioritized interrupts
to the 8088 if the 8259 interrupt mask bit in port 21h for that
type of interrupt is enabled. Pending interrupts are held until
the current interrupt has finished. A special end-of-interrupt
(EOI) signal must be sent to 8259 port 20h by an interrupt
routine to indicate that the next interrupt may be processed.
The 8259 prioritizes the types of interrupts so that the system
timer and keyboard have highest priority.

20   8253 Channel 0 System-Timer-Tick Attention (IRQ0)
INT 8, All PCs, Points: BIOS, Set: BIOS, Contents: FFEA5
Normally, 8253 channel 0 (see 8253 ports 40–43) causes an
IRQ0 interrupt every 54.936 milliseconds, which activates a

routine to update the system timer at 46C–470h, checks to see if the disk motor should be turned off, and drives INT 1C for user timer-tick tasks. See also INT 1A and INT 21 functions 2C–2Dh.

24 Keyboard Attention (IRQ1)
INT 9, All PCs, Points: BIOS/BASIC, Set: BIOS/BASIC, Contents: FFEA5/07D85, Jr=F1561/EABB2
PC 8259 causes this vector to be used to activate the keyboard handler routine whenever a key is pressed or released. PCjr uses 8088 NMI INT 2 to detect a keypress or release, INT 48 to map 62-key keyboard to 83-key keyboard equivalent; then this interrupt is called. PCjr Cassette BASIC uses a temporary INT 9 so that it can check for Ctrl-Esc or Esc as first key pressed after power-on. See also related memory usage starting at locations 417h and 480h; also ports 60–61h. Because of the large number of related memory locations, see Chapter 2.

28 Reserved for Future Use (IRQ2)
INT A, All PCs, Points: IRET, PC1=0, Set: BIOS, Contents: FFF23, PC1=0, Jr=FF815
Reserved for I/O expansion channel use.

2C Reserved for Communications COM2 (IRQ3)
INT B, All PCs, Points: 0, Jr=IRET, Set: BIOS, Contents: FF815 PCjr: Primary Serial Port.
See memory location 50h.

30 Reserved for Communications COM1, BSC, or SDLC (IRQ4)
INT C, All PCs, Points: 0, Jr=IRET, Set: BIOS, Contents: FF815 PCjr: Internal Modem Port.
See memory location 50h.

34 Hard Disk Attention (IRQ5)
INT D, XT, Points: Hard Disk BIOS, Set: Hard Disk BIOS, Contents: C8760
Used to signal hard disk BIOS that a hard disk controller interrupt has occurred; usually means that status information is now available.

34 Reserved for Hard Disk BIOS (IRQ5)
INT D, Not XT/PCjr, Points: 0, Set: BIOS, Contents: 00000

34 Vertical Retrace (IRQ5)

INT D, PCjr, Points: IRET, Set: BIOS, Contents: FF815
Available for user routine to synchronize palette register
modification with video vertical refresh. See Chapter 4 for
details.

38 Disk Attention (IRQ6)

INT E, All PCs, Points: BIOS, Set: BIOS, Contents: FEF57
Used to signal BIOS that a disk controller interrupt has occurred. This usually means that status information for the last
I/O request is now available. On the PCjr, the watchdog timer
(port F2h) is connected to this line to terminate the disk operation during a disk error. All other 8259 interrupts are disabled
during the disk function, causing a beep if a key is pressed.

3C Reserved for Parallel Printer (IRQ7)

**INT F, All PCs, Points: 0, Jr=IRET, Set: BIOS, Contents:
FF815**

BIOS Device Function Requests

The ROM BIOS provides service request routines for the
management of the attached peripheral devices. DOS provides
a higher-level interface to user programs for device requests,
but these BIOS routines are ultimately used by DOS routines
to satisfy requests for device services. See the ROM BIOS listing in the *Technical Reference* manual. Notice that PCjr
routines are not always at the same BIOS location as PC
routines. The use of these interrupt vectors to reach the desired routine is the key to upward compatibility with future
PCs. See Chapter 1 for a program that you can use in BASIC
to request DOS services.

40 Video Functions

**INT 10, All PCs, Points: BIOS, Set: BIOS, Contents: FF065,
Jr=F0D0B**
This routine provides a variety of video services. See Chapter
4, memory locations beginning at 74h, 7Ch, and 449h. Also
see INT 1D, INT 1F; DOS functions 2, 6, and 9; ports 3B0h,
3D0h, and 21h.

AH Function
00   Set mode
01   Set cursor type
02   Set cursor position
03   Get cursor position
04   Get light pen position
05   Set display page
06   Scroll up
07   Scroll down
08   Get attribute and character
09   Put attribute and character
0A   Put character
0B   Set palette
0C   Put dot
0D   Get dot
0E   Put TTY mode
0F   Get status: columns, mode, page
10   Set palette registers (PCjr only)

44 Equipment Determination
INT 11, All PCs, Points: BIOS, Set: BIOS, Contents: FF84D
The routine returns equipment configuration bytes originating
from ports 60–62h at power-on. See memory locations
410–411h for details of returned information.

48 Memory Size Determination
INT 12, All PCs, Points: BIOS, Set: BIOS, Contents: FF841
The total amount of usable memory (not including display
memory) in 1K blocks is returned. The PCjr includes only up
to 112K (128K–16K for video), no matter how much additional
memory is added. PCJRMEM.COM device driver supplied
with expansion memory alters to true total memory size or
memory size minus RAM disk space. See memory locations
413–414h and ports 60–62h.

4C Disk Functions
INT 13, Not XT, Points: BIOS, Set: BIOS, Contents: FEC59
The subject routine performs a variety of disk functions. See
also memory locations starting at 78h, 43Eh; ports 4, 21h, 40h,
41h, 60h, F0h (PCjr), and 3F0h.

AH Function
00   Reset controller
01   Get status
02   Get sectors
03   Put sectors
04   Verify sectors
05   Format track

4C Hard Disk Functions

INT 13, XT, Points: Hard Disk BIOS, Set: Hard Disk BIOS, Contents: C8256

Routine performs a wide choice of hard disk functions. Disk functions vector is relocated to INT 40. See ports mentioned above and 6, C2h, and 320h; see memory location 474h and routines starting at location C8000h.

AH Function
00   Reset controller
01   Get status
02   Get sectors
03   Put sectors
04   Verify sectors
05   Format track
06   Format track and bad sector flags
07   Format drive starting at specified sector
08   Return parameters from drive table
09   Initialize drive pair characteristics using INT 41
0A   Read long
0B   Write long
0C   Seek
0D   Alternate disk reset
0E   Read sector buffer
0F   Write sector buffer
10   Test drive read
11   Recalibrate
12   Controller RAM diagnostic
13   Drive diagnostic
14   Controller internal diagnostic

50 RS-232 Serial Communications Functions

INT 14, All PCs, Points: BIOS, Set: BIOS, Contents: FE739

For serial communications using a built-in modem or the asynchronous communications adapter for a serial printer or external modem. See ports starting at 2F8h for primary COM1, and 3F8h for alternate COM2. Pluggable shunt modules are provided on the adapter card to allow COM1 or COM2 selection. The PCjr Internal Modem is logically addressed as COM1, even though it physically uses ports starting at 3F8h. When the internal modem is not installed, COM1 is the RS-232 connection starting at port 2F8h. See associated locations 2Ch, 30h, 400h, 47Ch.

AH Function
00   Initialize port
01   Put character
02   Get character
03   Get port status

DB25
Pin   Usage
2   Transmitted data
3   Received data
4   Request to send
5   Clear to send
6   Data set ready
7   Signal ground
8   Carrier detect
20   Data terminal ready
22   Ring indicator

54 Cassette Functions

INT 15, All PCs, Points: BIOS, Set: BIOS, Contents: FF859
(The XT returns an *invalid cmd* error code if this vector is used.) All other 8259 interrupts are masked off while the cassette is being accessed, including the system timer. See related memory locations starting at 467h. The PCjr provides a mechanism to channel the cassette audio input to the TI CSG sound chip. See Chapter 3; see also ports 42h and 62h (bit 4).

AH Function
00   Motor on
01   Motor off
02   Get blocks (motor on, then off)
03   Put blocks (motor on, then off)

58 Keyboard Functions

INT16, All PCs, Points: BIOS, Set: BIOS, Contents: FE82E, Jr = F13DD
Provides a number of keyboard-related services. See Chapter 2, related memory starting at locations 24h, 417h, and 480h; INT 9, INT 21 functions 1, 6–8, A–Ch, INT 48–49; and ports 60–61h.

AH Function
00   Read key
01   Get character status
02   Get Shift status
03   Set typamatic rates (PCjr only)
04   Set keyboard clicker on/off (PCjr only)

5C Parallel Printer Functions
INT 17, All PCs, Points: BIOS, Set: BIOS, Contents: FEFD2
The BIOS routine provides several parallel printer services.
The DOS MODE command can be used to direct parallel
printer functions to a serial printer. Also see INT 5, F, 21 function 5, and DOS 3.0 INT 2F. See ports 21h, 278h, 378h, and
3BCh. Connector pin usage is contained at the latter port
descriptions.

AH Function
00   Put character
01   Initialize printer
02   Get status

BIOS Miscellaneous Interrupts
60 ROM-Resident BASIC Entry Point
**INT 18, Not PCjr, Points: Cassette BASIC, Set: BIOS, Con-
tents: F6000**
Entry point for ROM-resident Cassette BASIC.

60 ROM-Resident BASIC Entry Point
**INT 18, PCjr, Points: BIOS/Cartridge BASIC, Set:
BIOS/Cartridge BASIC, Contents: FFFCB/E8177**
This vector is set to point to a BIOS routine that will install a
temporary INT 9 vector to test for Ctrl-Esc and Esc as the first
keypress; it overlays this vector to point to the ROM-resident
Cassette BASIC at F6000h and issues INT 18 to go there. If
the BASIC cartridge is installed, the cartridge initialization routine during POST or system reset overlays this vector to point
to its own entry point at E8177h. See Chapter 1 for more details about BASIC, cartridges, and Cartridge BASIC.

64 Bootstrap Routine
**INT 19, All PCs, Points: BIOS, Set: BIOS, Contents: FE6F2,
XT=C8186, Jr=F0B1B**
The routine loads a sector from the disk or hard disk into loca-
tion 7C00 and executes the instructions loaded. Failure to read

224

the disk or hard disk causes INT 18 to be used to go to ROM
BASIC. See Chapter 1 for a full description of the system
bootstrap process.

68 System Timer Functions/PCjr Sound Source Functions
**INT 1A, All PCs, Points: BIOS, Set: BIOS, Contents: FFE6E,
Jr=F1393**
Provides system timer (location 46Ch) read/set services and
PCjr sound input selection. See also INT 1C and INT 8.

AH Function
00 Get clock
01 Set clock
80 Set sound multiplexor (PCjr only)
     Timer channel 2
     Cassette
     I/O channel
     TI CSG sound chip

See Chapter 3 for details of the PCjr sound selection function.

6C Keyboard Break User Routine
**INT 1B, All PCs, Points: IRET/BASIC, Set: BIOS/BASIC,
Contents: 840/7E30, Jr=840/EAC49**
Called by INT 9 routine to perform any user-desired actions
when Ctrl-Break or Fn-Break is pressed. See Chapter 2 for
additional details.

70 System-Timer-Tick User Routine
**INT 1C, All PCs, Points: IRET/BASIC, Set: BIOS/BASIC,
Contents: 840/6371, Jr=FF83C/E880B**
Called by INT 8 routine to perform any user-desired actions
when a system timer tick has occurred. See Chapter 3 for
additional details.

BIOS Tables
Vectors to system tables are provided so that the user can
copy the tables to RAM, modify them, then change the vector
to point to the customized version of the tables. See DOS
functions 35h and 25h for the supported upward-compatible
method of retrieving and changing the contents of a vector.

74   Video Parameter Table
INT 1D, All PCs, Points: BIOS, Set: BIOS, Contents: FF0A4
This vector points to a table containing four sets of 16 values
to be loaded into the 6845 registers for screen modes
corresponding to 40 × 25 (modes 0 and 1), 80 × 25 (modes 2
and 3), graphics (modes 4–6), and monochrome (mode 7 or
extended graphics modes 8–Ah on the PCjr). See Chapter 4
for more video mode details. See location 449h; INT 10, INT
1F; DOS functions 2, 6, and 9; ports 3B0h, 3D0h, and 21h.

78   Disk Parameter Table
INT 1E, All PCs, Points: DOS Data Area, Set: BIOS,
Contents: 522
The vector points to a table of disk operational characteristic
parameters copied from ROM BIOS (FEFC7, Jr=FEFB8) to the
DOS work area. The BIOS copy of the table is used during the
bootstrap process and later moved to 522h. See the XT *Tech-*
nical Reference manual, page A-44; PCjr, page A-80. Some
abbreviations need explanation: SRT=step rate time (expressed in 2 millisecond increments), HD=head, EOT=end of
track (number of last sector on the track), gap length=space
between sectors, DTL=data length of sector. If a hard disk is
present on the system, the disk parameter table is copied from
C8201 and the hard disk parameter table is pointed to by INT
41. The PCjr motor start-up time is enforced to a minimum of
0.5 seconds, regardless of any lower value that may be placed
in the table. See locations 522h, 43Eh, and port 3F0h (or port
F0h for the PCjr).

7C   Graphics Characters 128–255
INT 1F, All PCs, Points: Expansion ROM/0/BIOS, Set:
BIOS, Contents: F0000, PC1=0, Jr=FE05E
This vector points to a table of PEL maps for graphics characters 128–255. The PCjr provides these maps in ROM BIOS. In
the PC, this vector is to be set by the user. DOS 3.0 loads a
table of PEL maps, makes it resident, and modifies this vector
in response to the GRAFTABL command. See Chapter 4 for
additional information and instructions for creating PEL maps
for graphics characters 128–255 for the PC, similar to the way
used by DOS 3.0. A vector to PEL maps for the first set of
graphics characters (0–127) can be found at INT 44 in the
PCjr.

DOS Interrupts and Functions

See DOS 2.0, Appendix D, or DOS 2.10/3.0 *Technical Reference* manual, Chapter 5, for specifics of using these DOS services. The key to upward compatibility with future PCs is the use of these interrupt vectors to reach the desired routine. See Chapter 1 (Programs 1-13, 1-14, and 1-15) for programs that you can use in BASIC to request DOS services.

80   DOS Program Terminate

INT 20, All PCs, Points: DOS, Set: DOS, Contents: 1937, XT=19B7, Jr=19A7

Normal program exit return address. The interrupts saved in the PSP are restored for the terminating program. DOS functions 31h or 4Ch are preferred over using INT 20 since return codes may be passed. See Chapter 1 for additional details.

84   DOS Function Call

INT 21, All PCs, Points: Resident COMMAND.COM, Set: COMMAND.COM, Contents: 5580, XT=55A0, Jr=5530

Used to pass function requests to COMMAND.COM for routing to the appropriate routine in IBMDOS.COM. See Appendix D for a list of the interrupts and functions by type of device. The SRVCCALL program (Programs 1-13, 1-14, 1-15) in Chapter 1 can be used to call for DOS functions from your BASIC programs. An asterisk (*) is placed before the function number if the function was new in DOS 2.x or a dagger (†) if it was new in DOS 3.x.

AH   Function

00   Terminate program, same as INT 20
01   Keyboard input (with wait, echo, break)
02   Display character (with break)
03   Auxiliary input (with wait)
04   Auxiliary output
05   Printer output
06   Direct console I/O (no wait, break, or echo)
    DL=FFh return input character
    DL<>FFh output character
07   Direct console input (with wait, no echo or break)
08   Console input (with wait and break, no echo)
09   Display string till $ (with break)
0A   Buffered keyboard input (with wait, break)
0B   Check standard input character availability
0C   Clear keyboard buffer and do function 1, 6, 7, 8, or Ah

0D	Disk reset
0E	Select disk
0F	Open file FCB
10	Close file FCB
11	Search for first matching filename
12	Search for next matching filename
13	Delete file
14	Sequential disk read
15	Sequential disk write
16	Create file
17	Rename file
18	Reserved
19	Query current disk
1A	Set disk transfer area address
1B	Query drive allocation units and sectors by FCB
1C	Query drive allocation units and sectors by drive number
1D–20	Reserved
21	Disk random read by FCB
22	Disk random write by FCB
23	Disk file size to record number
24	Set disk random record number
25	Set interrupt vector
26	Create a program segment prefix
27	Random block read using FCB
28	Random block write using FCB
29	Parse filename
2A	Get date
2B	Set date
2C	Get time
2D	Set time
2E	Set disk write verify on/off
*2F	Get disk transfer area address
*30	Get DOS version
*31	KEEP, terminate process and stay resident
32	Reserved
*33	Get or set Break on/off
34	Reserved
*35	Get interrupt vector
*36	Get disk free space
37	Reserved
*38	Get country delimiter information
*39	MKDIR, create subdirectory using name
*3A	RMDIR, remove directory using name
*3B	CHDIR, change current directory using name
*3C	CREAT, create file using name
*3D	Open a file using name

228

* 3E   Close a file using handle
* 3F   Read file using handle, redirection if standard input device
* 40   Write file using handle, redirection if standard output device
* 41   UNLINK, delete file using name
* 42   LSEEK, move file pointer using handle
* 43   CHMOD, change or get file mode using name
* 44   IOCTL, perform get/put/status/device information by handle
* 45   DUP, get duplicate handle
* 46   DUP, point file handle at another file
* 47   Read directory for drive
* 48   Allocate memory in paragraphs
* 49   Free allocated memory in paragraphs
* 4A   SETBLOCK, change allocated paragraphs amount
* 4B   EXEC, load or execute program by name
* 4C   EXIT, terminate process with return code
* 4D   WAIT, get return code from process
* 4E   FIND FIRST, find first file and get information using name
* 4F   Find next file and get information using name
  50–53 Reserved
* 54   Get disk verify state
  55   Reserved
* 56   Rename file using name
* 57   Get/set file date/time using handle
†58   Reserved
†59   Get extended error code for INT 21 or 24
†5A   Create temporary file
†5B   Create new file, cannot previously exist
†5C   Lock/unlock file access
†5D   Reserved
†5E   Reserved
†5F   Reserved
†60   Reserved
†61   Reserved
†62   Get PSP address

88 DOS Program Terminate User Address
**INT 22, All PCs, Points: Resident COMMAND.COM, Set:
COMMAND.COM, Contents: 568C, XT=56AC, Jr=563E**
The routine that this vector points to is called by DOS when a
program ends so that any user-required cleanup may be done
by an invoking program. For example, modules under DEBUG
have this vector pointing back to DEBUG so that it will regain
control when the program ends. This vector is saved in the invoked program's PSP. DEBUG's INT 22 in its PSP points back
to COMMAND.COM. COMMAND.COM checks the integrity

of the transient portion and reloads it if needed. See Chapter 1 for more details on the transient portion of COMMAND.COM, invoking programs, and the PSP contents.

8C   DOS Break User Exit Address
INT 23, All PCs, Points: Resident COMMAND.COM/ BASIC, Set: COMMAND.COM/BASIC, Contents: 5689/623A, XT=56A9/625A, Jr=5649/E8157
This vector points to a user routine which is called by DOS when a Ctrl-Break or Fn-Break is entered so that the program will allow or disallow the termination of the current activity or the program. For example, for modules running under DE-BUG, this vector points back to DEBUG so that it will regain control when Break is entered. This vector is saved in the invoked program's PSP. DEBUG's INT 23 in its PSP points back to COMMAND.COM. See Chapter 1 for more details of invoking programs and the PSP.

90   DOS Fatal Error Handler Address
INT 24, All PCs, Points: Resident COMMAND.COM/ BASIC, Set: COMMAND.COM/BASIC, Contents: 58D2/67BE, XT=58F2/67DE, Jr=5892/E8DF6
This vector is used to point to the routine that DOS will call when an error occurs that DOS error recovery has been unable to correct. The routine will examine the error conditions and decide what action needs to be taken. The *Abort, Ignore, or Retry* message is indicative of the possible error choices. All programs, including those invoked by other programs, point by default to a routine in COMMAND.COM. BASIC attempts to handle its own errors, going to COMMAND.COM only in extreme cases. The original contents of this vector are saved in the current PSP to be restored when the program ends. The INT 24 vector saved in the PSP for COMMAND.COM points to the DOS entry point for a fatal error in COMMAND.COM. This entry point is at 19F3h, XT=1A13h, Jr=19B3h.

94   DOS Read Absolute Disk Sectors
INT 25, All PCs, Points: DOS, Set: DOS, Contents: 2210, XT=2290, Jr=2280

98   DOS Write Absolute Disk Sectors
INT 26, All PCs, Points: DOS, Set: DOS, Contents: 225E, XT=22DE, Jr=22CE

9C DOS Terminate But Stay Resident
INT 27, All PCs, Points: DOS, Set: DOS, Contents: 3543, XT=35C3, Jr=35B3

The terminating program is retained in memory with all further programs being loaded above the end of it. Function 31h serves the same purpose but allows a return code to be passed to the invoking program or batch file. See Chapter 1 for additional details about this feature. The "Video" chapter, Chapter 4, uses this call to cause PEL maps for graphics characters 128–255 to remain resident after the program ends.

A0 Used Internally by DOS
INT 28, All PCs, Points: DOS, Set: DOS, Contents: 1943, XT=19C3, Jr=19B3

Seems to be consistently used as a vector to an IRET instruction in COMMAND.COM.

A4 Used Internally by DOS
INT 29, All PCs, Points: IBMBIO.COM, Set: DOS, Contents: 82E

Seems to be consistently used as a vector to an INT 10 function Eh (put TTY) followed by an IRET.

A8–BB Reserved for DOS
INT 2A–2E, All PCs, Contents: Zeros

BC Print Queue Functions
INT 2F, DOS 3.x, Points: DOS

Reports status; submits or cancels print queue files.

AL	Function
00	Determine if queue handler installed
01	Submit file for printing
02	Cancel print of file
03	Cancel print of all files
04	Hold the print queue for scan
05	Activate the print queue after hold

BC Reserved for DOS
INT 2F, Not DOS 3.x, Contents: Zeros

C0–FF Reserved for DOS
INT 30–3F, All PCs, Contents: Zeros, Jr=FF815 (IRET)

100 Disk Functions
INT 40, Only XT, Points: BIOS, Set: Hard Disk DOS, Contents: FEC59
When the XT hard disk BIOS replaces the INT 13 disk functions vector with a vector pointing to itself for hard disk functions, it saves the old disk INT 13 vector here so that it may call INT 40 to perform disk functions. See locations 4Ch and 78h.

104 Hard Disk Parameter Table
INT 41, XT Only, Points: Hard Disk BIOS, Set: Hard Disk BIOS, Contents: C83E7
The vector points to a table of hard disk operational characteristic parameters in hard disk BIOS. You can copy this table to RAM, modify the parameters, and change this vector to point to your own version of the table. The hard disk BIOS copy of the table will be used during the bootstrap process. The hard disk parameters are used by the INT 13 routine to accomplish the hard disk functions. Four different hard disk drive types can be defined in the table entries. The contents and meaning of the table entries can be seen starting on page A-94 of the XT *Technical Reference* manual. The parameter table for disk is copied from hard disk BIOS at C8201h to location 522h and is pointed to by INT 1E. See ports 6, C2h, and 320h and memory location 474h; see hard disk BIOS routines starting at location C8000h.

108–10C Reserved for BIOS
INT 42–43, All PCs, Contents: Zeros, Jr=FF815 (IRET)

110 PCjr Graphics Characters 0–127
INT 44, PCjr Only, Points: BIOS, Set: BIOS, Contents: Jr=FFA6E
This vector points to a table of PEL maps for graphics characters 0–127. The PCjr provides these maps in ROM BIOS. In the PC, the PEL maps are always assumed to be located at FFA6Eh, making it impossible for the user to redefine these characters. See Chapter 4 for additional information about PEL maps. A vector to PEL maps for the second set of graphics characters (128–255) for all PCs can be found at INT 1F.

110 Reserved for BIOS
INT 44, Not PCjr, Contents: Zeros

114–11C Reserved for BIOS
INT 45–47, All PCs, Contents: Zeros, Jr=FF815 (IRET)

120 PCjr Keyboard Translation
INT 48, PCjr Only, Points: BIOS, Set: BIOS, Contents:
Jr=F10C6
The subject routine performs the needed translation from the
PCjr 62-key keyboard scan codes to the PC 83-key keyboard
scan codes so that the PC-style INT 9 keyboard attention rou-
tine may be used for compatibility purposes. Scan codes above
those generated by the keyboard are also processed by using
the table pointed to by INT 49.
See Chapter 2 for additional details.

120 Reserved for BIOS
INT 48, Not PCjr, Contents: Zeros

124 PCjr Nonkeyboard Translation Table
INT 49, PCjr Only, Points: BIOS, Set: BIOS, Contents:
Jr=F109D
Translation table for INT 48 to use in interpreting
nonkeyboard-generated scan codes (56–7Eh and D6–FEh). The
default table translates these scan codes into keyboard scan
codes of 48–69h. See Chapter 2, INT 48, INT 9, and *Technical
Reference* manual, page 5-42.

124 Reserved for BIOS
INT 49, Not PCjr, Contents: Zeros

128–17F Reserved for BIOS
INT 4A–5F, All PCs, Contents: Zeros, Jr=FF815 (IRET)

180–19F Reserved for User Interrupts
INT 60–67, All PCs, Contents: Zeros, Jr=FF815 (IRET)

1A0–1FF Reserved
INT 68–7F, All PCs, Contents: Zeros, Jr=FF815 (IRET)

200–217 Reserved for BASIC
INT 80–85, All PCs, Contents: Dynamic

218–3C3 Reserved for BASIC Interpreter
INT 86–F0, All PCs, Contents: Dynamic

3C4–3FF Reserved for Interproccess Communications
INT F1–FF, All PCs, Contents: Dynamic

Locations: 400–4FFh
256 Bytes for BIOS Data Areas

Starting with memory location 400h, we will no longer be discussing interrupt vectors but rather data storage areas. Thus, the "INT number, Points:, Set:, and Contents:" line is of no particular use. Since the data stored in these locations is often model-dependent, each entry will indicate which model the information applies to or does not apply to. If there is no indication, then it is used in the same way for all models.

Configuration Data
400 Asynchronous Adapter Port Addresses

Port addresses of up to four RS-232 asynchronous adapters (currently, only two supported). If two adapters are present, the first two bytes will contain F8 03 (3F8h) and the next two, F8 02 (2F8h). Any unused entries will contain zeros. The PCjr has 2F8h as the first address if the internal modem is not installed; otherwise, 3F8h, then 2F8h. The port address order corresponds to COM1 and COM2. See ports 2F8h and 3F8h and memory locations 50h, 2Ch, 30h, 526h, and 47Ch.

408 Parallel Printer Adapter Port Addresses

Port addresses of up to four parallel printer adapters (currently, only three supported). If three adapters are present, the first two bytes will contain BC 03 (3BCh monochrome/printer adapter), then 78 03 (378h), and the next two, 78 02 (278h). Any unused entries will contain zeros. The PCjr contains 378h in the first entry if the parallel printer adapter is installed. The port address order corresponds to LPT1, LPT2, LPT3. See ports 278h, 378h, and 3BCh, and memory locations 3Ch, 5Ch, BCh, and 478h.

410 Equipment Flags

These indicator flags are set by BIOS POST routines from configuration switches obtained through ports 60–62h. The PCjr sets these flags (to maintain compatibility) based on the equipment installed rather than using configuration switches. Use INT 11 to obtain this byte and the next (411h) in an upwardly compatible manner. See Chapter 1 for additional details. The configuration switches are used in the following arrangement:

234

Switch 1

Toggle	XT	PC1/PC2
1	POST loop	Drives with 7–8
2	8087	Same
3–4	Memory on system board	Same
5–6	Monitor type	Same
7–8	Drives available	Same

Switch 2

Toggle	XT	PC1/PC2
1–5	Not present	Memory options
6–8	Not present	Unused

bits 7–6 Number of disks present (if bit 0=1)
   00=1
   01=2
   10=3
   11=4

bits 5–4 Initial video mode
   00=None (or enhanced video adapter)
   01=40×25 color (PCjr default)
   10=80×25 color
   11=80×25 monochrome

bits 3–2 System board RAM

XT/PC2	PC1	PCjr
00=64K	16K	
01=128K	32K	
10=192K	48K	Entry level, 48K
11=256K	64K	Enhanced, 64K

bit 1 Not used
bit 0 1=Disk drive installed

411 Equipment Flag 2

This flag byte is set by the BIOS POST routines when examining the system for adapter cards. INT 11 should be used to obtain the contents of this byte in an upwardly compatible manner.

bits 7–6   Number of parallel printers (see location 408h)
bit 5   PCjr only: 1=serial printer in use (see location 400h)
           Unused by all PCs except PCjr
bit 4   1=Game adapter present (normally 1 on PCjr) (see port 200)
bits 3–1   Number of asynchronous adapters (see location 400h)
           (normally 1 on PCjr)
bit 0   PCjr only: 1=no DMA, 0=DMA on system (normally 1)
           Unused by all PCs except PCjr

412 PCjr: Count of Keyboard Transmission Errors
All PCs Except PCjr: Manufacturer Test Flags

413 Memory Size
Amount of memory available including system board and expansion memory in I/O channel, not including display memory. Expressed in terms of 1K blocks. Use INT 12 to obtain this value in an upwardly compatible method. See Chapter 1, ports 60–62h, and location 415h.

The PCjr includes only up to 112K (128K–16K for video), no matter how much additional memory is added. The PCJRMEM.COM device driver supplied with expansion memory alters this location to true total memory size or to memory size minus selected RAM disk space.

415 Expansion Memory
PC1/2: Number of 1K blocks of memory expansion in I/O channel, not including display memory.
PCjr: Number of 1K blocks of memory on system board and expansion in I/O channel, but not display memory.
XT: Manufacturer test routines work area.

Keyboard Data
417 Keyboard Flag
This flag of the keyboard state is maintained by the INT 9 (and INT 48 in the PCjr) keyboard attention routines. It, and location 418h, can be examined to determine the current Shift and toggle key settings. Note that only location 417h (not 418h) is returned in response to using the provided keyboard status function of INT 16, function 2. See Chapter 2 for additional information, related memory locations, and TRM references.

bit 7   Ins toggled
bit 6   Caps Lock toggled
bit 5   Num Lock toggled
bit 4   Scroll Lock toggled
bit 3   Alt pressed
bit 2   Ctrl pressed
bit 1   Left Shift pressed
bit 0   Right Shift pressed

418   Keyboard Flag 1
See the description above of the first flag byte.
See location 485h for PCjr-only additional keyboard data.

bit 7   Ins pressed
bit 6   Caps Lock pressed
bit 5   Num Lock pressed
bit 4   Scroll Lock pressed
bit 3   Ctrl–Num Lock or Fn-Pause toggled
bit 2   PCjr: Keyboard clicker on
bit 1   PCjr: Alt-Ctrl-Caps Lock (clicker) toggled

419   Alt-Keypad Accumulator
Accumulator for Alt-keypad (or Alt-Fn-N Alt-numbers on
PCjr) ASCII character number entry. See Chapter 2.

41A   Buffer Head
Pointer to the next character to be retrieved from the keyboard
circular buffer.
     The first entry in the buffer is 41Eh, but it's not necessar-
ily the head of the buffer, as explained in Chapter 2. The contents of these locations are actually not in the typical vector
format, but are a two-byte offset from 400h.
     All PCs except PC1: See 480h for keyboard buffer
start/end pointers.

41C   Buffer Tail
Pointer to the next unused entry in the circular keyboard
buffer.
     The last entry in the buffer is 43Ch, but it's not necessar-
ily the tail of the buffer, as explained in Chapter 2. The contents of these locations are actually not in the typical vector
format, but are a two-byte offset from 400h. If 41C–41Dh is
the same as 41A–41Bh, then the buffer is empty. If 41A–41Bh
is two more than 41C–41Dh, then the buffer is full. The keyboard buffer can be cleared by setting Buffer Tail to the same
value as Buffer Head or using DOS function Ch.
     All PCs except PC1: See 480h for keyboard buffer
start/end pointers.

41E   Keyboard Buffer
Circular keyboard buffer containing 16 entries (15 usable),
each with the ASCII code/scan code or zero/extended scan
code of a keypress. See locations 41Ah, 41Ch, 480h, 417h,
and Chapter 2.

Disk Data

See also INT E, 13, 1E; memory location 522h; and ports 3F0h (or port F0h for the PCjr), 4, 21h, 40h, 41h, 60h.

43E Seek Status

Drive needs recalibration (the head retracted to track 0) if drive number bit=0. Causes the next seek (positioning the head to the proper cylinder) to be preceded by a recalibrate operation. All set to zero with INT 13, function 0.

All PCs except PCjr: Bit 7=1 means INT E/IRQ 6 being processed.

bit 3 drive D
bit 2 drive C
bit 1 drive B
bit 0 drive A

43F Motor Status

The bit corresponding to the subject drive is set to zero if the drive motor is running. Bit 7 is set on if a write is currently being performed on any of the drives. See port F2h for the PCjr watchdog timer that monitors the motor status.

bit 7   1=Write occurring
bit 3   drive D
bit 2   drive C
bit 1   drive B
bit 0   drive A

440 Motor Count

Used as a counter to insure that motor turnoff occurs two seconds (default) after operation has completed.

441 Disk Status

Status of I/O request as interpreted by INT 13 (or INT 40 on an XT). If the carry flag is set on return from INT 13, AH contains the contents of this byte. See also location 442h.

bit 7=Time-out from disk drive
bit 6=Seek failed
bit 5=Controller failure
bit 4=CRC error on read

All PCs except PCjr: bit 3=DMA overrun
bit 2=Requested sector not found
bit 1=Write attempted to a protected disk
     All PCs except PCjr: with bit 3=DMA 64K boundary crossed
     Pcjr: with bit 0=Address mark not found
bit 0=Bad command given to disk controller

442 Controller Status/Hard Disk Command Block

This seven-byte area is used both as a storage area for status information returned from the disk and hard disk controller chip, and as a construction area for the command block to be sent to the hard disk controller. See XT *Technical Reference* manual, page 1-185, for the hard disk command block format and A-92 for the routine that sets the block. See TRM, page 1-164, for the possible disk status codes returned. The PCjr *Technical Reference* manual doesn't document the possible status bytes, so see A-79 for the routine that tests the results. The hard disk status bytes are shown starting on TRM page 1-181. See ports starting at 320h.

Video Data

See Chapter 4 for details of user and system usage. Also see INT 10, 1D, 1F; memory locations 410h, 449h, B0000h, B8000h; and ports 21h, 3B0h, 3D0h.

449 CRT Mode

ROM BIOS CRT mode value (as opposed to 6845 mode at location 465h). Use INT 10, function 0 to change the current video mode, and function Fh to request the current setting of the video mode.

Contents	Meaning	Screen/Width
0	40×25 b/w text	0/40 burst off
1	40×25 16-color text	0/40 burst on
2	80×25 b/w text	0/80 burst off
3	80×25 16-color text	0/80 burst on
4	320×200 4-color graphics	1/40, 2/40, 4/40
5	320×200 b/w graphics	3/40
6	640×200 b/w graphics	1/80, 2/80, 3/80, 4/80
7 All PCs except PCjr:		
7	80×25 mono text	any monochrome
8–A PCjr only:		
8	160×200 16-color graphics	3/20
9	320×200 16-color graphics	5/40, 6/40
A	640×200 4-color graphics	5/80, 6/80

44A CRT Columns
Width of display screen in columns. INT 10, function Fh returns the current number of video columns. Set with video mode using INT 10, function 0.

14h = 20 column PCjr mode 8
28h = 40 columns
50h = 80 columns

44C CRT Buffer Length
Length of the video buffer for the current video mode page. Set with video mode using INT 10, function 0.

Length	Use	Screen/Width	Mode	Pages in 16K
800h	Color text	0/40	0	8
1000h	Color text	0/80	2/3	4
4000h	Color graphics	1,2/40,80	4/6	1
4000h	PCjr only	3/20,40,80	8/5/6	1
4000h	PCjr only	4/40,80	4/6	1
8000h	PCjr only	5,6/40,80	9/A	half
4000h*	Monochrome			
	(All PCs except PCjr)	0,1,2/40,80	7	1

*Should be 1000h

44E CRT Start
The offset of the starting byte of the active page (see location 462h) in the display buffer. Can be any multiple (including 0) of CRT Buffer Length at location 44Ch. For example, the second page of a mode 0 screen would be at offset 1000h since the first page is at 0h. Set by implication with INT 10, function 5h, and determinable with function Fh.

450 Cursor Position
Cursor location for each of up to eight pages. Expressed in two-byte column, row format for each page. Set and obtained with INT 10, functions 2 and 3.

450–451h	page 0
452–453h	page 1
454–455h	page 2
456–457h	page 3
458–459h	page 4
45A–45Bh	page 5
45C–45Dh	page 6
45E–45Fh	page 7

240

460 Cursor Mode

Current cursor mode setting. Set with INT 10, function 1. Defaults would be expected to be 0706h (color) or 0C0Bh (monochrome), but they are observed to be 6700h (regardless of active monitor type in use) until set by user program.

460 Cursor end line
    0Ch monochrome default
    07h color default
461 Cursor start line
    Bits 7–6 Unused
    Bit 5   Cursor displayed, 0=yes
    Bits 4–0 Cursor start line
        0Bh monochrome default
        06h color default

462 Active Page

Which page in display memory is currently being shown, based upon the CRT Buffer Length and CRT Start values. INT 10, function 5 can be used to select the displayed page; function Fh is used to determine the current selection.

463 Address of Active 6845

Active display adapter index register port address.

    3B4h Monochrome
    3D4h Color

465 CRT Mode Setting

Current setting of the active 6845 mode register (3B8h or 3D8h) or the PCjr Video Gate Array, register 0. See also location 449h. For the PCjr, see also port 61h, bit 2 for alpha/graphics steering. INT 10, function 0 can be used to set the video mode; function Fh is available to determine the current setting.

bits 7–6 unused		bit: 543210	
bit	5 background intensity	101100	40×25 b/w
	becomes blink attribute	101000	40×25 16-color
bit	4 640×200 dimensions	101101	80×25 b/w
bit	3 enable video signal	101001	80×25 16-color
bit	2 select b/w mode	01110	320×200 b/w
bit	1 select graphics mode	01010	320×200 4-color
bit	0 80×25 text mode	11110	640×200 b/w

449h	Screen Characteristics	Screen/ Width/Burst	465h PC	PCjr	44Ch Length	462h Pages
0	40×25 b/w text	0/40/off	2Ch	Ch	800h*	8
1	40×25 16-col text	0/40/on	28h	8h	800h*	8
2	80×25 b/w text	0/80/off	2Dh	Dh	1000h*	4
3	80×25 16-col text	0/80/on	29h	9h	1000h*	4
4	320×200 4-col graphics	1,2,3,4/40/on	2Ah	Ah	4000h*	1
5	320×200 b/w graphics	1,2,3,4/40/off	2Eh	Eh	4000h*	1
6	640×200 b/w graphics	1,2,3,4/80/off	1Eh	Eh	4000h*	1
7	PCjr 80×25 monochrome text	any/any/any	29h	n/a	‡	1
8	PCjr 160×200 16-col graphics	3/20/on	n/a	1Ah	4000h*	
9	PCjr 320×200 16-col graphics	5,6/40/on	n/a	1Bh	8000h*	†
A	PCjr 640×200 4-col graphics	5,6/80/on	n/a	Bh	8000h*	†

*The PCjr may have up to eight display buffers of 16K, each segmented into screen pages of the appropriate length.
†Requires PCjr 64K display/memory enhancement.
‡Contains 4000h in error, should be 1000h.
n/a Not applicable.

466 CRT Palette

Current palette mask setting from port 3D9h (not on PCjr). Because of the significant differences in the method used to select colors on the PCjr from the PC, you should use INT 10, function Bh to select the color palette to maintain upward compatibility.

Text Modes
  bits 7–5 unused
  bit 4   intensity of background
  bits 3–0 screen/border IRGB

Graphics Modes
  bits 7–6 unused
  bit 5   0=green, red, and brown palette
             1=cyan, magenta, and white palette
             See third palette capabilities in Chapter 4.
  bit 4   unused
  bits 3–0 IRGB of background

Default Contents
  3Fh   640×200 b/w
  30h   every other mode
  00h   PCjr

Cassette Data

Cassette supported in PC1/2 and PCjr only. The next three entries therefore *do not apply to the XT*.

Used for POST routine work areas in the XT. See also INT 15 and ports 42h, 62h.

467 Edge Time Count
Amount of time spent at last data transition.

469 CRC Register
Work register for 256-byte data block CRC calculation and comparison.

46B Last Input Value
Last half-bit input value. A cassette bit is made up of two 250-microsecond halves.

Miscellaneous Data
46C Timer
A four-byte timer value, incremented by INT 8/IRQ 0. Left-to-right significance. See also INT 1A, which can set or get this value, INT 1C, DOS functions 2C–2Dh, and ports 21h bit 0, and 60h. For many purposes, the low-order byte can be used as a random number.

470 Timer Overflow
If nonzero, then the above timer has rolled over (24 hours have elapsed) since the last read.

471 BIOS Break
Bit 7=1 if Break key has ever been pressed.

472 Reset Flag
A value of 1234h, if Ctrl-Alt-Del detected by INT 9. POST and memory testing are skipped if 34h is found here. See Chapter 1 for a description of the system boot process.
PCjr only: Always 1234h so that cartridge removal/insertion won't cause POST routine execution.

474–4EF PC1/2 Unused Area
An unused area in the PC.

474 PCjr Disk Track Last Accessed
Four bytes used to note the number of the last track accessed on each of four possible drives. If the last track was zero, a seek need not be preceded by a recalibration.

474 XT Hard Disk Status
BIOS interpretation of hard disk controller status bytes. INT 13, function 1 obtains this byte for examination and zeros it. See TRM, page A-85, for contents meaning.

475 XT Hard Disk File Number
Number of hard disks found on system, including expansion unit. May contain a maximum of two.

476 XT Hard Disk Control Byte
Temporary holding area for hard disk control byte from sixth parameter table entry. See INT 13, location 104h, and TRM, page 1-186.

477 XT Hard Disk Port Offset
Which port relative to 320h is being accessed by INT 13.

478 Parallel Printer Time-out Values
All PCs except PC1: Four 0–255 second time-out values for parallel printers. Each set by the POST routines to 14h (20 seconds). This value explains why it takes so long for a BASIC program to determine that a parallel printer is not online.

47C RS-232 Time-out Values
All PCs except PC1: Four 0–255 second time-out values for RS-232 serial devices. Each set by the POST routines to 1 second.

480 Keyboard Buffer Start
All PCs except PC1: Offset from 400h where the circular keyboard buffer begins. Defaults to 1Eh. See location 41Ah.

482 Keyboard Buffer End
All PCs except PC1: Offset from 400h where the circular keyboard buffer ends. Defaults to 3Eh. See location 41Ch.

484–48F Unused Area in XT

484 PCjr Interrupt Flag
Flag used to indicate that a timer channel 0 interrupt occurred as expected in POST routines.

485 PCjr Current Character
Character to be repeated by typamatic keyboard function. See Chapter 2.

486 PCjr Variable Delay
Countdown of delay before typamatic key repeat. INT 16, function 3 can be used to indirectly adjust this value. See Chapter 2.

487 PCjr Current Function
Used by INT 48 as a flag to determine when the Fn key has been released so that multiple functions can be requested while the function key is held down.

488 PCjr Keyboard Flag 2
Third keyboard flag for the PCjr, used for the Fn key and repeating keys. See locations 417h and 418h, as well as details in Chapter 2. Not obtainable with provided interrupts.

bit 7 1=Fn currently pressed
bit 6 1=Fn key released
bit 5 1=Fn key seen, green labeled key next
bit 4 1=Fn key locked on
bit 3 1=Typamatic off
bit 2 1=Typamatic at half rate
bit 1 1=Typamatic delay is increased
bit 0 1=Typamatic delay elapsed, put out character

489 PCjr Horizontal Position of Screen
Current value of 6845 register 2 (horizontal synch) adjustable by five either way with Ctrl-Alt-cursor keys to center the screen. See Chapters 2 and 4, and port 3D5h.

48A PCjr CRT/CPU Page Register Image
Image of data in CRT/CPU page register. Specifies the memory pages being accessed by the 8088 processor and displayed on the monitor screen. See Chapter 4 and port 3DFh. The default contents for a 128K PCjr is 3Fh which causes 16K at 1C000h to be used by the processor as well as the display.

490–4EF Reserved for System Usage
Normally contains zeros.

4F0–4FF Reserved for User Interprocess Communications

Locations: 500–6FFh
512 bytes for DOS Data Areas
The following 512 bytes in the memory map (except for a few notable exceptions) are dynamically used by DOS and, in a few areas, by BASIC. The level of DOS and BASIC that is employed determines the exact manner in which these bytes are used, and there appear to be vast areas that are completely unused except by POST and diagnostic routines.

500–700   Disk Directory Buffer for Boot Process

The use of this area to contain the disk directory for the boot process explains the residual garbage left here.

500   Print Screen Status

Used by INT 5 to suppress a PrtSc request while processing a previous PrtSc request.

0 = not active or successful
1 = in progress
FFh = error

501–503   PCjr POST and Diagnostics Data Areas

504   Single Disk Drive Logical Drive

Indicator used by DOS to track the current logical disk drive being used on a single drive system.

0 = drive A
1 = drive B

505–50E   PCjr POST and Diagnostics Data Areas

50F   BASIC SHELL Flag

Set to 2 as a flag. Prevents another BASIC from being executed from the BASIC SHELL command. See Chapter 1.

510–511   BASIC Data Segment Storage

Contains the segment number of the beginning of the BASIC 64K workspace. Add 1000h (64K/16-byte segments) to find the end of the workspace. Multiply by 10h for absolute memory address. See Chapter 1 for BASIC data segment memory map.

512–515   BASIC Timer Interrupt Vector

BASIC's save area for the INT 1C vector.

516–519   BASIC Break Interrupt Vector

BASIC's save area for the INT 23 vector.

51A–51D   BASIC Fatal Error Interrupt Vector

BASIC's save area for the INT 24 vector.

51E–51F   BASIC Dynamic Use

520–521   DOS Dynamic Use

246

522-52C Disk Parameter Table

Pointed to by INT 1E, this is a table of disk characteristics copied from ROM BIOS and modified constantly to self-adjust the disk drive. The following table shows the location, typical adjusted value, and meaning of the parameter table entries.

Location	Value	Meaning
522 bits 7–4	D0	Step rate time in 2 ms increments
bits 3–0	0F	Head unload time in 32 ms increments
523 bits 7–1	02	Head load time in 4 ms increments
bit 0	01	1=non-DMA (used on PCjr)
524	25	Wait time before motor shutoff
525	02	Bytes per sector/256
526	09	Sectors per track
527	2A	Gap length between sectors
528	FF	Data length
529	50	Formatted gap length
52A	F6	Format fill byte
52B	0F	Head settle time in millisecond increments
52C	02	Motor start time in 1/8 second increments

52D-6FF DOS Unknown Use

Filling this area with zeros using DEBUG does not appear to have any disastrous consequences, nor do the zeros appear to be overlaid later.

Locations: 700-9FFFF
653,567 Bytes for Programs and Data Areas

See Chapter 1 for details of the partitioning of this area.

700-E2F IBMBIOS.COM in DOS 2.10

E30-4DB8 IBMDOS.COM in DOS 2.10

Memory storage block chain anchors (see Chapter 1):
EBC PC DOS 2.0 memory chain base
F28 PC DOS 2.1 memory chain base
F3C XT DOS 2.0 memory chain base
F98 PCjr DOS 2.1 memory chain base
FA8 XT DOS 2.1 memory chain base

4DB9–53EF Standard Device Drivers, Buffers, and File Control Entries In DOS 2.10

The size of this area will be changed when specifying values other than the defaults in CONFIG.SYS. The offsets of the following areas of memory will be correspondingly different from those shown.

53F0–5FCF Resident COMMAND.COM in DOS 2.10

5FD0–607F Default-Size Master Environment Area in DOS 2.10

6080–60AF Environment Area for Next Application Program in DOS 2.10

60B0–9FFFF Application Program Area

7C00 512-Byte Boot Sector Location

Locations: A0000–BFFFF

128K for Video Buffers

See Chapter 4 for details of the use of this area.

A0000–AFFFF Reserved for Future Video

All PCs except PCjr: Enhanced video adapters use this area.

B0000–B0FFF Monochrome Display Memory

All PCs except PCjr: 1000h 4096 bytes in length.
Pcjr: References to this area of memory are rerouted by the PCjr VGA, based upon the CRT/CPU register (see location 48Ah).

B1000–B7FFF Reserved for Future Video

All PCs except PCjr.

B8000–BBFFF Color Display Memory

All PCs except PCjr: 4000h 16384 bytes in length.
PCjr: References to this area of memory are rerouted by the PCjr VGA, based upon the CRT/CPU register (see location 48Ah.)

BC000–BFFFF Reserved for Future Video

All PCs except PCjr.

Locations: C0000–EFFFF
192K for Future ROM, PCjr Cartridges

See Chapter 1 for details on the partitioning of this area, cartridge fundamentals, and expansion ROM details.

An interrupt vector/function that references a routine in the following memory map entries is indicated after the description of the routine by the interrupt number and then any associated function number.

C0000–C7FFF	Reserved for future expansion ROM, PCjr cartridge
C8000	Hard disk BIOS through C87BB; XT only
C8005	Copyright; XT only
C8003	Initialization: Replace INT 13, 19, 40, 41 diagnostics for all drives; XT only
C8142	Diagnostics error handler; XT only
C8186	Bootstrap loader; XT only; 19
C8201	Disk parameter table; XT only; 1E
C820C	Exit housekeeping; XT only
C8256	Hard disk functions, high level; XT only; 13
C829C	Function table; XT only
C82CC	Port select, low level; XT only
C82EA	Hard disk functions, midlevel; XT only
C8337	Reset function; XT only; 13/00
C834D	Status function; XT only; 13/01
C8356	Read function; XT only; 13/02
C8360	Write function; XT only; 13/03
C836A	Verify function; XT only; 13/04
C8372	Format track function; XT only; 13/05
C8379	Format bad track function; XT only; 13/06
C8380	Format drive function; XT only; 13/07
C8390	Fetch parameter table byte; XT only; 13/08
C83E7	Parameter table for four drives; XT only; 41
C8427	Initialize drive pair function, high level; XT only; 13/09
C8444	Initialize drive, midlevel; XT only
C84C2	Initialize drive, low level; XT only
C84CF	Read long function; XT only; 13/0A
C84DD	Write long function; XT only; 13/0B
C84F2	Seek function; XT only; 13/0C
C84F9	Read sector buffer function; XT only; 13/0E
C8507	Write sector buffer function; XT only; 13/0F
C8515	Test drive ready function; XT only; 13/10
C851C	Recalibrate function; XT only; 13/11
C8523	Controller RAM diagnostics; XT only; 13/12
C852A	Drive diagnostics; XT only; 13/13

C8531	Controller internal diagnostics; XT only; 13/14
C8536	DMA setup, high level; XT only
C8562	Command block output to controller; XT only
C859C	Interpret sense bytes returned from controller; XT only
C861A	Bad controller, seek, or time-out; XT only
C8627	Bad address mark, ECC, or track; XT only
C866A	Bad command or address mark; XT only
C8677	Bad controller or ECC; XT only
C869F	DMA setup, low level; XT only
C8708	Wait for hard disk attention interrupt; XT only
C8771	Port select, high level; XT only
C878D	Find parameter table offset for drive; XT only
C87B3	ROM release date, eight bytes; XT only
D0000–D7FFF	Reserved for future expansion ROM, PCjr cartridge
D8000–DFFFF	Reserved for future expansion ROM, PCjr cartridge
E0000–E7FFF	Reserved for future expansion ROM, PCjr cartridge
E8000–EFFFF	Reserved for future expansion ROM, PCjr BASIC cartridge

Locations: F0000–FFFFF
64K for ROM BIOS, Diagnostics, Cassette BASIC

An interrupt vector/function (if any) that references a routine in the following memory map entries is indicated after the description of the routine by the interrupt number and then any associated function number.

F0000	ROM BIOS starts; PCjr only
F0000	ROM part number, eight characters, another at FE000; PCjr only
F0008	Copyright; PCjr only
F001B	Temporary return pointers; PCjr only
F0030	POST messages; PCjr only
F0043	Disable NMI, VGA, sound, cassette motor; PCjr only
F006D	8088 test; PCjr only
F00CA	8255 test and initialize; PCjr only
F0103	6845/VGA initialize; PCjr only
F0134	ROM BIOS/BASIC test; PCjr only
F015F	RAM test 0–2K and just below end (for video buffer); PCjr only
F01EB	INT 0–1F initialize; PCjr only
F0250	Configuration switch simulation; PCjr only
F0260	8259 initialize and test; PCjr only
F02A0	8253 timer test; PCjr only
F03B7	CRT initialize and test, put logo; PCjr only

F04CC Keyboard buffer parameters initialize; PCjr only
F0503 Memory size, test or clear; PCjr only
F05BC Memory K tested message to screen; PCjr only
F0640 Keyboard test; PCjr only
F0678 IR link test; PCjr only
F0703 Cassette port test; PCjr only
F0785 8250 serial printer test; PCjr only
F0796 8250 internal modem test; PCjr only
F07AD Set up hardware interrupt table; PCjr only
F07E0 Cartridge scan between C0000–F0000h; PCjr only
F0806 Disk control chip/watchdog timer test; PCjr only
F08E0 Printer/RS-232 base setup; PCjr only
F098C Burn-in loop check; PCjr only
F09AD Warm start INT 19 or cold start diagnostics; PCjr only
F09BC POST error handler; PCjr only
F0A61 Manufacturer test routine; PCjr only
F0AC4 8250 initialization; PCjr only
F0AF8 8250 test; PCjr only
F0B1B Bootstrap loader; PCjr only; 19
F0B59 Initialize or test memory; PCjr only
F0C21 Put logo on screen; PCjr only
F0D0B Video I/O; PCjr only; 10
F0DA5 Set mode; PCjr only; 10/00
F0F78 Keyboard read and deserialize NMI routine; PCjr only; 02
F1069 INT 48 tables; PCjr only
F109D INT 49 nonkeyboard scan code table; PCjr only; 49
F10C6 PCjr-to-PC scan code conversion, calls INT 9; PCjr only; 48
F11CB Break key test; PCjr only
F131E Typamatic key handler; PCjr only
F1393 Get/set time-of-day and audio source; PCjr only; 1A
F13DD Keyboard I/O; PCjr only; 16
F146C Scan codes; PCjr only
F1561 Keyboard interrupt routine (called by INT 48); PCjr only; 09
F1749 Break key test; PCjr only
F188D Manufacturer tick via INT 1C; PCjr only
F18A9 Display ASCII code; PCjr only
F18C3 Handle no-printer condition; PCjr only
F1937 Temporary INT 9, test for Esc or Ctrl-Esc; PCjr only
F1992 Write TTY; PCjr only; 10/0E
F1A0C Sound error beep; PCjr only
F2000 Keyboard adventure program; PCjr only
F6000 Cassette BASIC; 18
FE000 ROM part number, eight characters
FE008 Copyright
FE01B Set up permanent INT 9; PCjr only
FE021 Load manufacturer test routine; XT only

FE035 Keyboard error beeps; PCjr only
FE05B Test 8088; all PCs except PCjr
FE05E PEL maps for graphics characters 128–255; PCjr only; 1F
FE0AE 8255 initialize; all PCs except PCjr
FE0C3 Call for ROM checksum; XT only
FE0D3 Disable DMA; PC2 only
FE0D9 Disable DMA; XT only
FE0D7 Check timer channel 0; PC2 only
FE0E1 Check timer channel 0; XT only
FE10A Test and initialize DMA for memory refresh; PC2 only
FE112 Test and initialize DMA for memory refresh; XT only
FE14B Determine memory size and check memory in first 32K; PC2 only
FE165 Determine memory size and check memory in first 32K; XT only
FE1B4 Initialize 8259; PC2 only
FE1C4 Load manufacturer test routine; PC2 only
FE1CE Initialize 8259; XT only
FE1DE Set first 32 interrupts to temporary routine; XT only
FE1F7 Set first 32 interrupts to temporary routine; PC2 only
FE202 Save configuration switches in equipment flag; XT only
FE217 8259 test; XT only
FE242 Test and initialize 6845; XT only
FE2AD Test and initialize 6845; PC2 only
FE2C3 Jump to FF85F NMI parity error routine; XT only; 02
FE2F3 8253 test, setup; PC2 only
FE329 8259 test; XT only
FE35D 8253 test, setup; XT only
FE382 Check expansion box; PC2 only
FE3A2 Test keyboard; XT only
FE3DE Setup INT 0–15; XT only
FE43B Test keyboard; PC2 only
FE418 Check expansion box; XT only
FE45E Set cursor type; PCjr only; 10/01
FE46A Test memory above 32K; XT only
FE483 Cassette test; PC2 only
FE488 Set cursor position; PCjr only; 10/02
FE4B3 Set video page; PCjr only; 10/05
FE4BC Check ROM C8000–F4000h; PC2 only
FE4DB Read/set CRT/CPU register; PCjr only; 10/05
FE4DC Check BASIC ROM; PC2 only
FE4F1 Check disk; PC2 only
FE518 Check for ROM in C8000–F4000h; XT only
FE52D Read cursor position; PCjr only; 10/03
FE53B Check BASIC ROM; XT only
FE53C Set up printer and RS-232 base addresses; PC2 only

FE543 Set colors; PCjr only; 10/0B
FE551 Check disk; XT only
FE597 Set up printer and RS-232 base addresses; XT only
FE5B1 Read video status; PCjr only; 10/0F
FE5BC Enable NMI interrupts; PC2 only
FE5C2 Calculate display buffer address of character; PCjr only
FE5CD Branch to bootstrap loader; PC2 only; 19
FE5CF Error beep; PC2 only
FE5D3 Scroll up; PCjr only; 10/06
FE603 Beep; PC2 only
FE625 Convert and print ASCII; PC2 only
FE63F Scroll down; PCjr only; 10/07
FE643 Reset the keyboard; PC2 only
FE65F Enable NMI interrupts; XT only
FE66D Branch to bootstrap loader; XT only; 19
FE66F Subroutine to test RAM; XT only
FE675 Read 245 bytes in 512 bytes; PCjr only
FE684 Perform checksum and initialization of ROM modules;
           PC2 only
FE685 Set VGA palette registers; PCjr only; 10/10
FE6CB Print ROM checksum error message; XT only
FE6D8 Set manufacturer checkpoint; PCjr only
FE6E4 Bootstrap loader; PC2 only
FE6F2 Bootstrap loader; XT only
FE6F2 Redirection to bootstrap loader F0B1B; PCjr only; 19
FE6F5 8259 test conditions setup; PCjr only
FE706 8259 interrupt check; PCjr only
FE719 8250 interrupt clear; PCjr only
FE739 RS-232 I/O; 14
FE809 Print ROM checksum error message; PC2 only
FE81A Read timer 1; PCjr only
FE82E Keyboard I/O; 16
FE831 Test 8250; PCjr only
FE87E Keyboard tables; all PCs except PCjr
FE987 Keyboard attention routine; all PCs except PCjr; 09
FE98A Disk control chip test; PCjr only
FE9B4 Fetch values from disk parameter table; PCjr only
FE9E1 Set buffer for read/write/verify; PCjr only
FE9FB Seek track, optionally recalibrate; PCjr only
FEA6F Disk control chip attention handler; PCjr only
FEAA0 Read disk control chip interrupt information; PCjr only
FEAE1 Calculate sectors transferred; PCjr only
FEAFC Disable all 8259 interrupts except watchdog (INT 6);
           PCjr only
FEB09 Ctrl-Break test; all PCs except PCjr
FEB0B Enable all interrupts; PCjr only

FEB31 Wait for clock update on 8253; PCjr only
FEB45 Set drive bit mask for INT 13; PCjr only
FEB51 Check ROM C0000–F0000h; PCjr only
FEC59 Disk I/O; 13
FED4A Perform verify of disk I/O; all PCs except PCjr
FEE41 Disk control chip-output; all PCs except PCjr
FEE6B Fetch values from disk parameter table; all PCs except PCjr
FEE7D Disk seek; all PCs except PCjr
FEEC8 DMA setup for disk operation; all PCs except PCjr
FEF12 Handle disk attention; all PCs except PCjr
FEF33 Wait for disk attention to occur; all PCs except PCjr
FEF57 Disk attention handler; 0E
FEF69 Read disk control chip; all PCs except PCjr
FEFB8 Disk parameter table moved to 522h; see INT 1E; PCjr only
FEFC7 Disk parameter table moved to 522h; see INT 1E; all PCs except PCjr
FEFD2 Printer I/O
FF045 Video I/O; all PCs except PCjr
FF068 Save keyboard scan code during POST; save any keypresses during power-on sequence; PCjr only
FF085 Set 8250 parms; PCjr only
FF0A4 Mode parameter tables; 1D
FF0E4 Read attribute and character at cursor; PCjr only; 10/08
FF0FC Set mode; all PCs except PCjr
FF113 Write attribute and character at cursor; PCjr only; 10/09
FF12C Write character at cursor; PCjr only; 10/0A
FF146 Read dot at cursor; PCjr only; 10/0D
FF1CD Set cursor type; all PCs except PCjr; 01
FF1D9 Write dot at cursor; PCjr only; 10/0C
FF1EE Set cursor position; all PCs except PCjr
FF217 Set video page; all PCs except PCjr
FF239 Read cursor position; all PCs except PCjr
FF24E Set colors; all PCs except PCjr
FF259 Graphics scroll up; PCjr only; 10/06
FF274 Read video state; all PCs except PCjr; 10/0F
FF285 Calculate display buffer address of character; all PCs except PCjr
FF296 Scroll up; all PCs except PCjr; 10/06
FF305 Graphics scroll down; PCjr only; 10/07
FF338 Scroll down; all PCs except PCjr; 10/07
FF374 Read attribute and character at cursor; all PCs except PCjr; 10/08
FF3B9 Write attribute and character at cursor; all PCs except PCjr; 10/09
FF3EC Write character at cursor; all PCs except PCjr; 10/0A
FF3F1 Write graphics character; PCjr only

FF41E Read dot; all PCs except PCjr; 10/0D
FF42F Write dot; all PCs except PCjr; 10/0C
FF452 Calculate buffer location for dot; all PCs except PCjr
FF495 Graphics scroll up; all PCs except PCjr; 10/06
FF4EE Graphics scroll down; all PCs except PCjr; 10/07
FF531 Read graphics character; PCjr only
FF578 Graphics write character; all PCs except PCjr
FF629 Graphics read character; all PCs except PCjr
FF659 Expand medium color; PCjr only
FF67E Expand byte; PCjr only
FF6A0 Expand nybble; PCjr only
FF6AE Expand medium color; all PCs except PCjr
FF6C3 Expand byte; all PCs except PCjr
FF6C3 Read medium byte; PCjr only
FF6E5 Read medium byte; all PCs except PCjr
FF6FC Read medium byte; PCjr only
FF702 Calculate medium cursor position in display buffer; all PCs except PCjr
FF718 Write TTY; all PCs except PCjr; 10/0E
FF729 Calculate medium cursor position in display buffer; PCjr only
FF746 Read light pen; PCjr only
FF794 Read light pen; all PCs except PCjr; 10/04
FF815 Dummy interrupt intercept for unused INT vectors like 180h; PCjr only
FF83C IRET instruction for unused INT vectors; PCjr only
FF841 Memory size service; 12
FF84D Equipment determination; 11
FF859 Cassette dummy routine; XT only; 15
FF859 Cassette I/O; all PCs except XT; 15
FF85F NMI interrupt routine, parity check; XT only
FF8F2 ROM checksum subroutine; XT only
FF8FF POST error messages; XT only
FF93C Blink LED for manufacturer tests; XT only
FF953 Checksum optional ROM and initialize; XT only
FF98B Convert and print ASCII; XT only
FF9A9 Print message on screen; XT only
FF9D8 Error beep; XT only
FFA08 Beep; XT only
FFA2A Reset the keyboard; XT only
FFA5F Carriage return/linefeed to printer; PCjr only
FFA6E PEL maps for graphics characters 0–127; all PCs except PCjr
FFA6E PEL maps for graphics characters 0–127; PCjr only; 44
FFE6E Time-of-day read/set; all PCs except PCjr; 1A
FFE71 Checksum optional ROM and initialize; PCjr only
FFE9A Read 8250 register; PCjr only

FFEA5 8253 interrupt handler, timer tick
FFEEB Checksum ROM; PCjr only
FFEF3 INT 8–1F vector table
FFF23 Error messages; PC2 only
FFF23 Temporary interrupt service routine; XT only
FFF23 Print message on screen; PCjr only
FFF31 Sound beeper; PCjr only
FFF47 Temporary interrupt service routine; PC2 only
FFF54 Screen print; 05
FFFCB Set Cassette BASIC vector, then call via INT 18; PCjr only
FFFCB Carriage return/linefeed to printer; PC2 only
FFFDA Error messages; PC2 only
FFFDA Print segment as 20-bit address; XT only
FFFE0 Initialize timer; PCjr only
FFFF0 Power-on reset jump vector
FFFF5 ROM release date, eight characters
FFFFE Model values
       FF=PC, early XT
       FE=XT
       FD=Jr
       FC=AT

Appendix B
Port Map

Appendix B
Port Map

Using the same address and data lines as main memory, the
I/O port address space is segregated from main memory only
by the presence of a signal on a control line.

The architecture of the 8088 allows an I/O port address
space size of 1024, 400h, bytes (1K) since only ten bits are
used to derive the address of the port. The ports in this address space are accessed by using special IN and OUT assembler instructions (INP and OUT in BASIC programs, and I and
O in DEBUG).

The *Technical Reference* manual discusses ports for each
feature in the section devoted to that feature. Reading the
BIOS listing provides additional information about port usage.
This Appendix is the culmination of all the available information about port usage, presented in port number order for
ease of reference.

The PC implementation of the ports segregates them into
several usage groups: system board use only, system board
and I/O channel use (output only), and I/O channel use only.

These I/O ports cannot uniformly be used for both input
and output purposes. Some device ports are used for different
types of data in a flip-flop manner. Other ports are used for
different purposes depending on the current contents of a second port. The expected contents of a port as well as the I/O
directions supported are determined solely by the device connected to the port.

Figure B-1 summarizes the I/O port address space. Those
areas that are not used or reserved could be used by future
IBM products or another vendor's equipment.

Figure B-1. I/O Ports Map

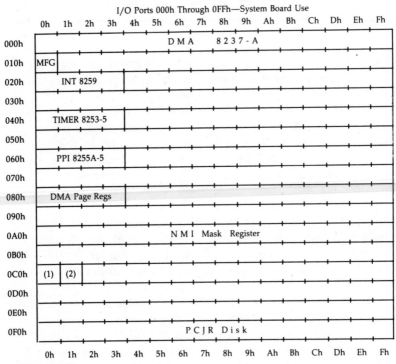

I/O Ports 000h Through 0FFh—System Board Use

(1) = PCjr sound chip
(2) = Non-PCjr DMA channel 3 connection selection

I/O Ports 100h Through 1FFh—System Board and I/O Channel Use
*** Restricted to Output-Only Use, Unused in PC ***

Port Map

I/O Ports 200h Through 3FFh—I/O Channel Use

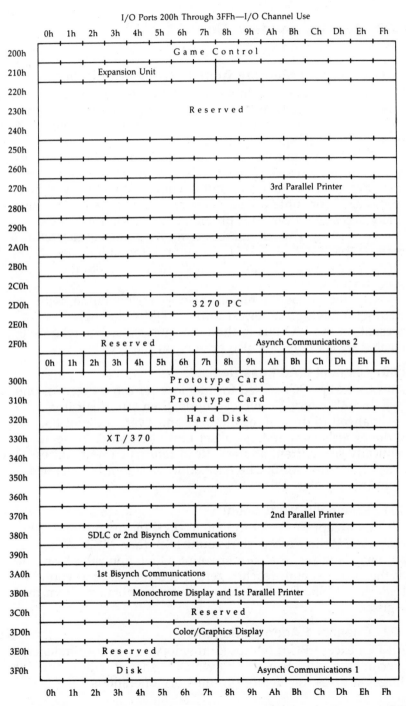

	0h	1h	2h	3h	4h	5h	6h	7h	8h	9h	Ah	Bh	Ch	Dh	Eh	Fh
200h				Game Control												
210h	Expansion Unit															
220h	Reserved															
230h																
240h																
250h																
260h																
270h								3rd Parallel Printer								
280h																
290h																
2A0h																
2B0h																
2C0h																
2D0h				3270 PC												
2E0h																
2F0h	Reserved								Asynch Communications 2							

	0h	1h	2h	3h	4h	5h	6h	7h	8h	9h	Ah	Bh	Ch	Dh	Eh	Fh
300h				Prototype Card												
310h				Prototype Card												
320h				Hard Disk												
330h		XT/370														
340h																
350h																
360h																
370h									2nd Parallel Printer							
380h	SDLC or 2nd Bisynch Communications															
390h																
3A0h	1st Bisynch Communications															
3B0h	Monochrome Display and 1st Parallel Printer															
3C0h	Reserved															
3D0h	Color/Graphics Display															
3E0h	Reserved															
3F0h	Disk								Asynch Communications 1							

0h	1h	2h	3h	4h	5h	6h	7h	8h	9h	Ah	Bh	Ch	Dh	Eh	Fh

000–0FF for System Board Only
Not for I/O Channel

8237A-5 Direct Memory Access (DMA) Controller
The 8237 provides four independent channels for fast data transfer of up to 64K between devices and memory, or memory to memory (using two channels). Memory-to-memory transfer is not supported on the PC.

The DMA controller accomplishes data movement using one-sixth of the clock cycles needed by the 8088. The *Technical Reference* manual does not document the inner workings of the 8237, or contain instructions for its use, as it is not normally accessible from user programs, and its correct operation is crucial to system activities. See the XT *Technical Reference* manual, page A-8 and A-41, for setup information. See INTEL *Microprocessor and Peripheral Handbook,* page 2-88, for specifications.

Channel 0 has the highest priority for operation, with channel 3 having the lowest priority. DMA channels 1–3 are present on the I/O bus to the expansion slots. The read-cycle created by channel 0 is also present on the I/O bus.

000 Channel 0 Address Register
All PCs except PCjr: Used for memory refresh by read of one byte in 64K every 15 microseconds, then automatically reinitialized to do it all again, over and over. See port 83. Write expects start address offset LSB, then MSB. Write automatically sets current address. Read returns current address offset LSB, then MSB. The base address cannot be obtained from this register.

001 Channel 0 Word Count
All PCs except PCjr: Set to FFFFh=64K for memory refresh purposes. Write expects start count LSB, then MSB. Write automatically sets the current count. Operation progresses until the current count reaches zero. Read returns start count LSB, then MSB. The base count cannot be obtained from this register.

002 Channel 1 Address Register
All PCs except PCjr: Not used; memory-to-memory transfer precluded on PC. See port 83 which is shared with channel 0. Target address for memory-to-memory operations.

262

003 Channel 1 Word Count
All PCs except PCjr: Not used; memory-to-memory transfer precluded on PC.

004 Channel 2 Address Register
All PCs except PCjr: Used for floppy disk data transfer; see port 81. Read/write data and sequences same as channel 0.

005 Channel 2 Word Count
All PCs except PCjr: Read/write data and sequences same as channel 0.

006 Channel 3 Address Register
All PCs except PCjr: Used for hard disk data transfer; see port 82 and C2. Read/write data and sequences same as channel 0.

007 Channel 3 Word Count
All PCs except PCjr: Read/write data and sequences same as channel 0.

008 Status/Command Register
All PCs except PCjr: Read returns status, write sets command. Status register bits:

> bit 7 channel 3 request pending
> bit 6 channel 2 request pending
> bit 5 channel 1 request pending
> bit 4 channel 0 request pending
> bit 3 channel 3 ended
> bit 2 channel 2 ended
> bit 1 channel 1 ended
> bit 0 channel 0 ended

Command register bits, initialized to 00

> bit 7 0=DACK sense active low
> bit 6 0=DREQ sense active high
> bit 5 0=select late write (do not change)
> bit 4 0=fixed priority (do not change)
> bit 3 0=normal timing (do not change)
> bit 2 0=controller enabled
> bit 1 unused on PC, should be zero
> bit 0 0=memory to memory disabled, unused on PC, should be zero

009 Request Register

All PCs except PCjr: Provided to generate DMA block mode
request by software. Unused on PC.

 bits 7–3 not used
 bit 2   1=set request bit
        0=reset request bit
 bits 1–0 00=channel 0
        01=channel 1
        10=channel 2
        11=channel 3

00A Mask Register

All PCs except PCjr: Selects DMA channel masks to enable or
disable the channel.

 bits 7–3 not used
 bit 2   1=set mask bit (disable), 0=clear mask bit (enable)
 bits 1–0 00=channel 0
        01=channel 1
        10=channel 2
        11=channel 3

00B Mode Register

All PCs except PCjr: PC uses "single" mode for all channels.
Initialization values: channel 0=58h, 1=41h, 2=42h, 3=43h.

 bits 7–6 00=demand mode
        01=single mode
        10=block mode
        11=cascade mode
 bit 5   0=address increment
        1=address decrement
 bit 4   1=automatic reinitialize
 bits 3–2 00=verify
        01=write
        10=read
 bits 1–0 00=channel 0
        01=channel 1
        10=channel 2
        11=channel 3

00C Clear LSB/MSB Flip-Flop

All PCs except PCjr: Write to here to reset to LSB first, then
MSB.

00D   Master Clear/Temporary Register

All PCs except PCjr: A write to this port causes all DMA activity to cease and an internal reset to be done; initialization will be needed. The readable temporary register is not used on the PC since it is used only in memory-to-memory operations.

00E   Clear Mask Register

All PCs except PCjr: A write to this port enables all DMA channels for interrupts.

00F   Multiple Mask Register

All PCs except PCjr: A write sets all mask register bits.

    bits 7–4   not used
    bit 3   1=set channel 3 mask bit, 0=clear
    bit 2   1=set channel 2 mask bit, 0=clear
    bit 1   1=set channel 1 mask bit, 0=clear
    bit 0   1=set channel 0 mask bit, 0=clear

Manufacturer Test Monitoring Device

010 POST Routine sends a test checkpoint number to this device during manufacturer burn-in loop testing.

011–01F not implemented

8259A Programmable Interrupt Controller

The 8259 prioritizes up to eight interrupts and presents them to the 8088 in their priority sequence. Pending lower priority interrupts are held until they may be processed. INT 08–0F are associated with the eight 8259 interrupts (IRQ 0–7). IRQ 0 is highest priority, while IRQ 7 is lowest. Interrupt types may be individually enabled or disabled by setting 8259 mask bits. The associated interrupt routine is responsible for notifying the 8259 when other interrupts may be processed by sending 20h to port 20h. See the preamble to INT 08 in the Memory Map Appendix for additional information.

    The *Technical Reference* manual does not document the inner workings of the 8259 or contain instructions for its use, as it is not normally accessible from user programs. See XT *Technical Reference* manual, page 1-9, or PCjr, page 2-15, for a list of the IRQ usage. PCjr TRM, page 2-16, offers some summary information about the PC usage of the device. TRM, page A-9 and A-12, or PCjr, A-11, shows the initialization routine for the 8259. See INTEL *Microprocessor and Peripheral Handbook*, page 2-120, for specifications.

Because of the complexity of the various options allowed in this device, we'll be focusing on how the 8259 is used in the PC models. Explanation of the full range of capabilities of the 8259 is beyond the scope of this section.

020 8259 Command Port

Send 20h here to signal end-of-interrupt (EOI). PC models use ICW1=13h here to set edge-triggered mode, eight-byte interrupt vectors, noncascade mode, and ICW4 required. Then, ICW2=8h is sent to port 21 to select INT 08–0F to correspond to IRQ 0–7. Next, ICW4=9h is set to port 21 to designate no nesting, buffered slave mode, no automatic end-of-interrupt (EOI), and 8088 mode.

021 Interrupt Mask Register

0=interrupt enabled, 1=interrupt disabled

bit 0=highest priority, bit 7=lowest
bit 7 IRQ 7 Parallel printer, on I/O channel
bit 6 IRQ 6 Disk controller, on I/O channel; all PCs except PCjr
bit 6 IRQ 6 Disk watchdog timer, every three seconds; PCjr only
bit 5 IRQ 5 Hard disk, on I/O channel; XT only
bit 5 IRQ 5 Available for I/O channel use; all PCs except PCjr
bit 5 IRQ 5 PCjr vertical retrace
bit 4 IRQ 4 COM1, on I/O channel
bit 3 IRQ 3 COM2, on I/O channel
bit 2 IRQ 2 I/O channel use, available for use
bit 1 IRQ 1 Keyboard, not on I/O channel; all PCs except PCjr
bit 1 IRQ 1 PCjr reserved (keyboard uses 8088 NMI)
bit 0 IRQ 0 System timer, not on I/O channel

8253–5 Programmable Interval Timer

The 8253–5 features three independently programmable timers with several modes of timing operations available. The *Technical Reference* manual does not document the inner workings of the 8253 or contain instructions for its use. Because of this, and the power of the 8253 in performing timing functions for your programs, an expanded discussion of the 8253 is offered here. See the INTEL *Microprocessor and Peripheral Handbook*, page 6-139, for specifications. See TRM, page A-13, or A-11 in PCjr TRM for the POST 8253 check-out routine. See also Chapter 3 for examples of using channel 2 of the timer.

266

The 8253 clock input of 1,193,180 hertz is derived from the 4,772,727 hertz system clock which is obtained from the system-board 14.3178 megahertz crystal. This frequency results in an interrupt frequency ranging between a high of every 838.0965152 nanoseconds (corresponding to one bus cycle, or four 8088 cycles) to a low of every 54.925493 milliseconds depending on the 1–65536 divisor selected. Use a divisor of 0 after 65535 to obtain 65536. Set the mode bits in port 43 to load the LSB/MSB divisor for the desired channel.

Load the divisor into the port for that channel (40–42) to set the interrupt rate. To calculate the divisor, divide 1,193,180 by the desired frequency. Or, the frequency per second equals 1,193,180 divided by the divisor. For example, BASIC uses a divisor of 16,384 to obtain 1,193,180/16,384=72.82592773 interrupts per second (an interrupt every 1/72.82592773= 13.731373 milliseconds) to time music functions.

Timer channel current contents may be obtained without affecting the current countdown in that channel by latching the channel using port 43, then reading LSB/MSB with INP instructions. *Both LSB and MSB must be read to insure proper operation.*

040   8253 Channel 0
Used for system timer INT 08 via 8259 IRQ 0. See INT 08. Uses a divisor of 0 (65536) to cause an interrupt 18.20648193 times per second, or 54.925493 milliseconds apart. The disk motor timing is also based on INT 08. Operates in mode 3; see port 43h. In its normal mode of operation, a pseudorandom number can be obtained by latching the counter with OUT &h43,0, then R=INP(&h40):R1=INP(&h40). Both INPs must be done. This latching of the counter does not affect its countdown.

041   8253 Channel 1
All PCs except PCjr: Used to time the memory refresh cycle. Operates in mode 2 with a divisor of 18, causing an interrupt to the 8237 DMA controller every 15.08 microseconds. Do not disturb.

PCjr only: PCjr uses for keyboard serial data timer and accumulator for clock ticks during disk I/O. Therefore, no keyboard during disk I/O.

042 8253 Channel 2

Used for cassette (not XT) and speaker functions. Connected to speaker by port 61h. See Chapter 3 for examples of use. See TRM, page 1-120, or PCjr, page 2-85.

043 8253 Mode Control

    bits 7–6 00=channel 0
                 01=channel 1
                 10=channel 2
    bits 5–4 00=latch present counter value
                 01=read/write only MSB
                 10=read/write only LSB
                 11=read/write LSB, then MSB
    bits 3–1 000=mode 0: countdown with optional inhibit (level output)
                 inhibit via count register reload
                 001=mode 1: countdown with optional restart (level output)
                 restart via count register reload
                 010=mode 2: generate one pulse out of N
                 all PCs except PCjr: used for DMA memory refresh by channel 1
                 011=mode 3: generate square wave
                 used for channels 0 and 2
                 100=mode 4: countdown with optional inhibit (pulse output)
                 101=mode 5: countdown with optional restart (pulse output)
    bit 0   0=binary, 1=BCD counter decrementing
                 binary counting always used in PC

8255A-5 Programmable Peripheral Interface

The 8255A-5 features three independently accessible I/O ports that interface external devices to the bus circuitry. These external devices are the keyboard, speaker, configuration switches, and cassette tape. The 8255 supports several modes of peripheral interfacing in addition to the mode used by the PC.

The *Technical Reference* manual does not document the inner workings of the 8255 or contain instructions for its use. A brief summary of the port allocation can be found on TRM page 1-10 (PCjr page 2-30). These are the first pages of a fairly complete explanation of port assignments. See the

INTEL *Microprocessor and Peripheral Handbook*, page 6-166, for specifications. See TRM, page A-7, or page A-8 in the PCjr TRM for the POST 8255 initialization routine. Also see Chapter 1 for explanations of the configuration switch usage.

Because each model of the PC family uses these ports in vastly different ways, their contents will be separately documented here, and PC1 switch meanings will be included. Be sure to use INT 11 to obtain the equipment configuration that is set in the switches. See memory locations 410–411. The following diagram summarizes switch usage on the PC1, PC2, and XT.

	XT	**PC1/PC2**
Switch group 1		
Toggle		
1	POST loop	Num. drives, also 7–8
2	8087	Same
3–4	Memory on system board	Same, but different meanings
5–6	Monitor type	Same
7–8	Num. drives	Same
Switch 2		Toggle
	Not present	1–5 Memory expansion
		6–8 Unused

060 Port A Input

PC1 and PC2 only: Used for keyboard scan code input or configuration switch group 1 input.

Keyboard scan code image if port 61 bit 7=0, or configuration switch group 1 image if port 61 bit 7=1. The configuration switches are presented in the following arrangement:

bits 7–6 sw 8–7 Number of disks
                           00=1
                           01=2
                           10=3
                           11=4
bits 5–4 sw 6–5 Type of display
                           00=reserved
                           01=color 40×25 b/w
                           10=color 80×25 b/w
                           11=mono

PC1 only:
    bits 3–2 sw 4–3 RAM on system board
                            00=16K
                            01=32K
                            10=48K
                            11=64K

PC2 only:
    bits 3–2 sw 4–3 RAM on system board
                            00=64K
                            01=128K
                            10=192K
                            11=256K
    bit 1   sw 2   Reserved for 8087
    bit 0   sw 1   Use disk to load system

060   Port A Input

XT only: Bits 7–0 keyboard scan code image or diagnostic monitoring output. See Chapter 2.

060   Port A Output

PCjr only: Used for keyboard scan code input simulation by INT 48 in the PCjr, and four hardware mode selection output switch bits. Bits 7–0 keyboard scan code image. See Chapter 1.

061   Port B Output

PC1 and PC2 only:

    bit 7 0=Keyboard enable, 1=clear keyboard and read switches
    bit 6 1=Keyboard clicking on, 0=off (see Chapter 2)
    bit 5 0=Enable parity error signals from expansion ports
    bit 4 0=RAM parity error enable
    bit 3 0=Cassette motor on
    bit 2 Select source for port 62 bits 0–3
           0=Read spare switches
           1=Read RAM size switches
    bit 1 1=Speaker enabled (see Chapter 3)
    bit 0 Speaker input gate (see Chapter 3)
           1=8253 channel 2 1.19318 megahertz clock input
           0=Direct speaker control via port 61 bit 1

061   Port B Output

XT only:

    bit 7 0=Keyboard enable, 1=acknowledge
    bit 6 1=Keyboard clicking on, 0=off (see Chapter 2)
    bit 5 0=Enable parity error signals from expansion ports

bit 4 0=RAM parity error enable
bit 3 0=Read high switches
       1=Read low switches
bit 2 Spare
bit 1 1=Speaker enabled (see Chapter 3)
bit 0 Speaker input gate (see Chapter 3)
       1=8253 channel 2 1.19318 megahertz clock input
       0=Direct speaker control via port 61 bit 1

061 Port B Output

PCjr only:

bit 7   Reserved
bits 6–5 Sound source multiplexor input selection
          (See Chapter 3)
          00=8253 channel 2 (power-on default)
          01=Cassette audio in
          10=I/O channel audio in
          11=TI76496 CSG
bit 4   Disable internal speaker and cassette motor
          (See Chapter 3)
bit 3   0=Cassette motor on if port 61 bit 4=0
bit 2   Text/graphics steerer (see Chapter 4)
          1=Text
          0=Graphics
bit 1   1=Speaker enabled (see Chapter 3)
bit 0   Speaker input gate (see Chapter 3)
          1=8253 channel 2 1.19318 megahertz clock input
          0=Direct speaker control via port 61 bit 1

062 Port C Input

PC1 and PC2 only:

bit 7   1=RAM parity error
bit 6   1=Error in expansion slots
bit 5   8253 channel 2 output signal (see Chapter 3)
bit 4   Cassette data input

Either

bits 3–0 Switch group 2, switches 4–1 if port 61 bit 2=1
          I/O channel expansion memory/32K
Or
bits 3–1 Unused
bit 1   Switch group 2, switch 5 if port 61 bit 2=0
          I/O channel expansion memory/32K

062 Port C Input

XT only:

bit 7   1=RAM parity error
bit 6   1=Error in expansion slots
bit 5   8253 channel 2 output signal (see Chapter 3)
bit 4   Unused spare

Either

bits 3–0 Switches 4–1 if port 61 bit 3=1
Bits 3–2 memory on system board
00=64k
01=128k
10=192k
11=256k
Bit 1 co-processor installed
Bit 0 loop in POST

Or

bits 3–0 Switches 8–5 if port 61 bit 3=0
Bits 3–2 disk available
00=1
01=2
10=3
11=4
Bits 1–0 initial monitor mode
00=reserved (used for enhanced graphics adapters)
01=color 40×25
10=color 80×25
11=b/w 80×25

062 Port C Input

PCjr only:

bit 7 0=Keyboard cable connected
bit 6 Keyboard data serial input
bit 5 8253 channel 2 output signal (see Chapter 3)
bit 4 Cassette data input or same as bit 5
bit 3 0=64k expansion installed
bit 2 0=Disk drive installed
bit 1 0=Internal modem installed
bit 0 1=Keyboard latched, cleared by read indicates missed
        key during disk I/O

063 Mode Control Register

Normally set to 99h to cause port B to be an output port (a read obtains the last value sent) and ports A and C to be input ports. PCjr sets this to 88h to cause ports A and B to be output ports and port A to be input.

bit 7	1=Active
bits 6–5	Port A mode
	00=Mode 0 (PC usage)
	01=Mode 1
	1x=Mode 2
bit 4	1=Port A 1=input, 0=output
bit 3	1=Port C (bits 7–4) 1=input, 0=output
bit 2	Port B mode
	0=Mode 0 (PC usage)
	1=Mode 1
bit 1	1=Port B 1=input, 0=output
bit 0	1=Port C (bits 3–0) 1=input, 0=output

DMA Page Registers

These page registers are provided to specify the high-order 4 bits to be used for the current DMA channel address register. The DMA address registers are only 16 bits wide, so 4 bits of these additional bytes are needed to form a 20-bit address. (These page registers are for all PCs except PCjr.)

080 unused
081 high-order four bits of DMA channel 2 address
082 high-order four bits of DMA channel 3 address
083 high-order four bits of DMA channel 1 address

NMI Mask Register
0A0　RAM Parity and Channel Error NMI Mask

All PCs except PCjr:

bit 7	1=enable NMI, 0=disable NMI

0A0　Latching Options, Read Operation Clears

PCjr only: See PCjr TRM, 2-35.

bit 7	1=NMI for keyboard enabled
	0=Disabled, used during disk I/O to sense ignored keypresses by examining port 62 bit 0
bit 6	1=8253 timer channel 2 (40 kilohertz) to IR diagnostic test

bit 5   8253 timer channel 1 input clock select
      0=1.1925 megahertz for keyboard deserialization
      1=Timer 0 output into timer 1 for timer 0 overflow
      detection during disk I/O for accurate time-of-day
      update (see 8253 timer)
bit 4   0=Enable 8088 HRQ line for future bus-attached
      DMA controller or alternate processors
bits 3–0 Unused

Complex Sound Generator

The sound chip incorporates three programmable tone generators (voices) that can produce tones through the entire range of human hearing, a programmable noise generator, a separate attenuation control for each voice, and simultaneous mixed output. Separate volume controls allow a range of 2 to 28 decibel attenuation, as well as settings for full and no volume. See Chapter 3 for a discussion of the use of this port.

0C0   T.I. SN76496 Programmable Tone/Noise Generator Access Port

Warning: The PCjr "hangs" if this port is read.
PCjr only:

bit 7   1=Bits 6–4 contain internal register number to select
      one of eight internal registers
      0=Second byte of multibyte sequence, used only for
      frequency specification continuation byte; bits 5–0 are
      most significant and first byte bits 3–0 least
      significant
bits 6–5 00=Voice 1 selected
      01=Voice 2 selected
      10=Voice 3 selected
      11=Voice 4 selected
bit 4   0=Voices 1–3 frequency in bits 3–0 and possibly another byte to follow
      1=Voices 1–4 attenuation in bits 3–0

Either

bits 3–0 Frequency or attenuation data as identified by bits
      6–5
      Frequency value: 3,579,540/(32 * desired frequency)
      (See bits 7=0 description above for continuation byte
      format)
      Attenuation: any combination of bits 3–0
      Bit 3=2 decibels
      Bit 2=4 decibels

Bit 1=8 decibels
Bit 0=16 decibels
All bits 0 = full volume
All bits 1 = sound off

Or

If bits 6–5 = 11 (voice 4)
bit 3   Unused
bit 2   0=Periodic noise, 1=white noise
bits 1–0   Frequency shift rate
            00=6991
            01=3496
            10=1748
            11=Voice 3 frequency

DMA Channel 3 Selector

See also ports 6 and 82h.

0C2   Selects Device to Be Attached to DMA Channel 3

All PCs except PCjr:

bits 7–6   11=DMA connected to DREQ3 and DACK3 on the bus
bits 7–6   10=DMA connected to hard disk

0E0–0EF Reserved

PCjr Disk Controller

See ports 3F0 for non-PCjr disk and 320 for hard disk.

0F0   Disk Controller

PCjr only:
See PCjr *Technical Reference* manual, page 3-13.

0F2   Control Port for the Controller

PCjr only:

bit 7   0=Reset the controller
bit 6   1=Start watchdog timer, followed by 0
bit 5   1=Enable watchdog timer; see port 21 bit 6
bit 0   1=Turn on drive motor and select drive

0F4   Status Register for Controller

PCjr only:

See also memory locations 43E–48, 78.

Either

Contents before request:
bit 7 1=Ready to communicate to controller
bit 6 1=Data direction from controller to processor
bit 5 1=Command in process, busy

Or

Contents after request:
bit 7 1=Time-out from disk drive
bit 6 1=Seek failed
bit 5 1=Controller failure
bit 4 1=CRC error on read
bit 3 1=DMA overrun
bit 2 1=Requested sector not found
bit 1 1=Write attempted to protected disk
        with bit 3=DMA 64K boundary crossed
        with bit 0=Address mark not found
bit 0 1=Bad command given to disk controller

0F5 Data Port for Controller
PCjr only:

See also INT 13.
Write: 1–9 byte command block; includes cylinder, head, sector, block, and control byte. Command class and operation:
02h=Read track
03h=Specify SRT, HUT, HLT, DMA
04h=Sense drive status
05h=Write data
06h=Read
07h=Recalibrate
08h=Sense interrupt status
09h=Write deleted data
0Ah=Read ID
0Ch=Read deleted data
0Dh=Format track
0Fh=Seek
11h=Scan equal
19h=Scan low or equal
1Dh=Scan high or equal

0100–01FF for System Board and I/O Channel

Restricted to output-only and so unused on PCs.

0200–03FF for I/O Channel, Not for System Board
Game Controller
See *Technical Reference* manual, page 1-204; PCjr, page 2-119. A read should be preceded by an initializing write of any data. The write will start the timing for the resistive values.

201
bits 7–4 Digital inputs
1=no contact, 0=pressed
    bit 7 joystick b, button 2
    bit 7 paddle d, button
    bit 6 joystick b, button 1
    bit 6 paddle c, button
    bit 5 joystick a, button 2
    bit 5 paddle b, button
    bit 4 joystick a, button 1
    bit 4 paddle a, button

bits 3–0 Resistive inputs
Length of pulse determined by 0–100K ohm resistive load.
Time=24.2 microseconds + (0.011 microsecond * resistance).
(1 is default bit setting, 0=timing active)
    bit 3 joystick b, y coordinate
    bit 3 paddle d, coordinate
    bit 2 joystick b, x coordinate
    bit 2 paddle c, coordinate
    bit 1 joystick a, y coordinate
    bit 1 paddle b, coordinate
    bit 0 joystick a, x coordinate
    bit 0 paddle a, coordinate

Expansion Unit
An optional expansion unit features a "receiver card" that communicates with an "extender card" in an I/O expansion slot of the system unit (PC). Switches on the card indicate the amount of expansion RAM in the expansion unit, and wait states are inserted for the RAM. The expansion unit ports discussed below apply to *all PCs except the PCjr* unless noted otherwise. See XT *Technical Reference* manual, page 1-71.

210–213 Extender Card Ports

210 write: latch expansion bus data
read: verify expansion bus data
211 write: clear wait, test latch
read: MSB of data address
212 read: LSB of data address
213 write: 00h=disable expansion unit,
01h=enable expansion unit
read: status
bits 7–4   switches
1=off
0=on
bits 2–3   not used
bit 1   wait state request flag
bit 0   enabled/disabled

214–215 Receiver Card Ports

214 write: latch data
read: data
215 read: MSB of address
next read: LSB of address

220–24F Reserved on All PCs

Third Parallel Printer
278–27F All PCs except PCjr: Third parallel printer (LPT3) if other two installed; otherwise, second or first. See second printer at 378–37F and the full description of parallel printer ports at 3BC.

2D0–2DF reserved for 3270PC
2F0–2F7 reserved

Second Asynchronous Adapter, PCjr: First
2F8–2FF Secondary Asynchronous Communications
All PCs except PCjr: See primary at 3F8–3FF for details of asynchronous ports. See also TRM, page 1-215.

2F8–2FF Primary Asynchronous Communications
PCjr only: See 3F8–3FF for details of asynchronous ports. See also PCjr TRM, pages 2-125 and 4-18. Note that the PCjr does not support user out1, out2, or ring indicator. When the internal modem is installed, it becomes COM1 but uses ports 3F8–3FF.

Prototype Card
300–31F All PCs except PCjr: Prototype experimentation card; see TRM, page 1-209.

Hard Disk Controller
See XT *Technical Reference* manual, pages 1-179 and A-86. See ports 3F0 for disk ports or F0 for the PCjr.

The descriptions of hard disk controller ports apply to all PCs except the PCjr.

320 Read/write from/to controller

Write: 1–9 byte command block includes cylinder, head, sector, block, and control byte.

Command class and operation:

00h	Test ready
01h	Recalibrate
03h	Sense
04h	Format drive
05h	Check track
06h	Format track
07h	Format bad track
08h	Read
0Ah	Write
0Bh	Seek
0Ch	Initialize drive
0Dh	Read ECC
0Eh	Read buffer
0Fh	Write buffer
E0h	Perform RAM diagnostics
E3h	Perform drive diagnostics
E4h	Perform controller diagnostics
E5h	Read long
E6h	Write long

Read: sense bytes when port 321 error bit on.

Byte 0:

bit 7	address valid
bit 6	spare
bit 5–4	error type (see TRM, page A-100)
bit 3–0	error code

Byte 1:

bits 7–6	zero
bit 5	drive number
bits 4–0	head number

Byte 2:
      bits 7–5   cylinder number high bits
      bits 4–0   sector number
Byte 3:
      bits 7–0   cylinder number low bits

321 read: controller status

      bit 5   drive number (0/1)
      bit 1   error occurred, read sense bytes
      write: controller reset

322 write: generate controller select pulse

323 write: pattern to DMA and interrupt mask register (see ports 0F, 21, and C2)

330–33F reserved for XT/370

Second Parallel Printer, PCjr First

378–37F All PCs except PCjr: Second parallel printer (LPT2) if primary installed; otherwise first. See third printer at 278–27F and the full description of parallel printer ports at 3BC. See TRM, page 1-107.

378–37F PCjr only: Parallel printer (LPT1). See the full description of the parallel printer ports at 3BC. See PCjr TRM, page 3-95.

Second Bisynchronous or Primary SDLC Adapter
380–389 Second Binary Synchronous Adapter

All PCs except PCjr: If primary installed at 3A0; otherwise primary. See primary adapter at 3A0–3A9 for the description of these ports. See TRM, page 1-245.

380–38C Synchronous Data Link Control (SDLC) Adapter

All PCs except PCjr: For the sake of anyone actually using this high-performance, expensive, mainframe communications adapter, a summary of port usage is included here. For more specific information see TRM, page 1-265. All references to 8253, 8255, and 8273 for the SDLC adapter refer to the on-board units and not to the system board devices.

    The descriptions below apply to all PCs except the PCjr.

380 8255 Port A, internal/external sense
381 8255 Port B, external modem interface
382 8255 Port C, internal control and gating
383 8255 Mode register
384 8253 Channel 0 square wave generation

385 8253 Channel 1 inactivity time-out
386 8253 Channel 2 inactivity time-out
387 8253 Mode register
388 8273 Read: status; Write: command
389 8273 Write: parameter; Read: response
38A 8273 Transmit interrupt status
38B 8273 Receiver interrupt status
38C 8273 Data

Primary Bisynchronous Adapter
3A0–3A9 Primary Binary Synchronous Adapter

A secondary adapter can be installed at port location 380–38C.
See TRM, page 1-245. Just in case you ever acquire this
adapter or use one in your business environment, here is a
summary of the adapter's port usage. Since it is rare to find
one in a PC, consult the TRM for more specifics. The 8253,
8255, and 8273 referenced in this section are present on the
adapter and are distinct from those on the system board.

The descriptions below apply to all PCs except the PCjr.

3A0/380 8255 Port A, internal/external sense
3A1/381 8255 Port B, external modem interface
3A2/382 8255 Port C, internal control and gating
3A3/383 8255 Mode register
3A4/384 8253 Counter 0 not used
3A5/385 8253 Counter 1 inactivity time-outs
3A6/386 8253 Counter 2 inactivity time-outs
3A7/387 8253 Mode register
3A8/388 8251 Data
3A9/389 8251 Command, mode, status register

Monochrome Monitor and Parallel Printer Adapter

This is the most popular adapter installed in non-PCjr models
of the PC. The clarity of the characters on a monochrome display, the relatively low cost of a monochrome monitor, and
the included connection for an inexpensive dot-matrix or letter-
quality printer combine to make this adapter an excellent
choice for word processing and nongraphics-display comput-
ing. The adapter is so popular that a whole industry has
formed to compete with the IBM version of the adapter, offer-
ing still more features packed into a single expansion slot.

The PCjr does not support this adapter. However, those
programs previously written for the monochrome display are

supported by the PCjr Video Gate Array (VGA); access intended for the monochrome display buffer is redirected to the PCjr's active display buffer. References to the monochrome display ports are, however, not redirected to the color display ports, proving once again that provided interrupts and functions are the necessary keys to upward compatibility.

See Chapter 4 for a full discussion of the port usage for the monochrome display. See also XT *Technical Reference* manual, page 1-113, ports 61/62, and memory locations B0000, 449–465, INT 10, and INT 1D. See color video ports starting at 3D0.

The descriptions below apply to all PCs except the PCjr.

3B0–3BB Monochrome Monitor Adapter

3B0–3B3 See ports 3B4 and 3B5.

3B4 6845 Index register, used to select register to be accessed with port 3B5. See the register numbers at that port. This port is not readable. The vector at 463h points here if monochrome is the current active display. Note that the address decode method used on the adapter allows port 3B4 to be addressed as 3B0, 3B2, 3B4, or 3B6.

3B5 6845 Data to be placed in the register selected by port 3B4. Only registers C–Fh may be retrieved; all others are write-only. If the adapter is not installed, FFh will be the result of a read from this port. Note that the address decode method used on the adapter allows port 3B5 to be addressed as 3B1, 3B3, 3B5, or 3B7.

Register	Use	Contents
0	Horz total characters −1 character clock cycles per horizontal line (size to screen)	61h
1	Horz displayed characters/line	50h
2	Horz synch position up/down centering	52h
3	Horz synch width in characters	0Fh
4	Vert total lines −1 int (lines * scan lines/char) −1	19h
5	Vert total lines −1 fraction of above	06h
6	Vert displayed rows	19h
7	Vert synch position row top to first row of chars	19h
8	Interlace mode	02h

9	Maximum scan line address	0Dh
	scan lines/character −1	
10	Cursor starting scan line	0Bh
	bit 7 unused	
	bit 6 blink rate, don't use	
	since hardware blinking	
	bit 5 0=display	
	1=no display	
	bits 4–0 starting scan line	
	0=top, 0D=bottom	
	BASIC LOCATE changes this register	
11	Cursor ending scan line	0Ch
	bits 7–5 unused	
	bits 4–0 ending scan line	
	0=top, 0D=bottom	
	BASIC LOCATE changes this register	
12	Memory address MSB	00 readable
	bits 7–6 unused	
	bits 5–0 half the offset for the	
	byte to be at top left	
13	Memory address LSB	00 readable
	half the offset for the	
	byte to be at top left	
14	Cursor address MSB	00 readable
	bits 7–6 unused	
	bits 5–0 half the offset for the	
	byte to be at top left,	
	plus cursor offset	
15	Cursor address LSB	00 readable
	half the offset for the	
	byte to be at top left,	
	plus cursor offset	
16	Reserved for light pen	
17	Reserved for light pen	

3B6–3B7 See notes for ports 3B4 and 3B5.
3B8 6845 Mode control register
    bit 5 enable blink
    bit 3 enable video signal (doesn't affect monochrome cursor)
    bit 0 80×25 text
3B9 Reserved for color select register on color adapter
3BA Status register, read-only
    bit 3 1=vertical retrace
    bit 0 0=video enabled

            1=horizontal retrace
3BB Reserved for light pen strobe reset

Primary Parallel Printer
3BC–3BF Parallel Printer Adapter
See ports 378–37F for second printer adapter (primary on PCjr) and 278–27F for third printer. See TRM, page 1-107; PCjr, page 3-95. Only ports 378 to 37F apply to PCjr.

3BC/378/278 Printer data out, also readable

    bit 7 pin 9 data bit 7
    bit 6 pin 8 data bit 6
    bit 5 pin 7 data bit 5
    bit 4 pin 6 data bit 4
    bit 3 pin 5 data bit 3
    bit 2 pin 4 data bit 2
    bit 1 pin 3 data bit 1
    bit 0 pin 2 data bit 0

3BD/379/279 Printer status register

    bit 7 0=busy, pin 11
    bit 6 0=acknowledge, pin 10
    bit 5 1=out of paper, pin 12
    bit 4 1=online (selected), pin 13
    bit 3 1=error, pin 15
    bit 2 0=unused
    bit 1 0=unused
    bit 0 1=time-out

3BE/37A/27A Printer control register

    bits 7–5 unused
    bit 4 0=disable, 1=IRQ7 enable for printer acknowledge
    bit 3 1=printer reads output, pin 17
    bit 2 0=initialize printer, pin 16
    bit 1 1=auto linefeed, pin 14
    bit 0 1=output data to printer, pin 1

3BF/37F/27F not used

3C0–3CF reserved

Color/Graphics Adapter
See Chapter 4 for a full discussion of the port usage for the color display. See also TRM, page 1-123; ports 21, 61, 62, 3DF; and memory locations B80000, 449-466, 489-48A, INT 10, INT 44, INT 05, INT 1F, INT 0D, and INT 1D. See monochrome video ports at 3B0.

3D0–3DC Color/Graphics Monitor Adapter

3D0–3D3 See ports 3D4 and 3D5.

3D4 6845 Index register, used to select register to be accessed with port 3D5. See the register numbers at that port. This port is not readable. The vector at 463h points here if color is the current active display. Note that the address decode method used on the adapter allows port 3D4 to be addressed as 3D0, 3D2, 3D4, or 3D6.

3D5 6845 Data to be placed in the register selected by port 3D4. Only registers C–Fh can be retrieved; all others are write-only. If the adapter is not installed, FFh will be the result of a read from this port. Note that the address decode method used on the adapter allows port 3D5 to be addressed as 3D1, 3D3, 3D5, or 3D7.

Register	Use	Contents Mode 40/80/Graph/ Jr Graph
0	Horz total characters −1 character clock cycles per horizontal line (size to screen)	38/71/38/61h
1	Horz displayed characters/line	28/50/28/50h
2	Horz synch position up/down centering	2D/5A/2D/52h
3	Horz synch width in characters	A/A/A/Fh
4	Vert total lines −1 int (lines * scan lines/char) −1	1F/1F/7F/19h
5	Vert total lines −1 fraction of above	6/6/6/6h
6	Vert displayed rows	19/19/64/19h
7	Vert synch position top to first row of chars	1C/1C/70/19h
8	Interlace mode	2/2/2/2h
9	Maximum scan line address scan lines per char −1	7/7/1/Dh
10	Cursor starting scan line bit 7 unused bit 6 · blink rate, don't use since hardware blinking bit 5 0=display 1=no display bits 4–0 starting scan line 0=top, 0D=bottom BASIC LOCATE changes this register	6/6/6/Bh

A

B	11	Cursor ending scan line	7/7/7/Ch

         bits 7–5 unused
         bits 4–0 ending scan line
                0=top, 0D=bottom
         BASIC LOCATE changes this register

C 12   Memory address MSB   0/0/0/0 readable
         bits 7–6 unused
         bits 5–0 half the offset for the
                byte to be at top left

D 13   Memory address LSB   0/0/0/0 readable
         half the offset for the
         byte to be at top left

E 14   Cursor address MSB   0/0/0/0 readable
         bits 7–6 unused
         bits 5–0 half the offset for the
                byte to be at top left,
                plus cursor offset

F 15   Cursor address LSB   0/0/0/0 readable
         half the offset for the
         byte to be at top left,
          plus cursor offset

10 16   Light pen MSB
11 17   Light pen LSB

3D6–3D7 not used; see notes for ports 3D4–3D5

3D8 control register
(Port access not honored by PCjr; see PCjr TRM, page 4-16, port 3DA.)

      bit 5 1=background intensity means blink
             0=background intensity for 16 colors
      bit 4 640×200 mode
      bit 3 enable video signal
      bit 2 select b/w mode
      bit 1 select graphics
      bit 0 80×25 text

The usage of the above control register for various modes is:

Bit:	5	4	3	2	1	0	mode
	1	0	1	1	0	0	40×25 b/w
	1	0	1	0	0	0	40×25 16-color
	1	0	1	1	0	1	80×25 b/w
	1	0	1	0	0	1	80×25 16-color
	x	0	1	1	1	0	320×200 b/w
	x	0	1	0	1	0	320×200 4-color
	x	1	1	1	1	0	640×200 b/w

3D9 color select register
(Port access not honored by PCjr; see PCjr TRM, page 4-16, port 3DA.)
For text modes:

    bits 7–5 unused
    bit 4   intensity of background
    bits 3–0 screen/border IRBG

For graphics modes:

    bits 7–6 unused
    bit 5   0=green, red, and brown palette
             1=cyan, magenta, and white palette
    bit 4   unused
    bits 3–0 IRGB for background
           3F 640×200 b/w
           30 every other mode

3DA Status register
PCjr uses this port for VGA access.
All PCs except PCjr:

    bits 7–4 not used
    bit 3 vertical retrace
    bit 2 light pen switch
    bit 1 light pen trigger set
    bit 0 display enabled

PCjr only:
Video Gate Array (VGA) control port; see PCjr TRM, page 2-63. The port functions in an address/data flip-flop mode, with a read setting the address mode and obtaining status bits. The addressing mode accepts the number of the register to be given the following data. Registers are numbered 0–1Fh. See also port 61, bit 2.
PCjr only:
Status register:

    bit 4 1=video dot information available, diagnostic function
    bit 3 1=vertical retrace active
    bit 2 0=light pen triggered
    bit 1 1=light pen trigger set
    bit 0 1=display enabled

PCjr only:

Register Use
00   Mode control register 1
           bits 7–5 unused
           bit 4 1=16-color graphics for 160×200 and 320×200
                modes
           bit 3 1=video enabled
           bit 2 1=color burst disabled, gray shades;
                no effect on RGB monitors
           bit 1 1=graphics, 0=text
           bit 0 1=64k expansion, high band width for modes
                80×25 text, 640×200 4-color, 320×200 16-color
01   Palette mask register
                A zero in the following bits causes the correspond-
        ing attribute bits 3–0 to be ignored.
           bit 3 palette mask 3 16-color mode
           bit 2 palette mask 2 16-color mode
           bit 1 palette mask 1 16/4 color mode
           bit 0 palette mask 0 16/4/2 color mode
02   Border color register
           bit 3 intensity
           bit 2 red
           bit 1 green
           bit 0 blue
03   Mode control register 2
           bit 3 1=two-color graphics
           bit 2 should be zero
           bit 1 1=enable blink
           bit 0 should be zero
04   Reset register
           Not usable to RAM-resident programs
           bit 1 synchronous reset
           bit 0 asynchronous reset
10–1F   Palette registers
                These registers allow the user to specify the colors to
        be generated by the matching attribute byte contents. For
        example, an attribute byte containing 6h would use pal-
        ette register 16h for the desired IRBG setting of the color.
           bit 3 intensity
           bit 2 red
           bit 1 green
           bit 0 blue

3DB Clear light pen latch by any write
3DC Preset light pen latch
3DF PCjr only: CRT/CPU page register; see also memory location
       48Ah.

bits 7-6 00=all text modes
    01=low-resolution graphics (160×200)
    11=high-resolution graphics (640×200)
bits 5-3 16K video page address for redirection of
B8000/B0000
bits 2-0 16K video page being displayed
The default contents for a 128K PCjr is 3Fh which means:
    bit: 7654 3210
      0011 1111=3Fh
    bits 7-6=00 text mode
    bits 5-3=111 = 7*16K = 114,688 = 1C000h = processor
    accessed page
    bits 2-0=111 = 7*16K = 114,688 = 1C000h = display
    accessed page

3E0-3E7 reserved
Disk Controller

See ports 0F0 for PCjr disk and 320 for hard disk; see TRM, page 1-151.

    The following description of the disk controller ports applies to all PCs except PCjr.

3F2 Control Port for the Controller
    bit 7 1=drive D motor enable
    bit 6 1=drive C motor enable
    bit 5 1=drive B motor enable
    bit 4 1=drive A motor enable
    bit 3 1=enable interrupt and DMA requests,
       0=disconnect from bus
    bit 2 0=reset the controller
    bit 1-0 drive select
      00=A
      01=B
      10=C
      11=D

3F4 Status Register for the Controller
    bit 7 1=ready to communicate to controller
    bit 6 1=data direction from controller to processor
    bit 5 1=non-DMA mode
    bit 4 1=command in process, busy
    bit 3 1=Drive D in seek mode
    bit 2 1=Drive C in seek mode
    bit 1 1=Drive B in seek mode
    bit 0 1=Drive A in seek mode

3F5 Data Register

See also INT 13.

Write: 1–9 byte command block; includes cylinder, head, sector, block, and control byte. Command class and operation:

02h =Read track
03h =Specify SRT, HUT, HLT, DMA
04h =Sense drive status
05h =Write data
06h =Read
07h =Recalibrate
08h =Sense interrupt status
09h =Write deleted data
0Ah =Read ID
0Ch =Read deleted data
0Dh =Format track
0Fh =Seek
11h =Scan equal
19h =Scan low or equal
1Dh =Scan high or equal

Primary Asynchronous Adapter, PCjr Internal Modem

3F8–3FF Primary Asynchronous Serial Communications

See secondary (PCjr primary) at 2F8–2FF.

See also TRM, page 1-215; PCjr TRM, pages 2-125, 3-33, and 4-18. Note that the PCjr does not support user OUT1, OUT2, or ring indicator. Also see memory locations 400, 50, 2C, 30, and 47C.

3F8/2F8 Read: transmit buffer. Write: receive buffer, or baud rate divisor LSB if port 3FB, bit 7=1.

PCjr baud rate divisor is different from other models; clock input is 1.7895 megahertz rather than 1.8432 megahertz.

3F9/2F9 Write: interrupt enable register or baud rate divisor MSB if port 3FB, bit 7=1.

PCjr baud rate divisor is different from other models; clock input is 1.7895 megahertz rather than 1.8432 megahertz. Interrupt enable register:

bits 7–4   forced to 0
bit 3   1=enable change-in-modem-status interrupt
bit 2   1=enable line-status interrupt
bit 1   1=enable transmit-register-empty interrupt
bit 0   1=data-available interrupt

3FA/2FA Interrupt identification register (prioritized)

    bits 7–3   forced to 0
    bits 2–1   00=change-in-modem-status (lowest)
    bits 2–1   01=transmit-register-empty (low)
    bits 2–1   10=data-available (high)
    bits 2–1   11=line status (highest)
    bit 0   1=no interrupt pending
    bit 0   0=interrupt pending

3FB/2FB Line control register

    bit 7 0=normal, 1=address baud rate divisor registers
    bit 6 0=break disabled, 1=enabled
    bit 5 0=parity disabled
           1=if bit 4-3=01 parity always 1
           if bit 4-3=11 parity always 0
           if bit 3=0 no parity
    bit 4 0=odd parity, 1=even
    bit 3 0=no parity, 1=parity
    bit 2 0=1 stop bit
           1=1.5 stop bits if 5 bits/character or
           2 stop bits if 6–8 bits/character
    bits 1–0   00=5 bits/character
               01=6 bits/character
               10=7 bits/character
               11=8 bits/character

3FC/2FC Modem control register

    bits 7–5 forced to zero
    bit 4 0=normal, 1=loop back test
    bits 3–2 all PCs except PCjr
    bit 3 1=interrupts to system bus, user-designated output: OUT2
    bit 2 user-designated output, OUT1
    bit 1 1=activate rts
    bit 0 1=activate dtr

3FD/2FD Line status register

    bit 7 forced to 0
    bit 6 1=transmit shift register is empty
    bit 5 1=transmit hold register is empty
    bit 4 1=break received
    bit 3 1=framing error received
    bit 2 1=parity error received
    bit 1 1=overrun error received
    bit 0 1=data received

3FE/2FE Modem status register

> bit 7 1=receive line signal detect
> bit 6 1=ring indicator (all PCs except PCjr)
> bit 5 1=dsr
> bit 4 1=cts
> bit 3 1=receive line signal detect has changed state
> bit 2 1=ring indicator has changed state (all PCs except PCjr)
> bit 1 1=dsr has changed state
> bit 0 1=cts has changed state

3FF/2FF Scratch pad register

Appendix C
Interrupts

Appendix C

Interrupts

Interrupts and Functions by Type of Service

See the Memory Map Appendix, Appendix A, for interrupts and functions in numerical order.

An asterisk (*) marks new DOS 2.0/2.10 interrupts and functions.
A dagger (†) marks new DOS 3.0/3.01 interrupts and functions.

Keyboard Services

09 BIOS keyboard interrupt vector
16 BIOS keyboard functions
    00 Read key
    01 Get character status
    02 Get shift status
    03 Set key repeat rates (PCjr only)
    04 Set keyboard clicker on/off (PCjr only)
21 DOS function request
    01 Keyboard input (with wait, echo, break)
    06 Direct console I/O (no wait, break, or echo)
    DL=FFh return input character
    07 Direct console input (with wait, no echo or break)
    08 Console input (with wait and break, no echo)
    0A Buffered keyboard input (with wait, break)
    0B Check standard input character availability
    0C Clear keyboard buffer and do function 1, 6, 7, 8, or A
48 BIOS cordless keyboard 62 to 83 key translation (PCjr only)
49 BIOS nonkeyboard scan code translation table (PCjr only)

Video Services

0D BIOS vertical retrace attention (PCjr only)
10 BIOS video functions
    00 Set mode
    01 Set cursor type
    02 Set cursor position
    03 Get cursor position
    04 Get light pen position
    05 Set display page

06 Scroll up
07 Scroll down
08 Get attribute and character
09 Put attribute and character
0A Put character
0B Set palette
0C Put dot
0D Get dot
0E Put TTY mode
0F Get status: columns, mode, page
10 Set palette registers (PCjr only)
1D   BIOS video parameters table vector
1F   BIOS 128–255 graphics character patterns vector
21   DOS function request
02 Display character (with break)
06 Direct console I/O (no wait, break, or echo)
    DL<>FFh output character
09 Display string till $ (with break)
44   BIOS 0–127 graphics character patterns vector (PCjr only)

Disk Services

0D   BIOS hard disk attention
0E   BIOS floppy disk attention
13   BIOS hard disk functions (XT only)
00 Reset controller
01 Get status
02 Get sectors
03 Put sectors
04 Verify sectors
05 Format track
06 Format track and bad sector flags
07 Format drive starting at specified sector
08 Return current drive parameters
09 Initialize drive pair characteristics using INT 41
0A Read long
0B Write long
0C Seek
0D Alternate disk reset
0E Read sector buffer
0F Write sector buffer
10 Test drive read
11 Recalibrate
12 Controller RAM diagnostic
13 Drive diagnostic
14 Controller internal diagnostic

13 BIOS disk functions
    00 Reset controller
    01 Get status
    02 Get sectors
    03 Put sectors
    04 Verify sectors
    05 Format track
1E BIOS disk parameters table vector
21 DOS function request
    0D Disk reset
    0E Select disk
    0F Open file FCB
    10 Close file FCB
    11 Search for first matching filename
    12 Search for next matching filename
    13 Delete file
    14 Sequential disk read
    15 Sequential disk write
    16 Create file
    17 Rename file
    19 Query current disk
    1A Set disk transfer area address
    1B Query drive allocation units and sectors by FCB
    1C Query drive allocation units and sectors by drive number
    21 Disk random read by FCB
    22 Disk random write by FCB
    23 Disk file size to record number
    24 Set disk random record number
    27 Random block read using FCB
    28 Random block write using FCB
    29 Parse filename
    2E Set disk write verify on/off
  * 2F Get disk transfer area address
  * 36 Get disk free space
  * 39 MKDIR, create subdirectory using name
  * 3A RMDIR, remove directory using name
  * 3B CHDIR, change current directory using name
  * 3C CREAT, create file using name
  * 3D Open a file using name
  * 3E Close file using handle
  * 3F Read file using handle, redirection if standard input device
  * 40 Write file using handle, redirection if standard output device
  * 41 UNLINK, delete file using name
  * 42 LSEEK, move file pointer using handle
  * 43 CHMOD, change or get file mode using name
  * 44 IOCTL, perform get/put/status/device-information by
      handle

* 45 DUP, get duplicate handle
* 46 DUP, point file handle at another file
* 47 Read directory for drive
* 4E FIND FIRST, find first file and get information using name
* 4F Find next file and get information using name
* 54 Get disk verify state
* 56 Rename file using name
* 57 Get/set file date/time using handle
†5A Create temporary file
†5B Create new file, cannot previously exist
†5C Lock/unlock file access

25   DOS absolute disk read
26   DOS absolute disk write
40   BIOS reserved for floppy disk I/O when hard disk installed
41   BIOS hard disk parameter table vector

Program Management Services

1B   BIOS user break routine vector
20   DOS program terminate, same as INT 21, function 00
21   DOS function request
     00 Terminate program, same as INT 20
     26 Create a program segment prefix
     * 31 KEEP, terminate process and stay resident
     * 48 Allocate memory in paragraphs
     * 49 Free allocated memory in paragraphs
     * 4A SETBLOCK, change allocated paragraphs amount
     * 4B EXEC, load or execute program by name
     * 4C EXIT, terminate process with return code
     * 4D WAIT, get return code from process
     †59 Get extended error code for INT 21 or 24
     †62 Get PSP address
22   DOS program terminate address
23   DOS program Ctrl/Break exit address
24   DOS critical error handler vector
27   DOS terminate program, stay resident

Clock/Date/Time Services

08   BIOS 8253 timer interrupt vector
1A   BIOS time-of-day clock functions
     00 Get clock
     01 Set clock
1C   BIOS user timer tick routine vector
21   DOS function request
     2A Get date

2B Set date
2C Get time
2D Set time
*38 Get country delimiter information
*57 Get/set file date/time using handle

Printer Services

05   BIOS print screen
0F   BIOS reserved for printer
17   BIOS printer functions
     00 Put character
     01 Initialize printer
     02 Get status
21   DOS function request
     05 Printer output
2F †DOS submit, cancel, or get printer status
     †00 Determine if handler installed
     †01 Submit file for printing
     †02 Cancel print of file
     †03 Cancel print of all files
     †04 Hold the print queue for scan
     †05 Activate the print queue after hold

RS-232 Services

0B   BIOS reserved for communications
0C   BIOS reserved for communications
14   BIOS RS-232 communications functions
     00 Initialize port
     01 Put character
     02 Get character
     03 Get port status

Cassette Services (Not XT)

15   BIOS cassette functions
     00 Motor on
     01 Motor off
     02 Get blocks
     03 Put blocks

Auxiliary Device Services

21   DOS function request
     03 Auxiliary input (with wait)
     04 Auxiliary output

Miscellaneous 8088 System Services

00   8088 Divide by zero
01   8088 Single step
02   8088 Non-Maskable Interrupt
03   8088 Breakpoint instruction
04   8088 Overflow

Miscellaneous BIOS System Services

11   BIOS get equipment status
12   BIOS get memory size
18   BIOS BASIC entry point
19   BIOS system boot
1A   BIOS
       80 Set sound multiplexor (PCjr only)

Miscellaneous DOS System Services

21   DOS function request
       25 Set interrupt vector
     *30 Get DOS version
     *33 Get or set Ctrl/Break on/off
     *35 Get interrupt vector
     *38 Get country delimiter information

300

Appendix D
DOS Versions

Appendix D
DOS Versions

This Appendix will help you determine which commands and functions are usable with the various versions of DOS. For example, as you can see below, VER was new in DOS 2. You will not be able to call it from a program designed for all versions of DOS unless you determine the DOS version from your program and have the program act accordingly.

Batch file commands were enhanced in DOS 2.0, so you will need to know the version of DOS before using those enhanced facilities. Programs 1-2 and 1-3, MEMDOSVR and MEMDOSVS, presented in Chapter 1 can be used as models for determining the version of DOS that is being used.

To further pursue the details of an enhancement made to a DOS command, you will need the DOS manual at the level of the enhancement. DOS changes are shown on page A-1 of the DOS manual, page E-1 of the DOS 2.10 manual, and page 1-4 of the DOS 3.0 manual.

File Sizes of DOS				
DOS level	3.0	2.1	2.0	1.1
IBMBIOS	8964	4736	4608	1920
IBMDOS	27920	17024	17152	6400
COMMAND	22042	17792	17664	4959
Approximate DOS Memory Usage				
DOS level	3.0	2.1	2.0	1.1
	36K	24K	24K	12K

DOS 1.1
New: EXEC2BIN, date/time stamping of files
Enhanced: COPY, DEBUG, DISKCOMP, DISKCOPY, FORMAT, LINK, MODE

DOS 2.0

New: ASSIGN, BACKUP, BREAK, CHDIR, CLS, CTTY, FDISK, FIND, GRAPHICS, MKDIR, MORE, PATH, PROMPT, PRINT, RECOVER, RESTORE, RMDIR, SET, SORT, TREE, VER, VERIFY, VOL, sub-directories, disk labels, Ansi.sys, redirection, piping, nine sectors/track, functions 2F–57h

Enhanced: CHKDSK, COMP, DEBUG, DIR, DISKCOMP, DISKCOPY, EDLIN, ERASE, FORMAT, Config.sys, directories, batch files, function 1Bh, INT 25

DOS 3.0

New: ATTRIB, COUNTRY, GRAFTABL, KEYBxx, LABEL, LASTDRIVE, SELECT, SHARE, VDISK, high-capacity drives, country-specific keyboard and graphics characters, extended error codes, unique filenames, INT 2F (printer queue functions), functions 45, 59–5C, 62h

Enhanced: BACKUP, DATE, DISKCOMP, DISKCOPY, FORMAT, GRAPHICS, PRINT, RESTORE, command path, INT21, INT24, functions 38h, 3Dh, 44h

Appendix E

BASIC Versions

Appendix E
BASIC Versions

This Appendix will help you determine which BASIC commands and functions are usable with the various versions of BASIC and DOS. For example, as you can see below, WINDOW was new in DOS 2, isn't present in Cassette or Disk BASIC, and in the PCjr version has enhancements. You can also see that LINE is supported in all versions of BASIC, but DOS 2 and the PCjr versions have enhancements. Obviously, enhancements are never reflected in Cassette BASIC or earlier versions of BASIC. Program 1-4, MEMBASVR, in Chapter 1 can be used as a model to determine which version of BASIC is being used. Programs 1-2 and 1-3 can be used to determine the DOS version.

    To pursue the details of an enhancement made to a BASIC command further, you will need the BASIC manual at the DOS level of that enhancement or above. The first part of the manual describes enhancements from the earlier level. BASIC 2.0 changes are shown on page vii of the BASIC manual, while BASIC 3.0 shows changes for 2.0 and 3.0 beginning on page v.

File Sizes of BASIC				
DOS level	3.0	2.1	2.0	1.1
BASIC	17024	16256	16256	11392
BASICA	26880	26112	25984	16768

Key: C=Cassette, D=Disk, A=Advanced, J=Junior
     1=DOS 1.1, 2=DOS 2.0, 3=DOS 3.0
See BASIC manual for BASIC compiler differences.

	Not in BASIC	New in Version	Enhanced in Version
atn			2
basic	C		2
bload			2
bsave			2
chain	C		

	Not in BASIC	New in Version	Enhanced in Version
chdir	C	2	
circle	C, D		J, 2
clear			J
color			J
com(n)	C, D		
common	C		
cos			2
cvd	C		
cvi	C		
cvs	C		
date$	C		
delete			2
draw	C, D		J, 2
environ	C, J	3	
environ$	C, J	3	
eof			2
erdev	C, J	3	
erdev$	C, J	3	
exp			2
field	C		
files	C		
get (files)	C		2
get (graphics)	C, D		
ioctl	C, J	3	
ioctl$	C, J	3	
key			2
key(n)	C		2
kill	C		2
line			J, 2
load			2
loc	C		2
lof			2
log			2
lset	C		
merge			2
mkd$	C		
mkdir	C	2	
mki$	C		
mks$	C		
name	C		2
noise	C, D, A	J	
on com(n)	C, D		
on key(n)	C, D		
on pen	C, D		

	Not in BASIC	New in Version	Enhanced in Version
on play(n)	C, D	2	
on strig(n)	C, D		
on timer	C, D	2	
open			1, 2
open "com...	C		
paint	C, D		J, 2
palette	C, D, A	J	
palette using	C, D, A	J	
pcopy	C, D, A	J	
play	C, D		J, 2
play(n)	C, D	2	
pmap	C, D	2	
point			2
preset			2
pset			2
put (files)	C		2
put (graphics)	C, D		
randomize			2
reset	C		
rmdir	C	2	
rset	C		
run			2
save			2
screen			J
shell	C, D, J	3	
sin			2
sqr			2
strig(n)	C		1
tan			2
term	C	J	
time$	C		
timer	C	2	
varptr$	C	1	
view	C, D	2	
window	C, D	2	J

Appendix F
BASIC Tokens

Appendix F

BASIC Tokens

BASIC Tokens in Numeric Order

00 End of line, zero line link is end of
    program
0B Two-byte octal integer
0C Two-byte hex integer
0D Two-byte line address −1 (after
    RUN)
0E Two-byte line number (before RUN)
0F One-byte unsigned integer (10–255)
11 Digit 0
12 Digit 1
13 Digit 2
14 Digit 3
15 Digit 4
16 Digit 5
17 Digit 6
18 Digit 7
19 Digit 8
1A Digit 9
1C Two-byte unsigned integer (0–32767)
1D Four-byte single-precision floating
    point
1F Eight-byte double-precision floating
    point
20–7F Printable characters, not used for
    tokens

Cassette Commands

81 END	92 CLEAR	A6 EDIT
82 FOR	93 LIST	A7 ERROR
83 NEXT	94 NEW	A8 RESUME
84 DATA	95 ON	A9 DELETE
85 INPUT	96 WAIT	AA AUTO
86 DIM	97 DEF	AB RENUM
87 READ	98 POKE	AC DEFSTR
88 LET	99 CONT	AD DEFINT
89 GOTO	9C OUT	AE DEFSNG
8A RUN	9D LPRINT	AF DEFDBL
8B IF	9E LLIST	B0 LINE
8C RESTORE	A0 WIDTH	B1 WHILE
8D GOSUB	A1 ELSE	B2 WEND
8E RETURN	A2 TRON	B3 CALL
8F REM	A3 TROFF	B7 WRITE
90 STOP	A4 SWAP	B8 OPTION
91 PRINT	A5 ERASE	B9 RANDOMIZE

BA OPEN	CC TO	DD OFF
BB CLOSE	CD THEN	DE INKEY$
BC LOAD	CE TAB(	E6 >
BD MERGE	CF STEP	E7 =
BE SAVE	D0 USR	E8 <
BF COLOR	D1 FN	E9 +
C0 CLS	D2 SPC(	EA −
C1 MOTOR	D3 NOT	EB *
C2 BSAVE	D4 ERL	EC /
C3 BLOAD	D5 ERR	ED ^
C4 SOUND	D6 STRING$	EE AND
C5 BEEP	D7 USING	EF OR
C6 PSET	D8 INSTR	F0 XOR
C7 PRESET	D9 '	F1 EQV
C8 SCREEN	DA VARPTR	F2 IMP
C9 KEY	DB CSRLIN	F3 MOD
CA LOCATE	DC POINT	F4 \

Disk Functions

FD 81 CVI
FD 82 CVS
FD 83 CVD
FD 84 MKI$
FD 85 MKS$
FD 86 MKD$

Disk Commands

FE 81 FILES	FE 8C CHAIN	FE 98 VIEW
FE 82 FIELD	FE 8D DATE$	FE 99 PMAP
FE 83 SYSTEM	FE 8E TIME$	FE 9A ERDEV
FE 84 NAME	FE 8F PAINT	FE 9B CHDIR
FE 85 LSET	FE 90 COM	FE 9C RMDIR
FE 86 RSET	FE 91 CIRCLE	FE 9D ENVIRON
FE 87 KILL	FE 92 DRAW	FE 9E WINDOW
FE 88 PUT	FE 93 PLAY	FE 9F PALETTE
FE 89 GET	FE 94 TIMER	FE A4 NOISE
FE 8A RESET	FE 95 IOCTL	FE A5 PCOPY
FE 8B COMMON	FE 96 MKDIR	FE A6 TERM
	FE 97 SHELL	

Cassette Functions

FF 81 LEFT$	FF 8D TAN	FF 9A HEX$
FF 82 RIGHT$	FF 8E ATN	FF 9B LPOS
FF 83 MID$	FF 8F FRE	FF 9C CINT
FF 84 SGN	FF 90 INP	FF 9D CSNG
FF 85 INT	FF 91 POS	FF 9E CDBL
FF 86 ABS	FF 92 LEN	FF 9F FIX
FF 87 SQR	FF 93 STR$	FF A0 PEN
FF 88 RND	FF 94 VAL	FF A1 STICK
FF 89 SIN	FF 95 ASC	FF A2 STRIG
FF 8A LOG	FF 96 CHR$	FF A3 EOF
FF 8B EXP	FF 97 PEEK	FF A4 LOC
FF 8C COS	FF 98 SPACE$	FF A5 LOF
	FF 99 OCT$	

BASIC Tokens in Alphabetical Order

D9	'	86	DIM
EB	*	FE 92	DRAW
E9	+	A6	EDIT
EA	−	1F	Eight-byte double-precision floating point
EC	/	A1	ELSE
E8	<	81	END
E7	=	00	End of line, zero line link is end of program
E6	>	FE 9D	ENVIRON
FF 86	ABS	FF A3	EOF
EE	AND	F1	EQV
FF 95	ASC	A5	ERASE
FF 8E	ATN	FE 9A	ERDEV
AA	AUTO	D4	ERL
C5	BEEP	D5	ERR
C3	BLOAD	A7	ERROR
C2	BSAVE	FF 8B	EXP
B3	CALL	FE 82	FIELD
FF 9E	CDBL	FE 81	FILES
FE 8C	CHAIN	FF 9F	FIX
FE 9B	CHDIR	D1	FN
FF 96	CHR$	82	FOR
FF 9C	CINT	1D	Four-byte single-precision floating point
FE 91	CIRCLE	FF 8F	FRE
92	CLEAR	FE 89	GET
BB	CLOSE	8D	GOSUB
C0	CLS	89	GOTO
BF	COLOR	FF 9A	HEX$
FE 90	COM	8B	IF
FE 8B	COMMON	F2	IMP
99	CONT	DE	INKEY$
FF 8C	COS	FF 90	INP
FF 9D	CSNG	85	INPUT
DB	CSRLIN	D8	INSTR
FD 83	CVD	FF 85	INT
FD 81	CVI	FE 95	IOCTL
FD 82	CVS	C9	KEY
84	DATA	FE 87	KILL
FE 8D	DATE$	FF 81	LEFT$
97	DEF	FF 92	LEN
AF	DEFDBL	88	LET
AD	DEFINT	B0	LINE
AE	DEFSNG	93	LIST
AC	DEFSTR	9E	LLIST
A9	DELETE	BC	LOAD
11	Digit 0	FF A4	LOC
12	Digit 1	CA	LOCATE
13	Digit 2	FF A5	LOF
14	Digit 3	FF 8A	LOG
15	Digit 4	FF 9B	LPOS
16	Digit 5	9D	LPRINT
17	Digit 6	FE 85	LSET
18	Digit 7	BD	MERGE
19	Digit 8	FF 83	MID$
1A	Digit 9	FD 86	MKD$

FE 96	MKDIR		BE	SAVE
FD 84	MKI$		C8	SCREEN
FD 85	MKS$		FF 84	SGN
F3	MOD		FE 97	SHELL
C1	MOTOR		FF 89	SIN
FE 84	NAME		C4	SOUND
94	NEW		FF 98	SPACE$
83	NEXT		D2	SPC(
FE A4	NOISE		FF 87	SQR
D3	NOT		CF	STEP
FF 99	OCT$		FF A1	STICK
DD	OFF		90	STOP
95	ON		FF 93	STR$
0F	One-byte unsigned integer (10–255)		FF A2	STRIG
BA	OPEN		D6	STRING$
B8	OPTION		A4	SWAP
EF	OR		FE 83	SYSTEM
9C	OUT		CE	TAB(
FE 8F	PAINT		FF 8D	TAN
FE 9F	PALETTE		FE A6	TERM
FE A5	PCOPY		CD	THEN
FF 97	PEEK		FE 8E	TIME$
FF A0	PEN		FE 94	TIMER
FE 93	PLAY		CC	TO
FE 99	PMAP		A3	TROFF
DC	POINT		A2	TRON
98	POKE		0C	Two-byte hex integer
FF 91	POS		0D	Two-byte line address −1 (after RUN)
C7	PRESET		0E	Two-byte line number (before RUN)
91	PRINT		0B	Two-byte octal integer
C6	PSET		1C	Two-byte unsigned integer (0–32767)
FE 88	PUT		D7	USING
B9	RANDOMIZE		D0	USR
87	READ		FF 94	VAL
8F	REM		DA	VARPTR
AB	RENUM		FE 98	VIEW
FE 8A	RESET		96	WAIT
8C	RESTORE		B2	WEND
A8	RESUME		B1	WHILE
8E	RETURN		A0	WIDTH
FF 82	RIGHT$		FE 9E	WINDOW
FE 9C	RMDIR		B7	WRITE
FF 88	RND		F0	XOR
FE 86	RSET		F4	\
8A	RUN		ED	^

Appendix G

ASCII Values

Appendix G

ASCII Values

Hex	ASCII	Character	Hex	ASCII	Character
0	000	(null)	20	032	(space)
1	001	☺	21	033	!
2	002	●	22	034	"
3	003	♥	23	035	#
4	004	♦	24	036	$
5	005	♣	25	037	%
6	006	♠	26	038	&
7	007	(beep)	27	039	'
8	008	■	28	040	(
9	009	(tab)	29	041	)
A	010	◙	2A	042	*
B	011	♂	2B	043	+
C	012	(form feed)	2C	044	,
D	013	(carriage return)	2D	045	-
E	014	♫	2E	046	.
F	015	☼	2F	047	/
10	016	►	30	048	0
11	017	◄	31	049	1
12	018	↕	32	050	2
13	019	‼	33	051	3
14	020	¶	34	052	4
15	021	§	35	053	5
16	022	▬	36	054	6
17	023	↨	37	055	7
18	024	↑	38	056	8
19	025	↓	39	057	9
1A	026	→	3A	058	:
1B	027	←	3B	059	;
1C	028	∟	3C	060	<
1D	029	↔	3D	061	=
1E	030	▲	3E	062	>
1F	031	▼	3F	063	?

Hex	ASCII	Character	Hex	ASCII	Character
40	064	@	60	096	`
41	065	A	61	097	a
42	066	B	62	098	b
43	067	C	63	099	c
44	068	D	64	100	d
45	069	E	65	101	e
46	070	F	66	102	f
47	071	G	67	103	g
48	072	H	68	104	h
49	073	I	69	105	i
4A	074	J	6A	106	j
4B	075	K	6B	107	k
4C	076	L	6C	108	l
4D	077	M	6D	109	m
4E	078	N	6E	110	n
4F	079	O	6F	111	o
50	080	P	70	112	p
51	081	Q	71	113	q
52	082	R	72	114	r
53	083	S	73	115	s
54	084	T	74	116	t
55	085	U	75	117	u
56	086	V	76	118	v
57	087	W	77	119	w
58	088	X	78	120	x
59	089	Y	79	121	y
5A	090	Z	7A	122	z
5B	091	[	7B	123	{
5C	092	\	7C	124	¦
5D	093	]	7D	125	}
5E	094	^	7E	126	~
5F	095	–	7F	127	⌂

Hex	ASCII	Character	Hex	ASCII	Character
80	128	Ç	A0	160	á
81	129	ü	A1	161	í
82	130	é	A2	162	ó
83	131	â	A3	163	ú
84	132	ä	A4	164	ñ
85	133	à	A5	165	Ñ
86	134	å	A6	166	ª
87	135	ç	A7	167	º
88	136	ê	A8	168	¿
89	137	ë	A9	169	⌐
8A	138	è	AA	170	¬
8B	139	ï	AB	171	½
8C	140	î	AC	172	¼
8D	141	ì	AD	173	¡
8E	142	Ä	AE	174	≪
8F	143	Å	AF	175	≫
90	144	É	B0	176	▒
91	145	æ	B1	177	▓
92	146	Æ	B2	178	█
93	147	ô	B3	179	│
94	148	ö	B4	180	┤
95	149	ò	B5	181	╡
96	150	û	B6	182	╢
97	151	ù	B7	183	╖
98	152	ÿ	B8	184	╕
99	153	Ö	B9	185	╣
9A	154	Ü	BA	186	║
9B	155	¢	BB	187	╗
9C	156	£	BC	188	╝
9D	157	¥	BD	189	╜
9E	158	Pt	BE	190	╛
9F	159	ƒ	BF	191	┐

Hex	ASCII	Character	Hex	ASCII	Character
C0	192	└	E0	224	α
C1	193	┴	E1	225	β
C2	194	┬	E2	226	Γ
C3	195	├	E3	227	π
C4	196	─	E4	228	Σ
C5	197	┼	E5	229	σ
C6	198	╞	E6	230	μ
C7	199	╟	E7	231	τ
C8	200	╚	E8	232	Φ
C9	201	╔	E9	233	θ
CA	202	╩	EA	234	Ω
CB	203	╦	EB	235	δ
CC	204	╠	EC	236	∞
CD	205	═	ED	237	$\emptyset$
CE	206	╬	EE	238	ϵ
CF	207	╧	EF	239	$\cap$
D0	208	╨	F0	240	$\equiv$
D1	209	╤	F1	241	$\pm$
D2	210	╥	F2	242	$\geq$
D3	211	╙	F3	243	$\leq$
D4	212	╘	F4	244	$\lceil$
D5	213	╒	F5	245	$\rfloor$
D6	214	╓	F6	246	$\div$
D7	215	╫	F7	247	$\approx$
D8	216	╪	F8	248	°
D9	217	┘	F9	249	•
DA	218	┌	FA	250	·
DB	219	█	FB	251	$\sqrt{}$
DC	220	▄	FC	252	n
DD	221	▌	FD	253	^{2}
DE	222	▐	FE	254	■
DF	223	▀	FF	255	(blank)

Appendix H
The Automatic Proofreader

Appendix H

The Automatic Proofreader

Charles Brannon

Now there's a way to banish practically all typing errors when you enter BASIC programs in this book. "The Automatic Proofreader" instantly checks your typing as you enter each line. The Proofreader works on any IBM PC or Enhanced Model PCjr with Cartridge BASIC.

The Proofreader lets you enter program lines as you normally do, but with an important difference. After you type in a line and press Enter, a pair of letters appears, inserted just before the line you've typed. This pair of letters is called a *checksum*. You compare the checksum to a matching code of letters in the program listing. *If the pair of letters on your screen matches the pair of letters in the program listing, the line was entered correctly.* A glance is all it takes to confirm that you've typed the line right.

Does it sound too good to be true? It isn't. Thousands of readers of our magazines, *COMPUTE!* and *COMPUTE!'s Gazette*, have been successfully using similar Proofreaders to type in program listings for their Commodore, Atari, and IBM computers.

Using the Proofreader

To get started, type in the Automatic Proofreader listing at the end of this Appendix and save a couple of copies. You'll want to use it whenever you enter a program from this book, *COMPUTE!* magazine, and future COMPUTE! books. Naturally, the Proofreader can't check itself, so you'll have to be extra careful when you type it in. Often, when readers experience difficulty with the Proofreader, the problem has been traced to improperly typing the Proofreader program. If it's not typed in correctly, you may receive the message *Error #2*. The Proofreader traps all errors, even syntax errors. Instead of getting the usual message, *Syntax error in ...*, you get the error number (2 is syntax error) with no hint as to where the error might be. To help you find your typos, change the 650 to 0 in line 140. This turns off the error trapping so that you'll get the usual error messages if you have any errors.

Before using the Proofreader to type in programs, it's a good idea to test all the Proofreader commands, especially the SAVE command, just to make sure there are no bugs lurking in some obscure place in the program. To test the Proofreader's SAVE command, run the Proofreader and type in one line, say, 10 REM. Now save this test program. If you didn't get an error message, you can safely type in a complete listing without fear of losing all your typing due to a bug in the SAVE command. When you think you have all the bugs out, type BASIC to exit the Proofreader, change line 140 back to normal, and save this bug-free version of the Proofreader.

When you run the Automatic Proofreader, the screen clears to white and the prompt *Proofreader Ready* appears. At this point, the Proofreader is ready to accept program lines or commands. You can just type in a program as you normally would.

Here's an example of how it works. Type in the following line:

120 RESUME 130

When you press Enter, there'll be a short delay and the checksum will appear:

BE 120 RESUME 130

The two letters *BE* are the checksum. Try making a change in the line, then press Enter. Notice that the checksum has changed. The slightest alteration to the line results in a different checksum.

Most of the BASIC program listings published in this book have a checksum printed to the left of each line number. Just type in each line (omitting the printed checksum, of course) and compare the checksum on your screen with the checksum in the listing. If they match, go on to the next line. If they don't match, there's a difference between the way you typed the line and the way it appears in the book. It might be a very slight difference that's hard to spot at first. When you find it, you can correct the line immediately with the cursor and editing keys instead of waiting to find the error when you run the program.

Although the Proofreader is an indispensable aid, there are a few things to watch out for. First, the Proofreader is *very* literal: It looks at the individual characters in a line. It makes a distinction between upper- and lowercase, so be sure to *leave Caps Lock on* while you type in a listing, releasing it when necessary to enter lowercase. For similar reasons, do not use the question mark (?) as an abbreviation for PRINT—they're not the same thing in the Proofreader's eyes. The Proofreader can even catch transposition errors—such as PIRNT instead of PRINT.

The Proofreader is also picky with spaces, since proper spacing is important to prevent syntax errors in IBM BASIC. Adding an extra space or leaving one out—even in places where it's normally permitted, such as within PRINT statements or comment statements—will result in a different checksum. If you want to modify something, we recommend that you first type the program exactly as it's published, verify that it runs, and *then* make your modifications.

Proofreader Commands

The Proofreader has many commands, almost identical in syntax to those found in IBM BASIC. In fact, the editing environment is so similar that you may forget you're using a BASIC program to enter other BASIC programs. If in doubt, remember that BASIC's prompt is *Ok* while the Proofreader says *Proofreader Ready.* Also, the screen is white when the Proofreader is active.

LIST works just like it does in BASIC. LIST 10 lists line 10 only. LIST 40–90 displays all lines between 40 and 90, inclusive. If you press any key while the program is listing, the listing will stop. Unless you are running the Proofreader under PCjr Cartridge BASIC or BASICA 2.0 or 2.1, do not press Break to stop the listing or you will exit the Proofreader. The Break key is trapped with Advanced BASIC 2.0 or 2.1, so you'll get the message *Stopped.*

CHECK is a special Proofreader command that acts like LIST, except it also displays the checksum for each line.

LLIST will list the program to the current printer device. It works as LLIST does in BASIC.

NEW clears out the program in memory—not the Proofreader, but the program you're typing. However, there's an extra safeguard built in. Unlike BASIC, the Proofreader will ask,

Erase program—Are you sure? You must enter Y to erase the program. Remember, this won't remove the Proofreader itself, but only the program held by the Proofreader.

FILES lists the disk directory on the screen. It lists only the directory for drive A.

BASIC exits the Proofreader. It returns you to BASIC's *Ok* prompt and returns the screen color to black, leaving the Proofreader still in memory. To be safe, always save your program on disk before leaving the Proofreader. If you accidentally exit the Proofreader by typing BASIC, you can reenter the Proofreader and retrieve your program by typing CONT. You'll get a syntax error message and the screen won't return to white, but the program you were typing will be intact.

SAVE and LOAD Commands

You can save a program at any point when using the Proofreader. Just type SAVE *"filename"*. As usual, the ending quote is optional. If you don't enter a period and a three-character extender, the extender .BAS will be automatically appended. Again, this is just like IBM BASIC.

Unlike IBM BASIC, the Proofreader always saves programs to disk in ASCII form. You can load this program from BASIC like any other. Since ASCII files take up more room on a disk than ordinary program files, later you may want to resave the program back to disk from BASIC in order to conserve disk space. (Be sure to type NEW before loading an ASCII file.)

You can reload programs into the Proofreader with the command LOAD *"filename"*. (As with the SAVE command, the extender .BAS is assumed if you don't enter an extension.) This way you can type in part of a long program, save it on disk, and load it again later to continue typing. But make sure the program you're loading was saved by the Proofreader. The Proofreader cannot successfully load a program file that's not in ASCII form.

Program H-1. The Automatic Proofreader

```
10 'Automatic Proofreader Version 2.00 (Lines
   270,510,515,517,620,630 changed from V1.0)
100 DIM L$(500),LNUM(500):COLOR 0,7,7:KEY OFF:
    CLS:MAX=0:LNUM(0)=65536!
110 ON ERROR GOTO 120:KEY 15,CHR$(4)+CHR$(70):
    ON KEY(15) GOSUB 640:KEY (15) ON:GOTO 130
```

```
120 RESUME 130
130 DEF SEG=&H40:W=PEEK(&H4A)
140 ON ERROR GOTO 650:PRINT:PRINT"Proofreader
    Ready."
150 LINE INPUT L$:Y=CSRLIN-INT(LEN(L$)/W)-1:LO
    CATE Y,1
160 DEF SEG=0:POKE 1050,30:POKE 1052,34:POKE 1
    054,0:POKE 1055,79:POKE 1056,13:POKE 1057,
    28:LINE INPUT L$:DEF SEG:IF L$="" THEN 150
170 IF LEFT$(L$,1)=" " THEN L$=MID$(L$,2):GOTO
    170
180 IF VAL(LEFT$(L$,2))=0 AND MID$(L$,3,1)=" "
    THEN L$=MID$(L$,4)
190 LNUM=VAL(L$):TEXT$=MID$(L$,LEN(STR$(LNUM))
    +1)
200 IF ASC(L$)>57 THEN 260 'no line number, th
    erefore command
210 IF TEXT$="" THEN GOSUB 540:IF LNUM=LNUM(P)
    THEN GOSUB 560:GOTO 150 ELSE 150
220 CKSUM=0:FOR I=1 TO LEN(L$):CKSUM=(CKSUM+AS
    C(MID$(L$,I))*I) AND 255:NEXT:LOCATE Y,1:P
    RINT CHR$(65+CKSUM/16)+CHR$(65+(CKSUM AND
    15))+" "+L$
230 GOSUB 540:IF LNUM(P)=LNUM THEN L$(P)=TEXT$
    :GOTO 150 'replace line
240 GOSUB 580:GOTO 150 'insert the line
260 TEXT$="":FOR I=1 TO LEN(L$):A=ASC(MID$(L$,
    I)):TEXT$=TEXT$+CHR$(A+32*(A>96 AND A<123)
    ):NEXT
270 DELIMITER=INSTR(TEXT$," "):COMMAND$=TEXT$:
    ARG$="":IF DELIMITER THEN COMMAND$=LEFT$(T
    EXT$,DELIMITER-1):ARG$=MID$(TEXT$,DELIMITE
    R+1) ELSE DELIMITER=INSTR(TEXT$,CHR$(34)):
    IF DELIMITER THEN COMMAND$=LEFT$(TEXT$,DEL
    IMITER-1):ARG$=MID$(TEXT$,DELIMITER)
280 IF COMMAND$<>"LIST" THEN 410
290 OPEN "scrn:" FOR OUTPUT AS #1
300 IF ARG$="" THEN FIRST=0:P=MAX-1:GOTO 340
310 DELIMITER=INSTR(ARG$,"-"):IF DELIMITER=0 T
    HEN LNUM=VAL(ARG$):GOSUB 540:FIRST=P:GOTO
    340
320 FIRST=VAL(LEFT$(ARG$,DELIMITER)):LAST=VAL(
    MID$(ARG$,DELIMITER+1))
330 LNUM=FIRST:GOSUB 540:FIRST=P:LNUM=LAST:GOS
    UB 540:IF P=0 THEN P=MAX-1
340 FOR X=FIRST TO P:N$=MID$(STR$(LNUM(X)),2)+
    " "
350 IF CKFLAG=0 THEN A$="":GOTO 370
```

```
360 CKSUM=0:A$=N$+L$(X):FOR I=1 TO LEN(A$):CKS
    UM=(CKSUM+ASC(MID$(A$,I))*I) AND 255:NEXT:
    A$=CHR$(65+CKSUM/16)+CHR$(65+(CKSUM AND 15
    ))+" "
370 PRINT #1,A$+N$+L$(X)
380 IF INKEY$<>"" THEN X=P
390 NEXT :CLOSE #1:CKFLAG=0
400 GOTO 130
410 IF COMMAND$="LLIST" THEN OPEN "lpt1:" FOR
    OUTPUT AS #1:GOTO 300
420 IF COMMAND$="CHECK" THEN CKFLAG=1:GOTO 290
430 IF COMMAND$<>"SAVE" THEN 450
440 GOSUB 600:OPEN ARG$ FOR OUTPUT AS #1:ARG$=
    "":GOTO 300
450 IF COMMAND$<>"LOAD" THEN 490
460 GOSUB 600:OPEN ARG$ FOR INPUT AS #1:MAX=0:
    P=0
470 WHILE NOT EOF(1):LINE INPUT #1,L$:LNUM(P)=
    VAL(L$):L$(P)=MID$(L$,LEN(STR$(VAL(L$)))+1
    ):P=P+1:WEND
480 MAX=P:CLOSE #1:GOTO 130
490 IF COMMAND$="NEW" THEN INPUT "Erase progra
    m - Are you sure";L$: IF LEFT$(L$,1)="y" OR
     LEFT$(L$,1)="Y" THEN MAX=0:GOTO 130:ELSE
    130
500 IF COMMAND$="BASIC" THEN COLOR 7,0,0:ON ER
    ROR GOTO 0:CLS:END
510 IF COMMAND$<>"FILES" THEN 520
515 IF ARG$="" THEN ARG$="A:" ELSE SEL=1:GOSUB
    600
517 FILES ARG$:GOTO 130
520 PRINT"Syntax error":GOTO 130
540 P=0:WHILE LNUM>LNUM(P) AND P<MAX:P=P+1:WEN
    D:RETURN
560 MAX=MAX-1:FOR X=P TO MAX:LNUM(X)=LNUM(X+1)
    :L$(X)=L$(X+1):NEXT:RETURN
580 MAX=MAX+1:FOR X=MAX TO P+1 STEP -1:LNUM(X)
    =LNUM(X-1):L$(X)=L$(X-1):NEXT:L$(P)=TEXT$:
    LNUM(P)=LNUM:RETURN
600 IF LEFT$(ARG$,1)<>CHR$(34) THEN 520 ELSE A
    RG$=MID$(ARG$,2)
610 IF RIGHT$(ARG$,1)=CHR$(34) THEN ARG$=LEFT$
    (ARG$,LEN(ARG$)-1)
620 IF SEL=0 AND INSTR(ARG$,".")=0 THEN ARG$=A
    RG$+".BAS"
630 SEL=0:RETURN
640 CLOSE #1:CKFLAG=0:PRINT"Stopped.":RETURN 1
    50
650 PRINT "Error #";ERR:RESUME 150
```

Index